DAVID W. PENNEY is Associate Director of Museum Scholarship at the National Museum of the American Indian, Washington, DC.

GEORGE HORSE CAPTURE played a major role in establishing and running the National Museum of the American Indian in Washington, DC, where he held a number of senior positions. He subsequently compiled the A'ani Tribal Archive Project, a vast digital collection of words, photographs and audio material recording his tribe's history and culture.

Thames & Hudson world of art

This famous series provides the widest available range of illustrated books on art in all its aspects.

To find out about all our publications, including other titles in the World of Art series, please visit **thamesandhudsonusa.com**.

187 illustrations, 80 in color

North American Indian Art

David W. Penney

 Thames & Hudson world of art

Foreword

It is always an education and a pleasure to work with David Penney. A perceptive and intellectual scholar in the field, he keeps up on the literature, the developing art scene, and evolving thoughts, and then develops a theory, detailing it with numerous examples, and articulating and solidifying it in his writing. That methodology is clearly at work here. The book is chock full of interesting stories and information, as well as bold declarative statements.

In the very first paragraph, Dr. Penney notes that American Indian people are still vibrantly alive and still creating their traditional art, as well as participating in age-old ceremonies. This enlightenment is a far cry from what it was like when I started in the museum field so many moons ago. Our standard approach then was to preserve those relics from a long ago time at all costs, perhaps even to the degree of sealing them away in the dark, far from prying eyes. No one was to touch them; their sole responsibility was to exist. On occasion the most popular items were allowed to be on display, but the vast majority were locked away. As a curator I was often scolded and instructed on how to properly handle these ancient things from the lost past, but something inside of me felt something was wrong. Isolation rendered the items lifeless, and the treatment of the objects often reflected how the Indian people themselves were viewed.

Years later I had the privilege of joining the National Museum of the American Indian and the earlier restrictive museum philosophy changed dramatically. In addition to caring for the collection, we invited people – the tribal members of the makers of the material – to have access to their artifacts, and suddenly the collection came alive. The tribes came in and met their items with great emotion. Instead of persisting with the older concept of "don't touch: this material is ours," we embraced the reality that the tribes' ancestors had created these objects, and that the collection was a living one that could become a "connector" between the ancestors, the descendants, and others. Over the years at this museum I have witnessed such joy, pain, happiness,

2 *Hamatsa* dancer wearing cedar bark clothing and a mask carved from red cedar at a potlatch ceremony given by Chief W. T. Cranmer in Alert Bay, British Columbia.

awe, and reverence when tribal people experience their living heritage. The step we took to respect the people and to better understand the art and the artist was a good one. It remains our goal to familiarize American Indians with their material, and to acknowledge their cultural and spiritual needs.

Dr. Penney expresses other "stages of growth" in this interesting book. One tragic limitation of ethnographic museums has been the anonymity of the artists that created the masterpieces on display. With rare exceptions their names are lost in time. Often we cannot even identify the tribe. Dr. Penney acknowledges that we don't know nearly enough about the art and the artist, and he also provocatively asks the question, "What is Native American?" He defines this in differing tiers that compel additional study, and he goes on to observe that the first step towards addressing the question is established on a local level. It is here that the essence of what will become art begins, and if it could speak we could all hear. Indian communities across the continent are similarly engaged, and as such are an equal part of this foundation. When all of the local presentations are viewed together, they form "Native America."

Dr. Penney suggests that the researcher not only study the art piece, but also find out all that is possible about the artist's life, thoughts, relationships, family, spirituality, and other essentials, because art is a testimony to existence. Together these tenets have formed a force that has guided the artist's hand, and they may allow us a greater understanding not only of the art, but also of the artist and their humanity.

This evolution of understanding is a far cry from long ago when many anthropologists and other collectors obtained ethnographic masterpieces from a suffering people for a few cents, without even troubling to obtain the artist's name.

But times are changing for American Indians, as life and intelligence are becoming "connectors" between us as well. We are grateful to David and to others who are recognizing these new "stages of growth" of understanding. David's perception is remarkable, coming from a non-artist, as his mind paints the items and interprets them in an insightful and helpful manner. It will make life easier as we all become more real.

George Horse Capture,
National Museum of the American Indian,
Washington, D.C.

Chapter 1   Introduction

American Indian art now

Artists of Native American ancestry are making art today, at this moment. All over the United States, countless dancers, singers, artists who will display their work in booths, T-shirt vendors, and fry-bread cooks prepare for a weekend of powwows. The on-line "Gathering of Nations" website lists thirty-six powwows for the Fourth of July 2003 weekend, among them the Navajo Fourth of July Powwow at Window Rock, Arizona, the 131st Annual Quapaw Tribal Powwow in Quapaw, Oklahoma, the 35th Annual Ute Fourth of July Powwow at Fort Duchesne, Utah, and the 8th Annual Eastern Woodlands Intertribal Powwow in Lebanon, Maine. At the beginning of each event, every dancer, dressed in regalia perfected to the best of their abilities and talents, will line up in order of seniority and parade into the arena led by military veterans carrying flags and accompanied by the singers of the lead drum in the heart-stopping spectacle known as "Grand Entry" [1].

In the town of Alert Bay, British Columbia, several families assemble gifts and goods to distribute at potlatches scheduled for later in the year. Some will feature masked dances presented as treasured family possessions [2]. Skilled carvers in the community, like Beau Dick, will receive commissions to carve new masks. Old ones preserved in family collections will be painted and refurbished so they look their best during the ceremony.

Outside Santa Fe, Nancy Youngblood, a descendant of a long lineage of potters including matriarchs Margaret Tafoya and her mother Sara Fina of Santa Clara Pueblo, builds and polishes vessels of clay. Her lustrous black jars, whose ribbed forms derive ultimately from the shapes of squashes and pumpkins, are highly sought-after by collectors and museums [3]. Many are sold before she finishes them. In the recent past, long lines of hopeful

3 Ribbed melon jar, made by Nancy Youngblood, c. 1995. Youngblood's art builds upon the blackware traditions of her ancestral home, Santa Clara Pueblo, in New Mexico. Her mother Mela Youngblood was a potter, as was Mela's mother, the great Margaret Tafoya, Margaret's mother Sara Fina, and very likely many mothers before that.

purchasers formed early in the morning in front of her booth at Indian Market in Santa Fe. Some walked away disappointed after she sold all she brought for the day.

In Washington, D.C., Ho-Chunk (or Winnebago) sculptor Truman Lowe, formerly the chair of the art department at the University of Wisconsin, Madison, now serves as the curator of contemporary art at the National Museum of the American Indian. Among his many plans for upcoming exhibitions is one that will feature Native American artists who work in electronic media.

Some Native Americans today criticize museum exhibits, popular media, and books like this one, because they often situate American Indian culture in a historical past, as if there is no Native American culture today. This failure to frame the past from the standpoint of the present is particularly unfortunate when considering Native American arts, since indigenous artists have always been, and still are now, among those who most actively reconcile the traditions of the past with the circumstances of the present. Art is, and has been, one of the principal strategies of Native American "survivance," to use writer Gerald Vizenor's term. While the word "survival" summons up images of last-gasp tenacity, the term "survivance" refers more to the wisdom of memory and adaptability, and the strategies of resistance, accommodation, and transformation. Histories of survivance connect the present with the past, linking the experiences of the aforementioned artists active today with those of countless forebears, the generations of Native American artists whose creations are the subject of this book.

Art and aesthetics
Readers of this book may be unaccustomed to thinking of art as a "strategy," which implies a social and political intention. We may be more accustomed to regarding art as a personal expression of an artist's creativity. Some may be comfortable with the notion of art as a collective expression of a worldview, particularly when considering religious symbols or the ritual role of art in religious ceremony. The term "art," as it will be used here, encompasses all these things. The artistic object is created within a cultural system of aesthetics. There is no single and universal system of aesthetics. There is no privileged standard for what can or cannot be called art. "Art" is a word used to name certain kinds of things and its definition changes all the time. Aesthetic expression, on the other hand, seems to be a human universal. Human beings all over the

world express values about what is good or bad, appropriate or inappropriate, beautiful or ugly, holy or profane, through a system of aesthetic valuation. Aesthetics shape the qualitative and ethical perceptions of social life. As such, aesthetics permeate the political, religious, and economic realms of every society.

Aesthetic systems are culture-bound. Cultural misunderstandings and conflict can stem from contesting aesthetic and ethical systems. For example, the Enlightenment-era judgment that contrasted European civilization with the "primitive savages" of the New World can be understood as an essentially aesthetic evaluation deeply rooted in European philosophical and religious thought [4, 5]. The eighteenth-century French philosopher Jean-Jacques Rousseau's appreciation of the "Noble Savage" represented a reversal of this aesthetic assessment, but his writing had more to do with a critique of European society than any real understanding of North American Indians.

Aesthetic systems change. They are permeable and easily absorb new ideas, attitudes, and shifting valuations. They are not always internally consistent. They are at once reenacted and reinvented by individuals, who, for the purposes of this book, are

4 Watercolor portrait of Jean Baptist Brouillette, painted by George Winter, c. 1863–71, based upon a sketch of 1837. The clothing worn by Brouillette, a Miami *metis* or mixed-blood of Indiana, merited the following comment in the artist's journal: "He wore a fine frock coat of the latest fashion. His 'pes-mo-kin' or shirt was white spotted with a small red figure, overhanging very handsome blue leggings, 'winged' with very rich silk ribbons of prismatic hues, exhibiting the [women's] skillful handiwork."

5 Godfried Maes, *America*, pen and ink with gray wash over black chalk, *c.* 1690–1700. Distinctions between broad categories of human beings, European and Native American, depend upon equally broad generalizations. Note that even in this extraordinarily early and allegorical representation of a Native American, the artist has included the stereotypical feathered headdress, bow, and quiver full of arrows.

artists and their audiences. For example, attitudes about media and design can change easily. In the eighteenth century women of the Great Lakes region quickly understood the aesthetic opportunities offered by trade goods such as cotton cloth, silk ribbon, and glass beads. They adopted new techniques to use these kinds of materials when decorating formal clothing. More impervious to change were the underlying ideas that valued formal clothing and its display during public events as an expression of self-worth. The powwows of today mentioned at the beginning of this chapter stand as a contemporary expression of that underlying aesthetic value. So at any particular time, aesthetic systems reach simultaneously back into the past and forward to the future. Some aspects of an aesthetic system respond to the topical and contemporary, others draw from the traditions of generations past. This perspective reveals to us the continuities and innovations visible in the many thousands of years of Native American art.

What is Native American art?

If art stems from an aesthetic system, and aesthetic systems develop and operate within the realm of culture, what, then, is Native American art? Native American aesthetics? Native American culture? The world of North America, prior to the identification of its inhabitants as Native Americans or American Indians, was a world unto itself. It had been home to human societies for at least 15,000 years before the voyages of Columbus. The breadth of its cultural diversity was equal to or surpassed that of any comparable landmass on the planet. At least 170 different languages were spoken in North America, probably more. The multitude of languages, life-ways, and conventions for understanding the world spawned as many understandings of art and aesthetics. Prior to contact with Europe, it would be difficult to imagine that any resident of North America thought self-consciously of him or herself as a Native American. People referred to their cultures by names that translate frequently as their language term for "the people:" *A'aninin*, "White Clay People" (later named the Gros Ventre by the French), for example, or *Mesquakie*, "Red Earth People" (later named the Renards, or Fox, by the French). The creation of a "Native American" identity was forced historically by the circumstances of North America's conquest. It is now common to speak of Native American culture, Native American art, or even a Native American perception of the world. My point is that this very human construct stems from a long and difficult history. And the implications of this history need some clarification because not everybody means the same thing when they speak of things "Native American."

The modern nations of the United States and Canada have invested a great deal of their cultural identities in the concept of "Native Americans." Images of Native people have decorated national currencies. "Red Skins," "Indians," and "Braves" are names of sports teams. The "Cherokee" is a popular automobile. Images of people dressed in buckskin and feathers, which everyone is supposed to recognize as "American Indian," are used to advertise products as varied as butter, fruit, and tobacco. It may be stating the obvious to say that these kinds of appropriations of names and images have little to do with the identities of real Native people. It may be less obvious to some, however, that the experiences of real Native people are lost from view when replaced by these images.

Today some artists of Native ancestry draw attention to the ironies inherent in this cultural image of the "Indian." David Bradley's *American Indian Gothic: Ghost Dancers* appropriates Grant Wood's iconic painting of American cultural identity [6]. Instead of the earnest prairie farmer with a pitchfork and his unmarried daughter, Bradley substitutes another couple presented in the guise of iconic Plains Indians with flowing hair, braids, beaded garments, and a tipi instead of a farmhouse in the background. The exchange of stereotypes might seem humorous, a sly nod to the recognition that Native people preceded the so-called pioneers of the plains. Those with more insider knowledge, however, might recognize the couple's garments as those worn by practitioners of the Ghost Dance mentioned in the title of the painting, a religious movement of revival and resistance that spread throughout several Plains reservations during the year 1889 and thereafter. At Wounded Knee, South Dakota, during the winter of 1890, the United States military confronted Lakota Ghost Dancers and killed more than three hundred of them, men, women, and children. Bradley's seemingly playful manipulations of stereotypes take on far more sobering ironies: the stark differences between stereotypes and the experiences of real people. One now thinks of the Grant Wood painting reminded of the fact that his stereotype of national character remains oblivious to the suffering that made the life of the prairie farmer possible.

So who are Native Americans? Ultimately, the identity of Native Americans stems from countless local cultures that, historically, have found themselves and their descendants bound together in the situation of contending with the consequences of conquest and colonial repression. Some authors of Native ancestry have attempted to contrast the essential differences between indigenous North American and European-derived cultures. It becomes obvious, however, that drawing these differences only becomes possible as the result of the encounter. The encounter and its historical consequences established the framework of difference on such a broad scale. The entire enterprise of cross-cultural reflection, us looking at them looking back at us, stems from a long history of such encounters and their consequences, and this book is a part of that. Native American art on the level of the *local* community is experienced through participation. When it is observed, recorded, translated, and analyzed, it becomes part of a cross-cultural discourse in which such broad terms as "Native American" might apply.

6 David Bradley, *American Indian Gothic: Ghost Dancers*, acrylic on canvas, 1989. Bradley's picture appropriates the famous Grant Wood composition, "American Gothic," replacing the farmer and his daughter with images of Plains Indians in Ghost Dance dress. The picture is a play on stereotypes, substituting one for another, and yet reminding the viewer of the very real, violent, and tragic events that stereotypes attempt to hide.

History and anthropology

Most of the objects illustrated in this book belong to museums. Some art museums now collect and display items made by Native American artists, but the largest collections of Native American "material culture" reside in natural history and anthropology museums, such as the American Museum of Natural History in New York, the Field Museum of Natural History in Chicago, and the National Museum of Natural History (Smithsonian Institution) in Washington, D.C. During the period between the end of the Civil War and the beginning of World War I, hundreds of thousands of objects were excavated from the ground or collected (purchased, gifted, stolen) from Native people and placed in museums. During the first years of the twentieth century, museum collecting among Native communities became so competitive that curators often ran into each other in the field, racing to procure artifacts before their colleagues could find them. A vast network of traders and field agents who collected items from Native communities waited for the parade of curators to line up at their door and purchase them. What did museums want with all these things?

The growth of American natural history museums and their collections of Native American "artifacts" during the nineteenth century is tied closely to the development of American ethnology and anthropology. Early in the nineteenth century most ethnological thinking about American Indians concerned itself with speculations about the origins of the New World races and their connection to Genesis (the divine origin of human beings according to Judaic-Christian traditions). There was an implicit question here: how did the societies of the world become so diverse, with such evidently disparate capacities for technological invention and social complexity? To put the question in the language of the time, if all mankind descends from a common Genesis, why are "we" so civilized while "they" are so savage? Lewis Henry Morgan, an extremely influential American anthropological theorist of the mid-nineteenth century, addressed this question when he reasoned that complex societies grew from simple ones. The differences between societies, he thought, lay in the fact that some had grown more complex than others. Therefore, these differences reflected stages of growth from simple to complex or, to use his terms, from "savage" to "civilized." Drawing upon the ideas of the English naturalist Charles Darwin, Morgan viewed social growth as a natural, almost biological process. He called it "social evolution." From his point of view, in its distant historical past European civilization had passed through a stage of "savagery" and now represented the uppermost stage of social evolution, which would continue to refine and improve itself through progress, while Native American societies remained at an abased evolutionary stage. Morgan and subsequent anthropologists reasoned that understanding processes of social evolution as a whole would profit from the study of what they considered to be living fossils of savagery: American Indians.

A society imagined to be stuck in an early stage of social evolution has no history. In fact, the only history of Native American societies that concerned many early anthropologists was their decline in the wake of American progress. These anthropologists, many of whom worked in the field and collected for museums, feared that Native American societies were destined to disappear altogether or would become so transformed by their contacts with civilization that they would no longer reflect accurately earlier stages of social evolution. They did not want their research tainted by "acculturation," a term that refers to changes resulting from contacts and interactions between Native American and European American

7 North Pacific Hall, American Museum of Natural History, c. 1910. The canoe full of figures is intended to represent the moment when a Chilkat Tlingit chief and his entourage arrive at a village as guests of a potlatch. Captives hold the canoe steady in the surf with poles as the nobles sing songs for those waiting on shore. The entire display freezes the customs of Northwest Coast natives in a timeless "ethnographic present."

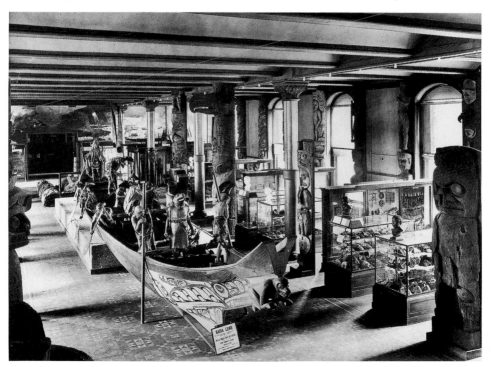

societies. During their fieldwork, these anthropologists interviewed elders and mined their memories for accounts of the old days before whites had come. When making their collections, they avoided "trinkets" made for sale because, as one anthropologist argued, "They chiefly embody the ideas of the white race and in no proper sense represent Indian arts." Anthropologists transcribed oral accounts of old ways and collected old things in order to preserve a record of Native American cultures in texts and museum collections that could be consulted long after Native societies had disappeared. When we read these older ethnographic texts or look at old museum representations of Native cultures (the North Pacific Hall at the American Museum of Natural History is a well-preserved example [7]), the cultures thus described seem situated in no particular historical moment, but timeless, forever enduring but, we know, enduring no more. We can call this conceptual moment of time without time, without history, the "ethnographic present."

More recent anthropology looks critically at this legacy of ethnographic research. Anthropologists today reject a model of unilinear social evolution. They remain interested in studying the dynamics of culture change but have become far more sensitive to the particularities of local histories. In this light, the history of the relations between Native communities and white outsiders becomes profoundly interesting: the histories of resistance, adaptation, and transformation (Gerald Vizenor's "survivance"). When earlier generations of anthropologists in the field failed to situate themselves historically within the context of the communities they studied, the texts they produced often failed to take notice of what was going on around them, how the acculturation they dismissed was part and parcel of a local history of culture change. As for those of us interested in the objects they collected for museums, we are less interested in them as examples of primitive technologies or design and more interested in the particular histories of their creation, use, and circulation. The so-called trinkets made for sale become extremely important in this regard, as artists adapted their craft to the possibilities of new consumers. And, not surprisingly, many of these kinds of objects ended up in museums when early anthropologists collected them while remaining ignorant of their local histories. Situating these objects historically dismantles the monolithic construct of the ethnographic present and restores the potential of a fuller understanding.

Artists

Individual artists are largely absent from the historical record of
Native America. Unlike the art histories of Europe, which are
largely biography-based, Native American art history has been
hard pressed to recover the names of the people who made
things. It is easy to see why. When objects were collected as
"artifacts," they were intended to be representative examples of
the kinds of things that the *culture* produced. With this emphasis
on culture, the identity of the individual is repressed.

Focusing on artists, however, their motivations, social
relations, and the cultural significance of the things they make,
brings into light the aesthetic system in which they operate. We
find culture through the individual, through personal experience,
not the other way around. The objects artists make are not simply
cultural expressions, but the creations of individuals intended to
fulfill cultural and social purposes. Their imagery, form, design,
symbolism, and iconography are intended to bring the ideas that
informed their creation into collective perception and help
motivate social action.

Consider for example, Big Plume, a Blackfeet man, and his
role in the creation of the "Lord's Shirt" now at the Denver Art
Museum [8]. Sometime before 1850, when Big Plume was on his
first war expedition and still quite young, he became separated
from his comrades. While lost and isolated, he dreamed of a
shining figure who comforted him each night for four successive
nights. On the last night, the shining figure wore a shirt pierced
with holes and instructed Big Plume to make one just like it. Big
Plume understood that the dream was in fact a spiritual encounter
and that the right to make the shirt had been given to him, along
with substantial spiritual powers. It was a common understanding
among the Blackfeet, and many other tribes as well, that dreams
sometimes offered such opportunities. Painted images for shield
designs or lodges (tipis), as well as designs for items of ceremonial
dress or special weapons, might be offered in dreams, and these
things held great potential for personal power and accomplishment.
Big Plume made the shirt, very likely with some help, and enjoyed
its benefits. But then, through a formal ritual of transfer, he gave it
to a man named Bear Chief. When Big Plume gave his shirt away,
he did not lose anything, because he retained the right to make
another. What he gained, in fact, was the formalized relationship
with Bear Chief and the social recognition of his spiritual power.
Big Plume made a second shirt and gave this one to Chewing
Black Bones. Bear Chief, who now also possessed the right to

reproduce the shirt, made a third version, which he gave to Albert Mad Plume. When this third shirt was destroyed in a fire, Albert Mad Plume made a fourth one. In the 1930s a fifth was made by a man named Three Calf, who had received the right to reproduce the shirt from Chewing Black Bones. It became known as the "Lord's Shirt," an awkward translation that refers to its spiritual origin. Potentially, many more shirts might have resulted from the original experience of Big Plume, but their proliferation depended upon formal rights of transfer that created indelible social bonds between those who owned them. The shirt, in fact, is simply the material expression of Big Plume's gift of spiritual power. The shirts were useless unless the spiritual and ritual knowledge remained tied to them, and this was accomplished through rituals of formal transfer from one recipient to another. The story of Big Plume and his shirt is useful to keep in mind since it illustrates a pattern of visionary origin and formalized circulation of art forms that seems to have recurred frequently in North America.

8 "Lord's Shirt," by an unknown Blackfeet artist, c. 1930. The shirt originated in a vision experienced by a man named Big Plume and was made in at least five different versions.

Art making, at some level, was a day-to-day activity for many in indigenous North America. Women of the Plains region customarily made and decorated clothing for their families. But there were always some who excelled. Among the nineteenth-century Kiowa of Oklahoma, it was customary to honor a favored child, an *auday*, with a cradle or baby carrier elaborately decorated with glass bead embroidery [9]. The parents might commission women widely recognized for their skills to make one for them. Or a female relation might be asked, if the family was fortunate enough to include a skilled beadworker among their kin. Over the years, such cradles have been separated from their families and found their way to museum collections. Barbara Hail, a scholar and museum curator, has been able to discover the names of several women who made cradles many years ago by interviewing their descendants and studying historic photographs.

The artists' experience reveals the family structure of support and lineage descent of training. In many instances, it was customary for artists to learn from elder relations, either biological or fictive. Excellence of artistic production led to personal and family prominence. Among many Native communities, the creation

9 Photograph of Lizzie Woodard (Kiowa) and child in a beaded cradle, c. 1890.

10 Headdress frontlet, attributed to Albert Edward Edenshaw (Haida), *c*. 1870. This carving tells the story of a man who captured and killed a sea-monster and now wears its skin. The man possessed the power to dive beneath the sea and hunt whales, like the one he holds in his hands.

and distribution of art were often tied to the obligations and potentialities of leadership.

In this regard, we might think about the life and art of Albert Edward Edenshaw, as brought to light by the research of art historian Robin Wright. Born sometime around 1812 in a small village on the Queen Charlotte Islands, also known as Haida Gwaii, Edenshaw grew up to be one of the most renowned chiefs of the nineteenth-century Haida. Like his maternal uncle and great-uncle, through which the name *7idansuu* (sic, later anglicized to "Edenshaw") had passed to him, Albert was also an artist. As Robin Wright explains, "Artists with a professional status on the northern Northwest Coast were usually members of the noble class who inherited their position and were trained as artists as well as leaders." Albert Edenshaw carved monumental memorial poles from great cedar logs for his wife's family, a customary obligation between clans joined by marriage. He trained himself as a blacksmith and, in one notable instance, salvaged guns burned in a fire on a shipwreck, repaired them, and sold them to increase his wealth. Some of his carvings survive today in museums. A frontlet (carved panel) for a headdress he made illustrates the Haida story of the young hero who killed a Wasgo, or sea-wolf [10]. In the carving, the hero wears its pelt like a headdress and holds a whale in his hands. Albert Edenshaw's skills and accomplishments as an artist were part and parcel of the obligations stemming from his noble status and they were critical to his success as a leader. As we shall see, art in indigenous North America frequently offered a path to social recognition and influence.

The perspective of the artist's experience also permits more insightful consideration of those artists who once negotiated between cultures through exchanges of gifts or sales to tourists, and those who operate in environments today that include both the art studio and local communities. The life of Albert Edenshaw's nephew, Charles Edenshaw, represents an important transition in this regard. Although he produced many objects customary to Haida social life, he is best known for his carvings of argillite, a black slate-like stone found on the Queen Charlotte Islands [11]. Charles trained under his uncle and assisted him with several important memorial poles in the villages of Skidegate and Masset, perhaps completing some commissions on his own. A number of frontlet headdresses are also attributed to his hand, but most of his known work was made for sale to outsiders. Charles also worked closely with ethnographers, making models of noble houses and house poles that accurately reproduced their complex designs for museum displays, and offered anthropologists invaluable detailed accounts of crest rights, genealogies, and

11 Charles Edenshaw (Haida), carving in his home, c. 1906. The argillite model of a memorial pole standing on the box in front of the artist is like the many he made for purchase by visitors to the Northwest Coast.

traditional stories. Late in his life, Charles lived and worked in Masset with his wife Isabella, herself an artist who wove baskets and hats of spruce root [12]. The argillite carvings, silver bracelets, painted hats and baskets they made could be purchased at a trading post at Port Essington and they often traveled to the larger towns and cities on the Northwest Coast – Juneau, Ketichican, and Victoria – to sell their work. Charles Edenshaw is considered today one of the most skilled, prolific, and influential artists of the Northwest Coast. He represents that historical moment, which occurred at many different times in many different places, as we shall see, when artists of indigenous America expanded their view from the local community to encompass the larger world that quickly came to surround them.

The expanse of that view, and its artistic potential when reconciling local with more worldly experience, is revealed in the biographies of many Native artists of the twentieth century. There is the case of the late George Morrison, who grew up with his Ojibwa family on the Grand Portage reservation on the Lake Superior shore of Minnesota. His paintings are best understood in the company of the Abstract Expressionist artists Franz Klein, Clyfford Still, and Jackson Pollock, who were his contemporaries and colleagues in New York City during the 1940s and 1950s. Late in his life, George Morrison told me that he "never used being Indian" in his work. There is no overt reference to American Indian themes, symbols, or stereotypes in any of his paintings, save perhaps for his focus on the subject of the northern Lake Superior shore which was the home of his childhood and the home of his senior years. Although active politically and culturally in Minneapolis, where he taught for many years, it is probably fair to say that Morrison's most powerful experiences of being "American Indian" stemmed from the sights, sounds, and feeling of his home community, Grand Portage. The paintings produced at Red Rock, his studio on Lake Superior, are profoundly authentic to that experience [172].

The lives of countless additional artists of Native American ancestry, active over a span that amounts to many thousands of years, remain hidden from view, but every object they made reflects the trace of their hands. With a focus on the artists and the social lives of the objects they made [13], even when their individual identities remain obscure, the significance of imagery, form, design, symbolism, and iconography becomes easier to grasp and understand. Although we can only approximate the meanings of many of the objects illustrated in this book, remembering that their meaning resides somewhere in the interplay between artist and audience provides us with a valuable starting point for interpretation.

13 Ceremonial feather belt made by a Maidu artist of California sometime between 1855 and 1870. Curator Stewart Culin purchased this belt for the Brooklyn Museum from Ann Barber in Chico, California, on 6 July 1908. The belt had been given to Mrs. Barber by her first husband, Pomaho, on the occasion of their marriage.

Chapter 2   Ancient Woodlands

Paleo-Indian origins

The character of the earliest art produced in North America is a matter of conjecture. Even the date of the earliest human habitation is a matter of some controversy. Many Native traditions of human origin recall the earliest ancestors emerging from the earth or descending from the sky. Others describe ancient migrations. The most widely accepted scientific view accounts for the peopling of the New World through migrations from Asia no more than 15,000 years ago when Siberia and Alaska were connected across the then-dry Bering Sea. Stone tools are the earliest objects that evidence human activity in North America. Archaeologists call the earliest Americans Paleo-Indians, from the Greek *palaios* for "ancient." Paleo-Indians may have woven baskets, painted hides, or worked with other kinds of ephemeral artistic media, but no evidence of such activity survives today. Archaeologists think they have identified some Paleo-Indian woodworking tools, such as scrapers, gravers, and adzes, but nobody knows what Paleo-Indians might have made of wood. The stone tools tell us, however, that these earliest Americans were consummate craftsmen and had a thorough knowledge of the sources and properties of the high-grade cherts they used to fabricate their tools and weapons.

Clovis culture, first identified at a site called Blackwater Draw near Clovis, New Mexico, represents the earliest, broadly based cultural pattern identifiable within the currently known archaeological record of North America. Clovis sites date from 13,500 to 12,900 years ago and they are scattered across much of North America, from Wyoming to New Mexico, from New York State to Florida. Although Clovis people made many different

kinds of tools of stone and bone, they are best known for the large, carefully made lance points with which they hunted Pleistocene mammoth and other now-extinct big game [14]. The blade's unique design, a narrow tapering profile with sharpened side edges and a technically challenging "flute" at the base for hafting, was intended to maximize the lance's ability to pierce the tough hides of big game prey. Their manufacture required a great deal of skill and flint-knappers today still disagree about the steps necessary to make one. Clovis blades have been recovered from kill sites where they are associated with the butchered carcasses of big game, from small village sites, and in various states of manufacture at quarry sites. In a few rare instances, groups of Clovis points have been discovered as isolated caches buried in the ground. The Fenn cache from an unknown site in southern Wyoming or northern Utah included a group of fifty-six high-quality bifaces, including many finished Clovis points, made of high-grade cherts, obsidian, jasper, and translucent quartz crystal. Here and in several other instances, the material used for Clovis blades had been quarried from sources hundreds of miles away from where the blades were eventually recovered. Who made these beautiful, technically challenging, and evidently highly coveted objects? Was it necessary to make one to own one, or was it possible or customary to procure them from others? How was the technical knowledge necessary for their manufacture passed on from one individual to another? What was the meaning of these objects when they were bundled together, covered with red ocher pigment (as was the case in some caches), and ceremonially buried in the ground? What did it mean to own such a collection

14 Clovis projectile points, c. 11,000 BC. These points, designed to hunt big game, are the earliest stylistically consistent, "culturally diagnostic" artifact type made in North America. The points are often made of materials that are high quality and difficult to procure, and that have strong visual qualities. Their design and techniques of manufacture would have required great skill to master. The creation, use, and circulation of the points by America's early peoples presage the importance of carefully crafted and highly valued material things in the social lives of Native Americans.

15 Wadlow blade of Burlington chert. Titterington focus, Late Archaic period, c. 1000 BC. Airport site, Springfield, Illinois. Groups of these long and elegant blades had been placed with burials at the site.

and how were such individuals regarded by others? In sum, what were the cultural values linked to such things, their manufacture, possession, and use, beyond and in addition to their technical utility? The evidence for Clovis points is just too scant for definitive answers, but the little there is hints at social roles for finely made objects among ancient North Americans, and this becomes far more clear in the archaeological record centuries later.

Implements, ornaments, and mortuary rituals of the Late Archaic

The Airport site, within present-day Springfield, Illinois, is located on an otherwise unremarkable sandy knoll produced by the outwash of retreating glaciers many thousands of years ago. Archaeological excavation has turned up three different episodes of cultural activity at the site, but in approximately 1000 BC thirteen individuals were buried here. Buried with them were thirteen extraordinary blades finely chipped of white Burlington chert [15]. They are long (the longest measures 9 in., or 23 cm), and thin, with graceful tapering shapes, and represent virtuoso flint-knapping skills. They are so delicate, however, that they are completely useless as tools or weapons and their surfaces show no signs of wear. Other blades of this shape and material have been found elsewhere in central Illinois, almost always with burials.

The burial component of the Airport site belongs to the Titterington focus of the Late Archaic period (3000–1000 BC). The Archaic period altogether (8000–1000 BC) represents a long era of slow population growth in Eastern North America, but the pace of growth and change quickened during the Late Archaic. By 5000 BC ground stone tools had entered into the archaeological record: grooved axes, adzes, and spear-thrower weights (atlatl weights). These were made with the peck-and-polish method: reductively hammering the surface of stone media into finished shape and then polishing the surfaces to a high luster. During the Late Archaic period, it becomes clear that some of these objects possessed significance beyond technological utility. Most of the evidence for this comes from the ways in which certain kinds of objects were treated during mortuary ceremonies.

The Indian Knoll site is all that remains of a large summer village near the banks of the Green River in central Kentucky. Evidently, hundreds of people gathered here every year during the Late Archaic period to harvest abundant freshwater mollusks and other summer foods, but also to bury their dead. Considering that

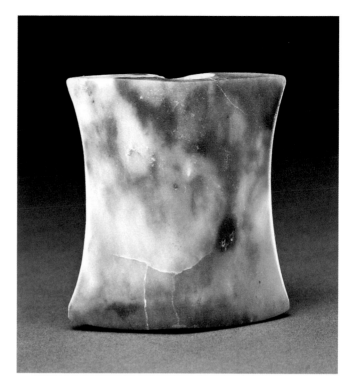

16 Bannerstone or atlatl weight of chalcedony. Late Archaic period, 3000–2000 BC. Indian Knoll site, Kentucky. The functional identity of this enigmatic, prism-shaped category of artifact was established at the Indian Knoll site, where archaeologists found bannerstones fitted on atlatls, or spear-throwers.

community members spent a good portion of the year dispersed into far-flung hunting territories as small family groups, the mortuary ceremony reinforced the identity of the larger group. The remains of ancestors resided at the Indian Knoll cemetery where their descendants would join them when their time came. It was customary for the living to place objects with the dead, most often weapons, tools, and ornaments. Several men were buried with atlatls, consisting of an antler handle, a straight wooden shaft, an antler hook at the end of the shaft, and a curious prism-shaped weight mounted in the center made of antler, shell, or stone. Indian Knoll atlatl weights of stone, sometimes called "bannerstones," are marvels of ground stone workmanship [16]. Their highly polished surfaces emphasize the textures and color of the granite, chalcedony, or banded siltstone chosen for material. Few of these varieties of stone are available locally and their procurement must have required special effort and knowledge of their sources. Furthermore, Indian Knoll bannerstones were not buried just with males of hunting age who may have used them. A few specially honored children and women also received them. One bannerstone was even strung on a necklace along with beads made of raw copper. Certainly, the totality of their meaning lay not only with their utilitarian purpose but also encompassed the skill and effort required to create them and the significance of possessing them, giving them away, or exchanging them with others.

Mortuary use of special categories of objects during the Late Archaic period anticipates the increasing importance of artful things in the social life of the Eastern Woodlands. We can only guess at the various occasions when members of the community recognized the efforts to procure visually arresting materials from distant sources and the skills that fashioned these media into significant form. We do not know what part these objects played in community life until such time when they were selected to accompany the dead during a mortuary ceremony. Here, as possessions of the dead, or gifts from survivors, they reflect a socially acknowledged identity. Perhaps control over these kinds of objects led to social prominence. For example, Indian Knoll residents sought out marine shell from sources on the southern Atlantic coast or Gulf of Mexico, which they carved into beads and pendants. Over time, analysis has shown, larger quantities of shell ornaments were concentrated among fewer and fewer individuals. One way to interpret the data is to posit that increased access to these valuables became concentrated within a smaller number of socially aspirant people.

Late Archaic peoples ranged across much of eastern North America to procure materials and objects. Doing so helped establish advantageous relations with distant neighbors as well as bring social recognition back home. And, always, these exotic materials were fashioned into significant form through the skills of artists. Around the Great Lakes and Midwest, burial sites were often located on the abundant natural elevations of this glacial terrain, distant from village sites. The Old Copper, Red Ocher, and

17 Three birdstones (atlatl bar weights?) of slate and porphyry. Late Archaic period, 1500–1000 BC. Red Ocher complex, Andrews site, Michigan. These three birdstones illustrate the range of visually resplendent materials used for sumptuary objects during the Late Archaic period.

18 Sandal sole gorget of marine shell. Late Archaic period, 1500–500 BC. Glacial Kame complex, William Spitzer Farm site, Ohio. The marine shell was imported from the southern Atlantic coast or the Gulf of Mexico. The animal, with its encircling tail and ear-like horns, resembles the Underwater Panther of later Great Lakes oral tradition (see figs 40, 50 and 175).

Glacial Kame burial complexes can be dated to the Late Archaic, but they are identified principally by the kinds of objects customarily found placed with the dead. Blades and implements hammered into shape from nuggets of copper (Ancient Woodlands peoples did not smelt copper) characterize Old Copper sites. Red Ocher burials are liberally sprinkled with this red pigment made of heated iron-based minerals. Individuals buried at the Andrews site, a Red Ocher site in Saginaw County, Michigan, possessed hundreds of oversized ceremonial blades made of fine Flint Ridge flint from Ohio, along with copper axes, awls, and beads. Four men were interred with effigy atlatl weights known today as birdstones due to the fact that they resemble seated birds with squared tails and pointed beaks [17]. Birdstone atlatl weights and marine shell ornaments known as sandal sole gorgets (pendants drilled with three holes for suspension or attachment to clothing) were favored objects at Glacial Kame sites. The distinctive shape of these latter ornaments were cut from large conch shells with sources ultimately along the southeast Atlantic shore or Gulf coast. Some rare sandal sole gorgets were carved with the images of animals [18] or with geometric, perhaps cosmologically inspired designs.

The Late Archaic Poverty Point culture of Louisiana imported Appalachian steatite from the east to make stone bowls, red

19 Jasper bead in the form of a locust or grasshopper, from Badlow Creek, Arkansas. Poverty Point culture, Late Archaic period, 1500–700 BC. Poverty Point artists developed a unique lapidary tradition, making exquisite effigy beads of imported jasper and other hard stone.

jasper for ornaments [19], galena from the upper Mississippi, and other exotic stone. Virtually nothing is known about Poverty Point burial practices, but some of their towns built massive earthworks. At one Poverty Point site, houses sat on six large embankments arranged as concentric semi-circles that stretched over an area of 500 acres. A massive earthen mound, 66 ft (20 m) high and 656 ft (200 m) long stands just to the west of the embankments. Archaeologists have long searched for evidence that this kind of town planning and the social organization required to construct such massive projects stemmed from Mesoamerican influence, but they have found nothing concrete to support this notion.

The Adena people
The Adena Mound, located just outside present-day Chillicothe, Ohio, had been the location of a circular enclosure made of upright wooden posts sunk into the ground. Inside, a modestly sized community or family group had gathered twenty-one of their dead, laying the bodies in carefully prepared tombs made of logs and lined with bark. At some point, they burned the structure and covered the charred remains with a mound of earth. Others, perhaps descendants of the original group, returned later, added more earth to the mound, and buried thirteen more members of the community.

Mortuary sites like the Adena Mound are found throughout south-central Ohio, northern Kentucky, and the upper watershed of the Ohio River to West Virginia. Their similarity of structural form and attributes of ritual practice suggest that the people who made them shared cultural attitudes, beliefs, and language. Archaeologists refer to them as Adena people. They also made a thick-walled, low-fired pottery, as did their neighbors to the west in present-day Illinois and elsewhere throughout the Mississippi valley. In the Eastern Woodlands region, the appearance of this kind of pottery marks the end of the Late Archaic period and the beginning of the Early Woodland, in about 1000 BC.

Copper bracelets and rings, blades made of fine Flint Ridge flint, ground stone ornaments, atlatl weights made of banded slate, and many other kinds of objects accompany Adena burials. Perhaps most extraordinary is an 8 in. (20 cm) pinkish stone effigy smoking pipe from the Adena Mound itself [20]. The pipe represents a man with an oversized head and short legs, standing in a slightly crouched position, arms held straight at his sides. He wears a garment around his loins, with large ornamental rings in his ears, and two crescent-shaped ornaments that curve back on either side of his head. Some of the people interred at the Adena Mound wore just such wrappers of woven fabric, and one wore a pair of crescent-shaped hair ornaments made of thin translucent mica. The sculptural image shows us, perhaps, the ceremonial dress of an Adena man. But the object is also a tubular smoking pipe, hollowed out on the inside. Tobacco was inserted at the bottom end and smoke drawn through a mouthpiece located on the top of the head. Two other smoking pipes without effigy carving, both elegant hollowed cylinders of the same pink stone with narrowed beveled mouthpieces, had been placed in two other tombs at the site.

Tobacco lies at the center of religious practice in Eastern North America. The origin stories for tobacco recall in oral tradition how it had been given to human beings by the Creator so that they, in turn, would have something to offer back to spirit beings in thanks for their blessings. Its ritual use addresses core values of giving, of offering, to spirits, ancestors, or any members of the unseen world whose influence or attitudes may affect the destinies of men and women. Carbonized remains of *Nicotiana rustica*, the most commonly used Native American tobacco, have been identified at North American sites dating from AD 100, but smoking pipes evidencing smoking technology enter into the archaeological record hundreds of years earlier, during the Late Archaic period. *Nicotiana rustica* had been domesticated as early as 3000 BC somewhere on the eastern slope of the Andes, in present-day Peru. The technology of its cultivation had spread subsequently through Mesoamerica and entered North America, perhaps through the Southeast via the Caribbean. For those Adena who possessed smoking pipes, knowledge of tobacco, the ability to cultivate it, the artistry required to fashion smoking pipes, and the performance of smoking rituals all contributed to their social distinction and very likely represented great power.

20 Effigy pipe of pipestone. Adena culture, Early Woodland period, *c.* 800–100 BC. Adena site, Ohio. This unique miniature sculpture functions as a tubular smoking pipe for tobacco. The ornaments and garments worn by the sculpted figure resemble those found at other Adena sites.

The many different kinds of objects placed with the dead during Adena burial rituals undoubtedly possessed other kinds of socially constituted significance, as gifts or possessions, representing wealth, knowledge, special abilities or statuses. Oversized ceremonial blades, ornaments and atlatl weights of ground and polished banded slate, distinctive copper ornaments, all testify to extraordinary artistic knowledge and skill. But we can only guess at the social roles of those who created them and the distinctions they enjoyed. Bone awls for leather-working and woven textiles hint at more ephemeral arts. Palette stones for grinding pigment suggest graphic art forms. Sandstone tablets carefully engraved with images of birds and composite human and animal figures may have been used for printing on textiles or hide garments [21].

If tobacco and smoking pipes were only one of several such bodies of specialized knowledge and skill, they were not shared with everyone. Only a few of the Adena possessed smoking pipes, and they were highly regarded if their treatment during burial offers a clue. How was such knowledge and skill passed from one person to another? What were the benefits of exchanging such

21 Wilmington engraved tablet of sandstone. Adena culture, Early Woodland period, c. 500 BC. Wilmington site, Ohio. This is one of several remarkable sandstone tablets recovered from Adena sites, engraved with strange images of animals and other creatures. Here, two bird heads with long, curved beaks face one another on the left-hand side. They also read as smiling faces with beard-like appendages curling beneath their chins.

knowledge? Did the power and social prestige for those who knew of pipes and tobacco, or the many other specialized Adena art forms for that matter, derive in part from the social ties that resulted when their knowledge was exchanged with others? Did the social fortunes of those who sought out such specialized knowledge rise within their own communities once they possessed it and initiated network exchanges of their own? Knowledge of Adena art forms, and many Adena objects themselves, spread east by some such mechanism of exchange, instruction, and emulation. Adena-style objects including tubular smoking pipes appear, albeit rarely, in the burials of the Point Peninsula people in present-day New York State. Some even penetrated as far east as the St. Lawrence river region and the Chesapeake Bay area.

Hopewell

The term Hopewell refers to a site in southern Ohio and is also used to describe the expansion of mortuary ceremonialism, inter-regional exchange, and startling artistic developments all across the Woodlands region. This episode of distinctive inter-cultural activity within the "Hopewell Interaction Sphere" defines the period known as Middle Woodland (200 BC to AD 400). The Ohio Hopewell people led the way in terms of the broad extent of their far-flung contacts and sources for materials and the energy invested in the creation of elaborate objects. They were the successors to the Adena in southern Ohio and evidently built upon their ritual accomplishments.

Over a period of some six hundred years, the Ohio Hopewell erected hundreds of large ceremonial structures along the terraces of the Scioto valley. Inside, they gathered the dead, laying some in log tombs or on raised platforms, and cremating others in carefully prepared basins excavated into the floor. Archaeologists call these buildings "charnel houses" or "great houses." They were made with support posts of wood and walls of bark or wattle and daub. Interior partitions created separate rooms and passageways. Once the appropriate rituals for the dead were complete, or triggered by some other unknown event or occasion, the great house was burned and a mound of earth piled over the remains. Some Ohio Hopewell sites include dozens of such structures and their subsequent mounds built sequentially over time. Monumental enclosures made of earth embankments marked the locations of the sites. Some of these earthworks include giant circles, squares, octagons, and avenues that spread across the

22 Circle and octagon earthworks at the Newark site, Newark, Ohio. Ohio Hopewell culture, Middle Woodland period, AD 1–200. Monumental earthworks marked the locations of charnel house sites of the Ohio Hopewell.

23 Great Serpent Mound, Ohio, c. AD 1070. Recent carbon 14 dates from Serpent Mound indicate a construction date consistent with the dates of the Fort Ancient culture, a people who built other, far less impressive serpent effigies of stone cobbles elsewhere in Ohio. These earth sculptures may have been inspired in part by earlier Ohio Hopewell earthworks.

landscape over thousands of acres [22]. Here people gathered regularly to reconnect with related families or clans, perform rituals for the dead, host visitors, feast, trade, build, repair or add additions to the great houses, and expand the earthen constructions.

As had been customary within the region for the previous thousand years, artistic objects accompanied the dead. But never before so many, made with such a broad variety of materials gathered from so many distant locations across the continent

24 Effigy platform pipe of pipestone. Ohio Hopewell culture, Middle Woodland period, 200 BC–AD 200. Tremper site, Ohio. This smoking pipe is designed so that tobacco can be inserted in the bowl within the bird's back and the smoke drawn from a hole drilled through to the front edge of the platform. The rear of the platform provides a handle that remains cool to the touch.

and fashioned with such artistry and skill. The knowledge and effort that led to their creation, and the distinctions that ownership bestowed, culminated in the mortuary ceremony and its significant moment of ritual consumption and separation from active social life. But it would be a mistake to assume that the ultimate purpose of these objects was simply to be buried with the dead. Like the Adena, members of Ohio Hopewell communities used objects and ritual knowledge to create and sustain social relationships with others and to build social recognition for themselves and their kin. The great mortuary ceremonies held at locations marked by massive earthworks [23] attracted guests from far and wide, to participate, to exchange objects and ritual knowledge, and to offer support and recognition to their socially aspirant hosts.

A mound community, meaning the social group or groups defined by their burial within a single mound, evidently possessed mastery over certain kinds of art forms and their attendant ritual significance. For example, hundreds of distinctive smoking pipes were burned and buried together with the individuals cremated at the Tremper site located in the southern Scioto valley. These diminutive "platform pipes" represent a startling innovation in smoking pipe design. Instead of the Adena hollowed cylinder, these have an upright bowl perched on a thin, squared, horizontal platform with a draw hole drilled into one end. Many of the pipe bowls at Tremper were carved with sculptural images of animals – birds, frogs, mammals – all finished with remarkable descriptive detail [24]. The hands of a small number of individual artists are visible among the set and the ensemble includes four or more different kinds of raw material for manufacture. It is plausible to believe that ownership of one of these pipes was part of the social bond that resulted in membership within the mound community. Their bodies and ceremonial possessions were eventually all gathered together for cremation in the Tremper charnel house.

Large collections of hundreds of closely related effigy platform pipes characterized the mound communities at Mounds 8 and 13 of the Mound City site, signaling their close ties to the community at Tremper. Effigy platform pipes also came into the possession of far more distant partners. Individual examples, rather than large collections, were included in the burial ceremonies of some prominent members of Havana communities resident in the lower Illinois valley, Crab Orchard communities of southern Illinois [25], and elsewhere more sporadically throughout the Southeast. The regional distribution of this unique art form can be read as a map of social relationships among and between communities that participated in effigy platform pipe ritualism.

Ohio Hopewell mound communities developed many additional specializations of ritual arts. Making objects of copper was one of the most significant. The charnel house beneath Mound 25, the largest of the Hopewell group, was filled with all manner of copper objects. A vast collection – 23 oblong-shaped copper plates and 66 copper "celt" axes, including one 23 in. (58 cm) in length and weighing 37 lb (17 kg) – had been arranged near two men on the charnel house floor. Nearby lay a collection of more than 120 copper stencils cut into the shapes of fish,

25 Conglomerate effigy platform pipe. Crab Orchard culture, Middle Woodland period, 200 BC–AD 400. Rutherford site, Illinois. When smoking tobacco in this small, intimately scaled pipe, the effigy carved on the bowl would have confronted the smoker face-to-face. An almost identical pipe, carved by the same maker from a brown pipestone, was buried with a prominent man of the Havana culture, who lived in the Illinois river valley to the north of Crab Orchard territory.

26 Falcon effigy cut-out of copper. Ohio Hopewell culture, Middle Woodland period, 200 BC–AD 400. Mound City site, Ohio. This is one of several copper cut-outs placed around the edges of a crematory basin in Mound 7, including another falcon effigy, a mask-like ornament, and a headdress with copper horns.

serpents, crosses, and other enigmatic patterns. Evidently these had been sewn to two elaborate ensembles of regalia that had been displayed on scaffolding inside the great house. Dozens of individuals, their bodies placed on low platforms, lay with copper plates placed beneath their heads and hips and distinctive "bi-cymbal" copper ear spools near their heads or hands. Some wore elegant copper headdresses. Ornaments of copper, mica, bears' teeth, and beads of shell and freshwater pearl were sewn to garments such as shirts, sashes, and belts. Other Ohio Hopewell mound communities possessed significant collections of copper ornaments as well, hinting at relationships between them. At Mound 7 of the Mound City group, a smaller number of individuals had been interred with copper headdresses, some fashioned with animal horns, ornaments, and copper plates cut into the silhouettes of falcons [26], patterns of eagles' heads and strange animal-like forms.

Copper itself, oral traditions inform us, possesses great spiritual significance. Its power stems from the earth and the underworld beneath it, the location for the ultimate destination of the dead. Some of the headdresses and ornaments of the Ohio Hopewell allude to the ritual treatment of corpses: images of torsos without heads, hands, or feet, and detached hands and heads. Mica appears important in this regard as well. The floors of some charnel houses had been laid with broad mosaics of cut

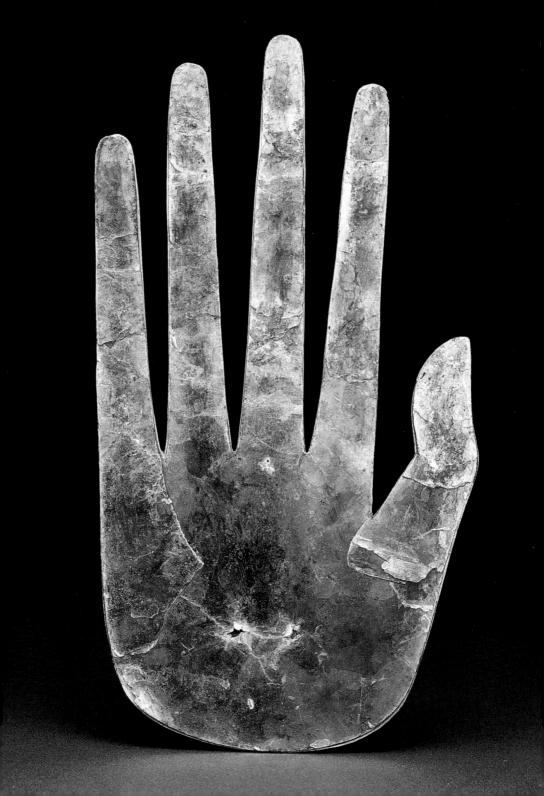

mica, or burial platforms covered with it. Some of the most artful of the Ohio Hopewell creations are graceful forms cut from thin delicate sheets of mica. They parallel the imagery of animals, animal parts, and ritually prepared human body fragments that predominate among copper objects. Mica cut-outs representing a human hand [27] and a headless torso came from Hopewell Mound 25.

While copper headdresses and stencil cut-outs were almost exclusive to Ohio Hopewell mound sites, bi-cymbal ear spools and copper panpipes, both sometimes combined with silver, circulated well beyond the Scioto valley. They were included in dozens of Middle Woodland period mortuary ceremonies dispersed from Florida to Ontario and as far west as Missouri. The forms originated among the Ohio Hopewell, but knowledge of them and the desire to possess them spread outward. Preliminary tests suggest that some from the Southeast are imitations made of locally quarried copper. In some manner, they all tie back to those powerful individuals with their hordes of copper and copper-decorated regalia belonging to the Hopewell and Mound City mound groups.

The flow of objects and ritual knowledge was not a one-way street, however. The diffusion of distinctive categories of ritual objects during the Middle Woodland period reveals several different conduits of cultural exchange. Finely made earthenware pottery incised with stylized images of birds links the Havana culture of the Illinois valley with the Marksville culture of the lower Mississippi. Small figurines modeled of terracotta evidence close relations between Middle Woodland societies of the Southeast with the Allison and Crab Orchard cultures of southern Indiana and Illinois. And marine shell from the Atlantic coast of the southeast and the Gulf region continued to circulate throughout the Woodlands region, as it had for centuries. The Middle Woodland period is best characterized as an extended episode of great inter-regional interaction, during which the exchange of exotic raw materials, finished objects, and ritual knowledge established social ties between geographically disparate communities. Within these societies, artists, entrepreneurs, and ritual specialists, characteristics perhaps combined in many socially ascendant individuals, enjoyed great prestige and social recognition.

It would be a mistake to think of the Hopewell Interaction Sphere as a comprehensive network of trade or the diffusion of a unified religious movement. More accurately, it can be

27 Hand effigy cut-out of muscovite mica. Ohio Hopewell culture, Middle Woodland period, 200 BC–AD 400. Hopewell site, Ohio. This and other Ohio Hopewell art works allude to how the heads and hands of the dead were sometimes privileged for special treatment during mortuary ceremonies.

characterized by the interplay between many different episodes of inter-regional interaction. Even Ohio Hopewell mortuary sites show shifts of emphasis over time, although the historical relationships between sites and the historical development within large, complex mound sites themselves are not well understood. It is clear, however, that by AD 400 inter-regional activity had diminished. The large earthwork sites on the Scioto river terraces had become inactive, with the exceptions of "Intrusive Mound" burials resulting from sporadic visits to these sacred sites by later peoples to bury their dead. The flow of exotic materials from distant locations also declined. A similar insularity is visible in the cultures descendant from other Hopewell Interaction Sphere participants. Mound burial continued in the Illinois valley, but without evidence of strong contacts with outsiders. The decline of the Hopewell Interaction Sphere and the circulation of the distinctive objects linked to it marked the end of the Middle Woodland period and the onset of the Late Woodland (AD 400–900).

It is a good bet that leadership among Middle Woodland societies derived from control and mastery of ritual knowledge, particularly tied to mortuary ceremonialism, strong ties to extra-regional partners, and the skills of artistic manufacture. The efforts made by individuals and their families to excel among their communities resulted in the achieved status of leadership. Artistic objects and the ideas they evoked were the palpable evidence of the powers the leadership controlled. A similar role for artistic objects developed among the far more hierarchical societies of the Mississippian chiefdoms that arose in the Woodlands region after AD 900.

Mississippian arts of leadership

The technologies of agriculture became the principal engine of culture change leading to the development of complex chiefdoms during the Mississippian period (AD 900–1600). Knowledge of corn, first domesticated in Mesoamerica, entered into North America via the Southwest during the first millennium BC and had been introduced to the Woodlands region by the second century AD. But corn agriculture played practically no role in the societies of the Hopewell Interaction Sphere. Knowledge of and dependence upon corn agriculture, supplemented by the cultivation of beans and squash, expanded during the Late Woodland period. The growing populations that agriculture supported, and the increasing need for effective social organization necessary to cultivate and defend prime agricultural lands, created opportunities for the emergence of Mississippian chiefdoms.

Centralized power required monumental symbols to sanction its authority. These appeared with startling abruptness at Cahokia, indigenous North America's largest town [28]. Cahokia is located in one of North America's most fertile regions, the American Bottom, where the Missouri, Illlinois, and Mississippi rivers come together to deposit rich alluvial soil. Agricultural communities had farmed the region since AD 600, but the resident population coalesced into powerful political unity in about AD 1050. The town of Cahokia, located in present-day East St. Louis, became established as a capital that dominated a hierarchy of surrounding settlements scattered over a region, according to some estimations, of some 60 to 90 square miles (95–145 km). The leaders of Cahokia directed the construction of enormous platform mounds made of earth that raised their chiefly residences and temples high over the surrounding countryside. The platform mounds flanked a large open plaza designed for the performance of public ritual. An encircling stockade built of upright logs defended this administrative and sacred core of the extended Cahokia community.

28 Artist's rendering of the town of Cahokia, East St. Louis, Illinois. Mississippian culture, AD 1200. Surrounded by a wood stockade, the political and religious center of the town was the central plaza, dominated by Monks Mound, a monumental, four-tiered platform mound. A court for playing chunkey, a game linked to divination, was located in the middle of the plaza, as marked by two striped poles.

The platform mound became the principal symbol of Mississippian chieftaincy. The chiefs of Cahokia renewed and enlarged the town's central mound, called Monks Mound today, several times between the years AD 1050 and 1200, until it rose over 100 ft (30 m) high. The pattern of renewal and growth resembles in part Ohio Hopewell great house ceremonies. Some of the temples were in fact charnel houses for the elite where priests, who themselves were members of high-ranking lineages, cared for the remains of Mississippian chiefs and their relations. Marking an interval of renewal, temples were customarily burned and their contents interred under a fresh mantle of earth which enlarged the mound. A new structure was then built on top, renewing the cycle. Platform mounds supporting residences of chiefs were also periodically destroyed and renewed. As the pattern of Mississippian chieftaincy established at Cahokia and elsewhere in the Mississippi valley spread throughout the broader Southeast over subsequent centuries, platform mound architecture spread with it. Often, smaller Mississippian towns built two mounds, one for the residence of the ruling lineage and one for the temple where their physical remains were cared for after death. These mounds represented simultaneously the political and religious center of the community.

The structure of Mississippian chieftaincy did not expand so much by conquest and migration as by emulation. Cahokia in fact succumbed to internal dissention (the site was all but abandoned during the fourteenth century). Meanwhile other town centers with platform mound architecture emerged all across the Southeast. The Mississippian pattern offered a kind of template for social organization, with a core ideology and symbols of power that could be adapted in slightly variant forms by ethnically diverse groups throughout the Woodlands region.

The sacred origins of the ruling lineage lay at the center of Mississippian thought. According to the Natchez of the lower Mississippi valley, Mississippian chiefs traced their descent from the sun. Each living chief was a personification of this originating power. The remains of sacred ancestors cared for in charnel houses and subsequently interred within a platform mound traced back ultimately to the lineage's sacred point of origin. Living Mississippian chiefs reinforced this notion with large-scale sculptures installed in their temples thought now to represent origin ancestors. Some of the most impressive of these were created for the temple of Mound C at Etowah, a Mississippian town located in northwest Georgia. Several massive stone figurines have been excavated from the mound. They had been housed in the temples on top of the mound, but when the temples were ritually destroyed, their contents had been buried during episodes of mound expansion. The largest temple figures from Etowah, a male and female couple carved from white marble and painted, exhibit a stolid monumentality [29]. They sit in poses that emphasize gender, the man with his legs crossed in front and the woman seated on her calves. He wears a close-fitting cap, while her tresses, gathered and loosely wrapped, fall between her shoulders. The faces of both are painted with broad bands of dark indigo pigment ranging across the eyes. Similarly conceived temple figures have been excavated from several other Mississippian sites.

29 Seated male and female effigies of marble. Mississippian culture, c. AD 1400. Etowah site, Georgia. This impressive couple were carved and painted to resemble the appearance of Mississippian chiefs, but they are also intended to evoke the sacred origins of Mississippian leadership by representing the primordial couple who originated the ruling lineage.

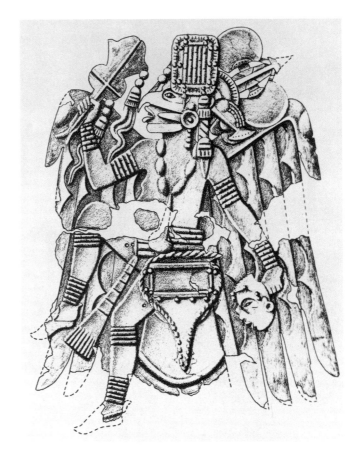

30 Rogan plate of copper. Mississippian culture, AD 1200–1450. Etowah site, Georgia. This copper plate, probably intended to fit on a headdress, represents a member of the Mississippian elite dancing in a costume with the attributes of a falcon. The falcon was revered by Mississippian warriors due to its aggressive attacks on flying prey while hunting.

The necessity of defense and the advantages of conquest reinforced strong military values among Mississippian towns. Some Mississippian ornaments show warriors with their faces decorated with the distinctive forked-eye markings of the peregrine falcon (*Falco peregrinus*), one of the most aggressive raptors of North America. Other warriors possess the attributes of eagles. One such image of a dancing warrior dressed with the mask and wings of a raptor was worked with repoussé technique upon a thin copper plate from Etowah where it probably functioned as part of a headdress [30]. The warrior holds a mace aloft in one hand and a decapitated human head in the other. While the image suggests a kind of mythic half-man, half-bird, almost every detail of the elaborate regalia worn by the dancing figure is replicated by artifacts and ornaments recovered during the excavation of Mound C, including a cloak-like armature to support costume wings. The image evidently represents a ritual performance in which the intimidating powers of predatory birds were evoked through costume and dance as a prerogative of Mississippian leadership.

Disk-shaped marine shell gorgets worn on the breast distinguished social roles and status in many Mississippian communities. Etowah evidently supported a particularly accomplished artist or workshop that produced marine shell gorgets for use there but also for trade, since several closely related examples found their way to Mississippian towns in eastern Tennessee. Many of the Etowah gorgets were carved with variants of the bird-warrior theme [31]. Their designs are crafted with delicate engraving combined with filigree-like carving. The production and distribution of prestige goods, like marine shell gorgets, supported the legitimization and expansion of Mississippian social hierarchies. Local aspirants to power sought links to established leaders and access to the powerful symbols of authority they controlled. It is plausible to believe that the artists, with their mastery over sacred materials and imagery, were drawn from the ranks of elite lineages or, perhaps in some cases, were the chiefs themselves. At Moundville, an important Mississippian ceremonial center in Alabama, waste from shell carving suggests that mound-top temples also functioned as workshops.

31 Marine shell gorget. Mississippian culture, c. AD 1400. Hixon site, Tennessee. The image carved on this circular gorget seems to represent a pair of falcon warriors locked in ritual combat. This ornament of the elite was worn suspended on the breast.

32 "Craig-style" design from an engraved shell cup. Caddoan culture, Mississippian period, AD 1100–1350. Spiro site, Oklahoma. This is a design from one of hundreds of cups made from conch shells interred in the "Great Mortuary" at the Spiro site.

The Craig Mound of the Spiro site, located in northeastern Oklahoma, contained the "Great Mortuary," an enormous assemblage of ancestral relics and artistic prestige goods that had been gathered from temples throughout the Caddoan territories for ultimate deposition there. The objects included hundreds of marine-shell cups engraved with images, shell gorgets, copper plates (probably for headdresses), wooden temple figures, stone smoking pipes and figurines, and a vast array of ornaments and ceremonial weapons. Many of these items had been imported from other distant Mississippian centers. Two very distinct styles of shell engraving have been identified, the "Craig style" [32], perhaps local, and the "Braden style" [33], with clear links to objects from the vicinity of Cahokia well to the north. Artists engraved large cups made from entire conch shells (*Busycon sp.*) with images of mythic beings and ritual performances. The corpus represents a virtual encyclopedia of Mississippian iconography, or what some archaeologists call the "Southeastern Ceremonial Complex."

In addition to Braden-style engraving, the Spiro assemblage suggests other links to Cahokia. Some of the most remarkable sculpture assembled at Spiro had been created by a workshop at or near Cahokia. These are figurines and large-scale smoking

33 "Braden-style" design from an engraved shell cup. Cahokia culture, Mississippian period, AD 1000–1250. Spiro site, Oklahoma. Braden style relates to engraved designs produced in the vicinity of Cahokia, well to the north of Spiro where this shell cup was found. Note the otter skin turban worn by the figure and the bird-head designs painted or tattooed on his body.

pipes made with locally quarried soft fine-grained red stone that is perfectly adaptable to carving. One figurine found in the greater vicinity of Spiro (not included in the Great Mortuary assemblage) shows a man playing the game of chunkey [34]. Chunkey play involved rolling a small stone disk on end down a prepared playing field, and then casting darts to land where the players predicted the chunkey stone would stop. In Mississippian thought, the game was linked to the arts of divination and was considered another important attribute of chiefly power. The open plazas situated between Mississippian platform mounds often included chunkey courts. Several shell engravings and gorgets also show chunkey players or include images of the distinctive barber-stripe poles that mark chunkey courts. A large collection of exquisitely crafted chunkey stones (archaeologists call them discoidals) accompanied the burial of a powerful chief at Cahokia, testifying to the chiefly significance of the game. Other red stone figurines and pipes from the Cahokia workshop represent Mississippian warriors, seated chiefs wearing impressive regalia, and mythic characters linked to agricultural fertility. They have been found at sites scattered throughout Illinois, at Spiro in Oklahoma, and even at Moundville, in south-central Alabama.

34 Bauxite chunkey player, from the Arkansas River valley, Oklahoma. Mississippian period, AD 1200–1350. This is one of several red stone figures and pipes made by an artist or group of artists near Cahokia, but circulated out to several distant communities, including Spiro in Oklahoma and Moundville in Alabama.

35 Ceramic bottle (Avenue polychrome), from Arkansas. Late Mississippian period, AD 1400–1600. The images of the sun painted on this bottle refer to the celestial origins of Mississippian chiefs, who traced their lineages back to this most powerful spirit-being of the sky world.

36 Ceramic head effigy jar (Carson red on buff), from Missouri. Late Mississippian period, AD 1400–1550. This jar probably represents an ancestral Mississippian chief whose remains, principally the head, hands, and leg bones, would have been kept preserved in a temple placed high on a platform mound. Archaeologists have found head effigy vessels like this one among the contents of such temples after they had been buried in the mounds during a ritual of renewal.

Trade in Mississippian prestige goods continued up and down the Mississippi valley long after the decline of Cahokia and the end of activity at Spiro (approximately AD 1400). The fertile territories flanking the river supported several Mississippian towns and their tributary settlements, each characterized by platform mound architecture and protected by encircling stockades. Many towns produced highly decorated or sculptural pottery vessels and traded them with other communities. Their designs often employ cosmological symbols: a cross within a circle as a reference to the four cardinal directions and the circular horizon of the terrestrial earth; images of the sun [35]; spirals that suggest the vortices of the watery underworld. Sculptural vessels represent animals, mythic creatures, or strange human figures with hunchbacks, bloated torsos and withered limbs (some archaeologists see these features as signs of a certain variety of tuberculosis). Rare jars skillfully modeled as images of human heads represent preserved relics of ancestral chiefs, whose actual remains resided within the community temple [36]. These evocative ceramic wares ultimately accompanied the burials of the elite, either in temple mounds or nearby community cemeteries.

Despite the fact that Mississippian cultures had evolved the most complex and populous societies of indigenous North America, few seem to know that fact today. And yet the earliest European visitors to the Southeast contended with the Mississippians. Hernando de Soto's expedition across the Southeast in 1540 to 1542 encountered many of the dominant Mississippian chiefdoms of the time. De Soto's army traversed Coosa, a complex chiefdom that had eclipsed and absorbed Etowah, by kidnapping the paramount chief and his sister, mother of the heir. Later De Soto's army fought a terrible battle at Mabila, a large Mississippian town in the vicinity of Moundville in Alabama. The Powhatan chiefdom that faced English settlement in Virginia was organized essentially along the lines of the Mississippian pattern. The Natchez of the lower Mississippi was the longest enduring Mississippian chiefdom until it succumbed to the French during their war of 1730. But the most devastating enemy of Mississippian social organization was European disease. Terrible epidemics decimated its chiefdoms and large nucleated settlements for a century after initial contact with Europeans. Nearly all of the towns encountered by De Soto along the Mississippi River in 1542 had been abandoned by the time French fur trader Louis Jolliet and Jesuit missionary Father Jacques Marquette descended the great river from the Upper Great Lakes in 1673. The descendants of the Mississippians re-organized. They include Muskogeans (Creek, Seminole), Cherokees, Choctaws, Chickasaws, Caddos, Chiwere Sioux (Winnebago, Oto, Iowa), Degiha Sioux (Iowa, Osage, Ponca, Quapaw), and others. Although the structures of Mississippian societies faded from the practice of community organization, Mississippian art and ideology stamped an indelible impression on subsequent traditions of the woodlands, prairies and plains.

Chapter 3   Eastern Woodlands

Visitors from another world

The first encounters between Native people of the northeast and European visitors began slowly and cautiously. The Norse attempted a short-lived settlement in Newfoundland at L'Anse aux Meadows (the "Vineland" referred to in Norse sagas) just after AD 1000 but it proved too difficult to support logistically and was quickly abandoned. Norse parties from the far more successful Greenland settlements occasionally ventured westward to North America thereafter, searching for timber and walrus ivory but wary of aggressive Inuit. Basque whalers and French cod fishermen worked the waters off Newfoundland after AD 1500. When they put to shore to process their catches, Native people approached to trade. Settlements up the St. Lawrence, and in Virginia and New England, followed later during the sixteenth century. While European interests in North America were varied and complex, Native willingness to engage their early visitors was motivated largely by opportunities to acquire the marvelous things they brought with them: metal tools and implements, glass and silver ornaments, and cloth. From a North American standpoint, the opportunities for trade represented the principal motivation for tolerating the newcomers. The realization that the threat of European force of arms required careful and accommodating diplomacy came afterward, quickly for some, more slowly for others.

The trade in animal pelts for products of European manufacture dominated the first few centuries of relations between indigenous North Americans and Europeans. The trade had profound effects upon the organization of Native social life, inter-tribal relations, and, certainly, the complexion of Native arts.

In the previous chapter, we saw how, for thousands of years, the procurement and circulation of precious materials and highly crafted and symbolic objects had been intertwined thoroughly with indigenous values of wealth, influence, leadership, and access to spiritual power. Trade with Europeans offered these same opportunities, but with novel and invaluable materials and things. During the first centuries of encounter, Native communities absorbed the new offerings of the trade into longstanding systems of indigenous aesthetics and understandings of the world.

Most immediately, the potentialities of European technologies provoked profound changes. Over a period of centuries, many tribes of the Northeast abandoned the production of pottery in favor of brass kettles. The gun revolutionized hunting and warfare. Iron and steel tools altered the practice of basic tasks. Consider, for example, Iroquois hair combs carved of moose antler in the sixteenth and seventeenth centuries. The nations of the Iroquois (or Haudenosaunee) confederacy, Mohawk, Oneida, Cayuga, Onondaga, and Seneca, had grown in prominence and population for centuries prior to European contact. Spread from east to west across what is now central New York State, their access to European trade had been indirect during the sixteenth century, from the French in the St. Lawrence region to the northeast. The founding of Dutch settlements during the early seventeenth century on the upper Hudson near present-day Albany changed all that. When moose antler combs had been carved with blades made with sharpened beaver incisors, they had no more than three or four tines and rudimentary if any decorative carving on the crest. Steel blades made possible such elaborate carvings as can be seen on a comb recovered by archaeologists from the remains of a Cayuga village of the mid-seventeenth century. The extended row of narrow parallel tines and fine carving reflect the carver's mastery of metal tools. Most remarkable is the intricate rendering of two men on horseback wearing brimmed hats, images of Dutch, French or English neighbors (the English seized New Netherlands in 1664) [37]. Some propose that this image commemorates a visit by English dignitary Wentworth Greenhalgh in 1677, but the several images of riders on horseback that grace Iroquois combs during this period may refer more generally to powers and wealth which the outsiders seemed to possess in such great abundance.

The notion that Native peoples were irresistibly drawn to trade goods due to their technical superiority conceals the fact that only some of the objects sought by Native trade partners –

iron axes, steel knives, brass kettles, and guns – contributed to any increased productivity or security. Over time, as the market became saturated with these kinds of goods, the far larger proportion of trade supplied raw materials of dress and ornament – wool and cotton cloth, silk ribbon, glass beads, silver ornaments. Native traders evaluated these things from within a frame of reference that recognized in them familiar symbolic and spiritual properties. For example, the white, red, and blue glass beads that dominated early trade corresponded to earlier Native ornaments of white shell, red catlinite (stone), and blue-green copper. The possession, circulation, and display of these materials played to longstanding indigenous values that extolled them as expressions of success, wealth, and leadership. Artists, principally women, began to innovate techniques that transformed trade materials into ensembles of formal dress and regalia.

37 Comb of moose antler, carved by a Cayuga man, 17th century. The carving on this comb shows two European riders wearing their characteristic hats. These images are among the earliest Native representations of European visitors.

Artificial curiosities

The bygone world of early European and Native relations is revealed to us today through a filter governed by the historical events of collecting and preservation. Excavations of old village sites recover only the most durable of objects and materials but, on occasion, European visitors took things home with them that came from the hands of Native people they encountered. We value these earliest, precious few objects preserved in museums, but it would be a mistake to think of them as unmediated by the circumstances of their collection. Within encounters where the character of relations would be managed, to a large degree, through the exchange of things (trade), one must look critically at the objects selected by Native peoples for Europeans to collect.

Consider, for example, the object known today as "Powhatan's mantle," preserved in the Ashmolean Museum in Oxford, England [38]. It is, in fact, four deerskins stitched together with sinew to create a large oblong mat of some 7 by 4 ft (2.1 by 1.2 m). Finely worked shell beads are sewn to one side of the deerskins to create a design that shows a full-length human figure flanked by two long-eared animals and surrounded by thirty-four disks. John Tradescant (1570–1638), gardener to the King of England, assembled the collection that would become the present-day Ashmolean Museum. As a student of botany, he collected plants from all over the world and many other exotic things as well. The earliest description of the collection comes from a German traveler named Georg Christoph Stirn, who reported in 1638 such exotica as "a bat as large as a pigeon, a human bone weighing 42 lbs, Indian arrows such as are used by the executioners in the West Indies... some very light wood from Africa, the robe of the King of Virginia...." A later catalogue of 1656 refers to this latter object as "Pohatan [sic], King of Virginia's habit all embroidered with shells, or Roanoke." There is no record of when the object entered the collection, although John Tradescant the Younger (1608–1662) had traveled to Virginia in 1637. One hundred English settlers had established England's first permanent North American settlement in Jamestown, Virginia, in 1607, right in the middle of an extensive chiefdom ruled by a paramount chief named Powhatan. By 1637, when Tradescant the Younger arrived, the Powhatan chiefdom was in a state of collapse after disease and warfare with the English had decimated the population. But the thirty years previous had been marked by strategies that alternated belligerence with diplomacy as first Powhatan, and then his successors, struggled to incorporate

38 Large mat made of deerskin and ornamented with shell beads. The object was collected before 1638 when it appears in an inventory of John Tradescant's collection in England as the "robe of the King of Virginia." Through some unknown circumstances it had been acquired by colonists of Jamestown (established 1607) from the highest-ranking leaders of the Powhatan chiefdom. Powhatan chiefs had the exclusive power to distribute shell ornaments to peers, allies, and rivals.

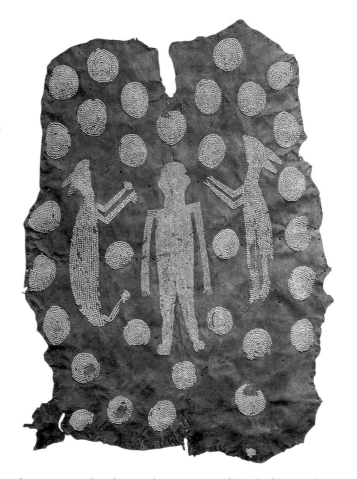

Jamestown within the social organization of the chiefdom, at first as a tributary town, then alternately as ally and enemy.

In one effort to establish formal relations, Powhatan directed his daughter, the famous Pocahontas, to "rescue" John Smith from execution as a precursor to formal adoption. It was customary for chiefs to shore up alliances by means of the exchange of family members through adoption or marriage. The exchange of gifts also established social bonds. Powhatan and his successors controlled the distribution of sumptuary goods, particularly copper and shell beads. They received them as payment from tributary villages or presented them as gifts to forge alliances. The so-called "Powhatan's mantle" is not a "habit" or a garment, but a mat, very likely of the type that observers reported functioned as a kind of throne for chiefs. Covered with precious shell beads, it represents the highest level of gift between peers of leadership,

39 Pouch customarily worn suspended against the chest with a cord around the neck, made of painted deerskin and decorated with porcupine quills. The pendants hanging from the bottom edge are cut from deer hooves.

and thus acts as a dynamic vehicle of diplomatic potential. We can only speculate that its presentation to an official of Jamestown represented a political strategem of alliance and accommodation, a gambit that ultimately failed.

It was also the habit of some wealthy aristocrats and merchants of European descent, like John Tradescant, to assemble "cabinets of curiosities" both natural and artificial. "Natural" refers here to things of nature – sea shells, exotic minerals, and stuffed animals like the "bat as large as a pigeon" listed in the Tradescant collection. "Artificial" means man-made – "curious" (interesting but unfamiliar) things made by human beings. As learned Europeans broadened their horizons to survey their world during the seventeenth and eighteenth centuries, collections demonstrated knowledge of and implied mastery over that world. The "artificial curiosities" they brought home and preserved in their collections provide us today with invaluable material documents, but it is important to keep in mind that they do not offer an impartial view. Their collection and preservation met the purposes of those involved with these transactions, not ours.

Mementos of service and travel

The royal cabinet of curiosities originally established in the fourteenth century by Henri IV of France became the repository of many things brought back by French explorers and traders and presented to the king, including "pouches, leggings, and belts made in the fashion of Barbary" obtained by Jacques Cartier (voyages in 1534, 1535 and 1541), and wampum belts – sashes of shell beads customarily exchanged to seal agreements and alliances – presented to Samuel Champlain by Huron emissaries in 1611. By the 1770s, through additional contributions by officials of New France and other visitors, the collection had grown considerably. In 1796, the post-revolution republic combined the royal collection with the collections of other aristocrats at the Bibliothèque Nationale for the education of the people of France. This is the origin of the present-day Musée de l'Homme in Paris. Today, sorting out where these things came from and who collected them is an almost impossible task. But there are some remarkable objects in the collection.

A deerskin pouch with a decorative panel made of a fine net of deerskin thongs wrapped with dyed porcupine quills from the Musée de l'Homme still has a precious hand-written label attached: "hide tobacco bag for the Indians of Canada 1721" [39]. The soft deerskin portion of the bag is painted with designs in red and black, including two circles with equal-armed crosses inside. These ancient symbols are also found in Mississippian art (see p. 50). The circle and cross motif refers in a very broad way to the terrestrial earth: a circular horizon and the four cardinal directions. The directional symbolism plots the daily course of the sun from east to west while the axis of north and south charts the slower ebb and flow of the seasons – the sun's journey southward, with winter on its heels, and its return in the spring. These general observations serve as the foundations for a complex series of spiritual reflections pertaining to the course of life, death, and rebirth, in short, an understanding of the way the world works. The netted quillwork panel suspended below the bag is worked with a pattern that represents a stylized bird with an hourglass-shaped body, triangular wings, and a small pointed head. This is an image of the Thunderbird, a widespread concept across North America that conceives of powerful thunderstorms as a monstrous, eagle-like bird whose flapping wings create thunder and whose flashing eyes produce lightning. While several of the cultural traditions of the Eastern Woodlands and Plains recognized the possibility that individuals may form powerful relations with thunder spirits through visions and dreams, here the design is far more likely a more general reference to powerful cosmological forces.

Images of the Thunderbird, the equal-armed cross, and the Underwater Panther [40] are often found in Eastern Woodlands art in ways that suggest a kind of cosmological diagram. The

40 Bag of nettle fiber and wool, made by an Odawa woman of Cross Village, Michigan, c. 1830. The design on this side of the bag represents two Underwater Panthers (see also figs 50 and 175). The other side, not visible here, features a Thunderbird.

Underwater Panther is the Thunderbird's nemesis yet compliment. They are enemies in constant conflict. The Underwater Panther dwells at the bottom of lakes and rivers, where its thrashing, serpent-like tail creates dangerous storms dreaded by canoe travelers. All three symbols together describe basic structures of the larger cosmos, the terrestrial earth bracketed by the sacred and powerful realms of sky and water above and below. Human beings, suspended amidst these powerful forces, strive to live within their precarious yet potentially rewarding state of balance.

The Musée de l'Homme bag resembles what are later called "fire-bags," sometimes worn around the neck of Ojibwa and Cree men of the Upper Great Lakes, or the tobacco bags of Plains people. The distinctive features in both instances are a soft, flexible, sleeve-like pouch (cloth was used in later Cree versions), with a stiff decorative panel suspended below. Successive generations of women artists continued to make variations of this form, incorporating new materials and new designs, for very many years after 1721. A new style of pouch began to appear in European collections drawn from the Great Lakes region after 1750 or so, and its design stems from the

41 Shoulder bag, in the form of a pouch worn against the hip with a strap around the shoulder, made of deerskin stained dark brown with dye from black walnut hulls, and decorated with porcupine quills. The pendants suspended from the bottom are made of tin wrapped around tufts of deer hair dyed bright red. Two Thunderbirds are featured in the design. The bag was reportedly presented in 1760 by "Iroquois" to Lord Jeffrey Amherst, commander of the British army in North America between 1758 and 1763.

military bandolier bags for powder and ammunition belonging to European soldiers. These pouches are almost square in shape and are worn suspended against the hip by means of a broad shoulder strap [41]. Their well-prepared deerskins are dyed dark brown (resulting in what is often called "black buckskin") and they are heavily ornamented with porcupine quill appliqué. Many of the designs employ images of Thunderbirds, equal-armed crosses, or Underwater Panthers.

These highly embellished objects represent tremendous artistic skill and mastery of difficult quill-working techniques. Clearly, European visitors sought them out and some had been presented as gifts to important officials. Closely related examples were brought back to Europe by Lord Jeffrey Amherst, commander in chief of the British forces in North America from 1758 to 1763, Sir Frederick Haldimand who served in Canada from 1760 to 1784, and Sir John Caldwell, posted in Detroit and Mackinac between 1768 and 1785, and there are many others. Other categories of objects, moccasins and knife cases for example, all decorated with closely related techniques, similarly returned to Europe as mementos of service in the North American colonies. Although it has been tempting to view these as early examples of a broadly based material culture (and there is much debate about the "tribal styles" they represent), it is far more likely that they are the products of a relatively modest number of skilled artists whose work was accessible for purchase near the major centers of Native and European interaction, such as Niagara, Detroit, and Mackinac. This is not to say that Europeans were the exclusive clients. Joseph Brant, the royalist Mohawk leader, founder of the Six Nations Reserve in southeastern Ontario, and namesake of Brantford, Ontario, wears a black buckskin shoulder bag in his portrait of 1807 by Canadian painter William Berczy.

There are tantalizing hints in contemporary memoirs and travel literature as to where such things could be found. The Huron of Lorette, Catholics who resettled outside Montreal in 1697 after the Huron and Iroquois wars of the earlier seventeenth century, are the well-documented creators of black buckskin bags and moccasins decorated with elaborate moose hair appliqué. Visitors purchased objects from their settlement at Lorette, or at Niagara Falls where Huron artists traveled to sell their creations. Memoirist John Long also reported moccasins of "superior workmanship and taste" made by Mohawk women from the Six Nations Reserve for sale at Niagara Falls just after the

Revolutionary War. Decades later, Samuel Keating remarked on the skills of Menominee women of Green Bay, Wisconsin, and "their mode of preparing belts, garters, sheaths for knives, moccasins, &c. and of ornamenting them with beads, and with the coloured quills of porcupines," while he was accompanying the exploratory expedition of Major Stephen Long in 1823. The Menominee lived along the major portage route for travelers between Lake Michigan and the Mississippi, and several of their creations of black buckskin and porcupine quills now reside in museums [42]. A rare glimpse of the domestic circumstances of artistic production is provided in the 1855 travel memoir of Johann Georg Kohl. At Sault Sainte Marie, the conduit of travel between Lakes Huron and Superior, Kohl visited the home of a mixed-blood pipe carver and his Ojibwa wife who worked with

42 Knife case of darkened deerskin and porcupine quills, made by a Menominee woman, Wisconsin, c. 1820. Several creations of Menominee women like this one were acquired by travelers.

porcupine quills. "The whole house was an atelier…. Red and black pipe-stones, half or quite unfinished pipe-bowls, with little engraving tools, lay in one corner of the room, and in the other portion…were clean birch bark and elegantly carved miniature canoes and children's pouches…or that fantastic and gay embroidery which Indian women prepare so cleverly out of porcupine quills."

New materials, new techniques
When European officials, visitors, and travelers sought out objects from Native people to purchase and own, they tended to privilege those things that seemed, to them, untainted by the circumstances of their encounter and authentic to their perception of what was distinctive and different about Native Americans, things made of natural materials like deerskin and porcupine quills, or distinctive weapons and implements such as ball head clubs (see p. 72) and smoking pipes. Certainly, artists like those among the Huron of Lorette, strived to meet these expectations. At the same time, however, the fashions of dress, design, and decorative technique throughout the Eastern Woodlands altered, as makers responded with vigor and creativity to the opportunities of new media offered by trade. Glass beads, silk ribbon, wool and printed cotton cloth, silver ornaments, and other materials required new techniques and working methods, and offered new possibilities for design and ornament.

Watercolor portraits of a Mohawk man and woman by an anonymous English or French artist of the late eighteenth century illustrate distinctive styles of dress made and decorated almost exclusively with imported materials [43]. The woman wears a printed cotton blouse that fits loosely over a wrap-around skirt of wool cloth edged with silk appliqué. She also wears a woolen robe with silk edging under one arm and over the other shoulder. Strips of more silk appliqué, probably supplemented with glass beads, descend down either side of her wool leggings and edge the hem just above her moccasins. Only the moccasins are made of deerskin, very likely with porcupine quill and glass bead ornament. She supports a pack or a baby carrier on her back by means of a tumpline or burden strap across her forehead. Burden straps of this type, made of twined nettle fiber and decorated with exquisite geometric designs of colorfully dyed moose hair, can be found among collections today. Textile garments like those the woman wears in the painting, however, survived far more rarely. Few collected them.

43 Watercolor of an Iroquois woman, painted during the late eighteenth century by an unknown English or French artist. The woman's wool fabric wearing blanket, skirt, and leggings are sumptuously decorated with silk ribbon appliqué.

A similarly constructed skirt with extremely complex ribbon appliqué was preserved in a trunk of heirlooms that had descended through several generations of a Miami family of Peoria, Indiana, until it was sold to a collector sometime around 1915 [44]. The skirt itself is a simple garment, an oblong length of dark wool cloth that would have been wrapped around the waist and tied with a belt. The bottom of the cloth is decorated with a broad band of silk ribbons of yellow, white, red, green, and blue, meticulously cut with scissors, folded, and stitched down along the edges of every detail of the pattern with cotton thread to create an intricate design of interlocking diamonds. Another panel of similarly fabricated "ribbonwork" decorates one side of the oblong cloth so that it descends down the front of the skirt when it is wrapped around the waist. Hundreds of small circular brooches of silver arranged in a broad pattern above the ribbonwork hem complete the decoration. The skirt would have been worn with a long, loose-fitting cotton or silk blouse, with similar lavish use of silver brooches for ornament. Indiana artist

George Winter painted images of Miami women wearing such garments decorated in this fashion during the 1830s.

The wealth that such a garment represented stemmed from the fur trade, in which Native women played a central role. As they converted animal hides into highly valued commodities (the quality of Native processed furs and deerskin had no parallel in Europe), they also transformed manufactured trade goods into Native expressions of wealth, success, and social prominence as formal dress or regalia. The vital role of their artistic skills and industriousness recast the raw materials of trade into items of social value for both parties of the transaction. While Native and European men worked the logistical side, assembling materials and arranging for their transport, the transformative powers of women artists provided the alchemy that made trade desirable and lucrative. Little wonder that both Native and European men, ambitious for the wealth and prestige that trade brought, sought out such women as marriage and business partners.

While the decoration of formal clothing often involved stitching silk ribbon, glass beads, and silver brooches directly upon cloth garments, women also adapted a number of weaving techniques to make sashes, garters (wrapped around the leg just under the knee), pouches, and shoulder bags. They used fine worsted wool yarns, often strung with glass beads, for finger-woven (braided) and twined textiles. Simple tension looms, sometimes employing a wooden heddle, made "woven beadwork" possible. When women wove sashes and shoulder bag panels with wefts strung with varied color glass beads, they invented startlingly new and intricate patterns [46]. And yet, many of the geometric designs are organized by a principle of quadrilateral symmetry, meaning that they are composed of four equivalent quadrants. No matter how complex, they can be read as variations on the theme of the equal-armed cross with its reference to the terrestrial earth and the four cardinal directions. Color asymmetry, often developed by alternating color or design from one side of a pattern to the other, restates the polar contrasts of Sky and Underworld. There is not much evidence that such design conventions represent a consciously narrative symbolism. Rather, these basic cosmological notions seem to inform aesthetic perceptions of what constituted proper and appropriate design. The women of each generation built upon the aesthetic traditions of the past, but with vigorous freedom of expression.

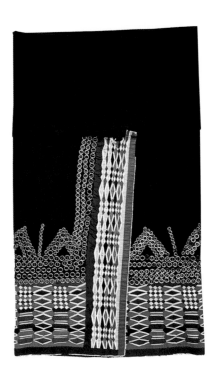

44 (above) Skirt of wool fabric, silk ribbon, and silver brooches, made by a Miami woman of Indiana, c. 1830. Note the intricate pattern of silk ribbon appliqué, referred to as "ribbonwork."

45 (above right) Shoulder bag of wool and cotton fabric, glass beads, and silk ribbon, made by a Creek woman during the 1830s or 1840s. The circle and cross pattern in the center of the design is an ancient Mississippian symbol. Note the printed cotton lining visible on the back-side of the strap. Other patterns on the bag may have been inspired by printed cotton cloth.

46 (right) Sash of glass beads, cotton twine, and wool yarn, made by an Ojibwa woman, c. 1850. This sash illustrates a technique of woven beadwork that made extremely intricate patterning possible.

47 Man's shirt of elaborately
patterned printed cotton calico,
made by a Seminole or Creek
woman during the 1830s.

Floral design

Decorative patterns of flowers first appeared within the vocabulary of Native dress as printed cotton fabrics used for shirts and blouses. Few of these garments survive, unfortunately, as the close study of imported fabrics might have offered some fine-grained detail about the dynamics of the trade. In light of twenty-first-century globalism, it is interesting to note that the plethora of inexpensive printed floral textiles (often called "calicoes" in trade documents) brought to North America resulted more or less directly from English and French colonial interests in India, both as a direct source of textiles but also as inspiration for competitive textile industries in Europe. Women of the Southeast seem to have been particularly attuned to the decorative possibilities of their printed patterns, as attested by a spectacular Seminole or Creek shirt obtained in Washington, D.C. by the German valet to the French ambassador sometime before 1846 when he presented it to the Royal *Kunstkammer* of Prussia [47]. So-called "patchwork" clothing of more modern-day Seminoles derives directly from this tradition.

This kind of florid sensibility is visible among Creek versions of the shoulder bag, created during the first decades of the nineteenth century. Made with wool fabric trimmed with silk, the straps, pouches, and distinctive triangular flaps of such bags are decorated with colorful glass bead appliqué applied in free-form designs that seem to draw equally from calico patterns and indigenous imagery. A particularly fine undocumented example combines elements that suggest floral blossoms and leaves, paisley-like forms, and sun disks, one with an equal-armed cross, just like those visible on examples of Mississippian pottery [45].

In 1830, President Andrew Jackson signed into law the Indian Removal Act and over the next twenty years the federal government and state militias uprooted tens of thousands of Native people from their homelands in the east and removed them to reservations west of the Mississippi River in Kansas, Nebraska, and Oklahoma. Here they joined tribes already resident on the prairies. Some avoided removal by hiding in remote locations, fleeing to Canada or, more rarely, by giving up their tribal status. The Eastern Band of Cherokee and the Seminole of Florida are two such nations that avoided removal, but most had to go. Many died en route. Among the reservations of these displaced peoples, a new style of clothing decoration emerged, one that combined abstract floral forms brought by the Cherokee and Creek to Oklahoma with Great Lakes and

Midwestern traditions of organizing designs with quadrilateral symmetry and color asymmetry. Broad and colorful patterns of ribbonwork and glass bead appliqué, often contrasted against heavy dark cloth, reasserted cultural values of Native identity through the traditions of artistic production, gift exchange, and the display of regalia. This late nineteenth-century, pan-tribal style of clothing decoration is sometimes referred to as "Prairie style" due to the prairie locations of post-Removal reservations.

Mission schools were another source of floral imagery, and their effect is first visible in the productions of Catholic converts: the moose hair embroidery of the Huron of Lorette, for example, or the Catholic Odawa of Michigan who decorated the birch-bark boxes they made to package and sell maple sugar with floral patterns done in porcupine quill during the first decades of the nineteenth century. Several accomplished woman artists of Michigan and southeastern Ontario carry on this tradition today [48], but now collectors desire the boxes, not the maple sugar. By the 1880s, pictorial floral designs with tulips, roses, peonies, and other recognizable blossoms dominated the decorated regalia of Northern Minnesota Ojibwa [49]. Ojibwa beadworkers told the anthropologist Sister Bernard Coleman that the floral designs they used to decorate formal clothing and beaded shoulder bags derived from the embroidery, cross-stitch, and lace patterns they had learned in government schools.

The tradition of using floral images for the decoration of regalia resonated far to the north and west during the 1800s. Families descendant from the unions of French, Scots, and English fur traders and Ojibwa and Cree women, called Metis, brought floral decoration out to the farthest reaches of the trade in northern Canada and the American Rockies. By the 1880s, Ojibwa families used the Northern Pacific Railroad to travel west and market floral shoulder bags and other beaded items. The "floral style" developed many regional variations as local beadworkers incorporated images into the repertoire. We will pick up the thread of the floral style in Chapter 8.

Telling stories: objects and pictographs
Agawa Rock is a sheer cliff of granite that descends directly into the water on the treacherous eastern shore of Lake Superior north of Agawa Bay. An Ojibwa artist or artists stood upon a narrow ledge just above the splashing waves and painted a series of evocative and seemingly mysterious images upon the raw stone cliff. Among the several painted sections there is an impressively

48 Box of birch bark and porcupine quill, made by Yvonne M. Walker Keshick (Odawa), Michigan, 1990s. Keshick is one of the greatest living makers of quilled boxes, a tradition that stems back hundreds of years in Michigan.

49 Family of Minnesota Ojibwa, photographed by D. F. Barry of Minnesota, print dated 1890s. In this staged photograph, the two men wear shoulder bags and leggings beaded with floral patterns.

large image of an Underwater Panther with long arched horns accompanied by two serpents swimming below [50]. A canoe containing five figures follows behind. Henry Rowe Schoolcraft, the Indian agent for northern Michigan stationed at Sault Sainte Marie between 1822 and 1841, learned about this image from a Sault Sainte Marie band chief whose name he recorded as Chingwauk. The chief told Schoolcraft that the painting commemorated the occasion when a man named Myeengun had led a party of war canoes across Lake Superior to join the Ojibwa of Agawa Bay and fight the Iroquois. The wind, rocks, currents, and threat of fierce storms make this an especially perilous passage under any circumstances, but Myeengun had successfully propitiated the dangerous spirits of the lake, the Underwater Panther and horned serpents, and brought his warriors across safely. This was possible, Chingwauk said, because Myeengun was a noted priest of the Midewiwin, a religion widespread among the Ojibwa and several other Great Lakes tribes. We can assume that Chingwauk had seen the painting on the rock and been told the story, and now, with the help of a drawing he made from memory, he told the story to Schoolcraft. The story of Myeengun's accomplishment was worth remembering and retelling. The painting, in bold red mineral pigment, served both as the mnemonic device to prompt the story and, located at the water's

50 Painted figures at Agawa Rock, Lake Superior, Ontario. This is one of several series of figures painted in red mineral pigment at the water's edge at Agawa Rock. This composition shows a great Underwater Panther accompanied by two serpents and a canoe conveying five figures behind.

edge, a humble and grateful acknowledgment of the lake's power to spare or destroy.

Men of the Eastern Woodlands frequently employed a pictorial language of images as a means of recording and remembering significant events. War parties might leave a pictorial account of their experiences along major trails as a kind of publication of the episode: how many in their party, the number of the enemy, the number killed or captured. Pictures employed to convey information in this way are called "pictographs" and their artful creation has resulted in a number of powerful graphic images preserved in a variety of media today.

Warriors sometimes engraved images tabulating war records or describing spiritual experiences upon their wooden clubs, some shaped like a lightning bolt, called descriptively a "gunstock" club, others carved of a single piece of wood with a curved handle and a heavy ball on the striking end, called a "ball head" club. Antoine Denis Raudot wrote from Quebec in 1705, "A man puts on it [his club] his divinity...the symbol of his name...the number of men he has killed, and the prisoners he has taken." Raudot added, "For their own glory he [a warrior] leaves such war clubs where he has been on some expedition in order that his enemies may know who killed their people and what nation he was." It is interesting to be reminded of this custom when considering a particularly beautiful ball head club carved of maple with what appears to be a head of a bear worked upon the end of the handle, preserved today at the Denver Art Museum [51]. It had been found, perhaps left as a reminder, at the site of Britain's most notorious defeat at the hands of warriors from the combined tribes of the central Great Lakes when the army led by Major

51 Ball head club of maple, recovered near the site of the "Battle of the Wilderness," where in 1755 the army led by Major General Edward Braddock was defeated at the hands of Odawa and Potawatomi. Western Iroquois, Delaware, and Shawnee also joined the fight, and the club may have belonged to a warrior of any one of these nations.

52 Gunstock club of wood and metal, observed in the possession of a young Ojibwa man at L'Anse, Michigan, in the 1840s. He said it was engraved with an image inspired by a vision in which his spirit guardian had showed him the Thunderbird seated in its nest.

General Edward Braddock was ambushed and routed just outside Fort Duquesne in 1755, near present-day Pittsburgh, Pennsylvania.

There are several such clubs preserved in collections both in North America and Europe, many engraved with images that tell of accomplishments in battle. Many collectors were eager to have them and they appear in early cabinets of curiosities under the popular category of arms and armor. For those who sold them, perhaps the honor of broadcasting one's accomplishments outweighed the trouble of making another. In the 1840s Johann Georg Kohl, the travel memoirist mentioned earlier, had the opportunity to discuss designs engraved upon a gunstock club with a young Ojibwa man he met at L'Anse, the site of a mission on Keweenaw Bay on the south shore of Lake Superior [52]. Two figures, the young man explained, represented himself and his guardian spirit who had come to him in a dream. Pointing to the image of a bird contained within a crescent, the young man said that the guardian spirit had instructed him to look upward and there he saw a giant eagle sitting in its nest with the moon and stars above. Kohl asked about the figures and crosshatched bands on the handle. These represented war expeditions against the Sioux but the young man said he had no knowledge of them. An elderly man who knew of these events had made these marks on the weapon. Kohl evidently did not purchase the club. It surfaced in Michigan more than one hundred years later. Considering the testimony, perhaps the elder man made it (he used a cut piece of an eighteenth-century mason's square for the blade) or at least engraved the pictographs. Perhaps it was customary for some elderly men, past their active years as warriors, to turn their attention to making weapons for others, interpreting what they were told with the pictorial language of pictographs and, in this case, recounting old and noteworthy battles for posterity.

Clearly, objects could become vessels of memory. Knowledge of history and the sources of spiritual power are preserved not by oral tradition alone, but by objects with their attendant rituals that prompt memories and stage occasions for passing that knowledge along to others. A small smoking pipe bowl carved of catlinite is all that remains of an assemblage of objects that provided power and protection in battle for generations of Miami warriors [53]. The objects, which included a necklace with small packets filled with spiritually charged substances, rattles, and the pipe and stem, customarily kept wrapped in a piece of deerskin when not used for rituals, can be referred to collectively as a "war bundle." The owner brought the bundle along on war parties he led and performed rituals with the contents that contributed to his party's safety and success. The sacred knowledge of how to use these things for such a purpose was a gift from spirit beings experienced as a dream or a vision. But the oral tradition of the bundle also recalled how it had been passed from one owner to the next, from elder to promising youngster, until it had been destroyed by accidental fire sometime around 1900. Only the stone pipe bowl and the story survived, although the ritual knowledge was lost. The objects themselves might have been periodically renewed or replaced during the life of the bundle. It is thought that the pipe was carved sometime during the eighteenth century, but it is impossible to determine the origin date for the bundle itself. When the man experienced the vision and sought to assemble the objects necessary for the bundle, who did he approach to make the pipe?

There are many scattered references to quarries of pipestone in the Lake Superior region, and attendant pipe carvers. The source of red catlinite used for the Miami war bundle pipe is well known and will be discussed in Chapter 5. The quality and

53 Catlinite pipe bowl, once part of a war bundle that had descended through the family of Camilius Bundy, a Miami of Peru, Indiana. The style of the pipe suggests it was carved during the 1700s.

54 Pipe bowl of stone and shell inlay, carved by an Odawa or Ojibwa man who has been identified by artist Paul Kane as Aubonwaishkum of Manitoulin Island. Kane sketched the pipe during his visit of 1845.

workmanship of many exquisitely carved pipe bowls testifies to specialized and highly developed artistic skills, but it is rare to match a pipe to a particular maker. An exception is a man of Manitoulin Island identified as Aubonwaishkum by Canadian artist Paul Kane in 1845. Kane drew a picture of a pipe of black stone he had purchased, its upright bowl carved as a human head with eyes inlaid with shell, and the figure of a woman seated on a chair on the shank [54]. Kane asked the artist about the meaning of the sculpted images, but Aubonwaishkum replied that his forefathers had made similar pipes with the same shaped head for the bowl, testifying to the continuity of his training through the generations. The pipe is preserved today in the collection of the Royal Ontario Museum in Toronto.

The carver's art

Arthur C. Parker, an Iroquois who became a notable anthropologist and folklorist, wrote, "Food tastes much better eaten from an *atog'washa* [wooden ladle]." It was customary throughout the Eastern Woodlands to use carved wooden bowls and ladles for meals. Families might possess a small collection and travelers took a bowl and spoon with them. The handles of ladles and the edges of bowls were sometimes delicately carved with

animal or human figures [55]. Prior to the accessibility of steel tools, men hollowed out wooden burls with hot coals, scraping the charred wood out with blades made of beaver incisors. Later, the farrier knife used by blacksmiths to shoe horses was adapted into what is now known as a "crooked knife," a carving tool with a curved blade useful for hollowing out the concave interiors of bowls and spoons. The wooden handles of crooked knives were sometimes imaginatively carved as well [56]. John Lawson, who published a history of Carolina in 1715, reported that Native men not particularly skillful in hunting for the deerskin trade fashioned spoons and bowls of tulipwood instead, trading them to hunters for deerskins.

One such master woodcarver, John Young Bear, was born in 1883 in Tama, Iowa, the settlement purchased by the Mesquakie after Removal. He was well known in the community as a carver of bowls, spoons, heddles used by Mesquakie beadworkers, and other kinds of wooden objects. His father was a carver as well and at least one massive feast bowl, hollowed from a maple burl with the head of an eagle rearing up from one end, has been documented to him [57]. The descendants of the Young Bear family were and are artists, historians, and writers. The Mesquakie Young Bears exemplify the lineage descent of Native artists, the roles they play within their communities, and how, with the products of their hands and their intellects, they create and nurture ties between themselves, their communities, and others.

55 Wooden *atog'washa*, or spoon, carved by an Iroquois man, perhaps during the 1800s. The image on the handle shows a waterfowl sleeping with its head tucked under its wing.

56 "Crooked knife" of wood, steel, and leather, made by an Ojibwa or Odawa man during the 1800s. A "crooked knife" is an all-round carving and fabricating tool.

57 Maple feast bowl, identified by Mesquakie carver John Young Bear (b. 1883) as having been made by his father. The head rising up from one edge represents an eagle, or the Thunderbird.

Chapter 4　Southwest

A visitor to Santa Fe today encounters perplexing combinations of an ancient past and a topical present. The Plaza, established in outline when the Spaniard Pedro de Peralta founded the city in 1610, flocks with teenagers in T-shirts on skateboards. Tourists dine in a walled courtyard where, during the late 1770s, refugees from the outlying towns camped to escape the sustained campaign of raids organized by Comanche war chief Cuerno Verde. In late May and June, giant thunderheads build in the western skies and bring brief drenching downpours in the late afternoon, as they have done in answer to the rituals and prayers of Pueblo agriculturalists for as many as fifteen hundred years. History and culture are the stock-in-trade of Santa Fe. And it makes perfect sense that works of art are the widely traded tender of these more elusive concepts. On the streets, in the gallery windows, American Indian art, or what passes for it among the uninitiated, appears at every turn. From the galleries on Canyon Road to the phenomenon of the Santa Fe Art Market that takes place every August, people come and go to Santa Fe to buy or sell art, a good deal of it made by artists who call one of the Southwest's pueblos or reservations home. In the context of the greater Southwest, Santa Fe has been around for a relatively short period of time. But the notion of a place where strangers come together to trade and exchange objects is an ancient one here, long predating the arrival of the Spanish and their town. The Spanish, however, quickly understood the value of the great trade fairs of Taos and Pecos pueblos, where visitors from the Plains brought buffalo hides and other valuables to trade. The Great Houses of Chaco Canyon, such as Pueblo Bonito built during the tenth century, functioned in part as great centers of ritual and exchange. Geographically, the

58 Pictograph in the Sutherland Wash Rock Art District, Pima County, Arizona, near the city of Tucson. Some of the abundant pictographs at this site are affiliated to pre-pottery Archaic cultures and can be dated as early as 500 BC. Others can be linked stylistically to the Hohokam culture.

Southwest seems isolated from the rest of the North American continent, bounded by formidable mountain ranges and inhospitable deserts. And yet, within this topographical setting, peoples who spoke different languages, stemming from many different cultural origins, knit together relations of mutual dependence that made coexistence possible. Within this great cultural mix, the production and circulation of art has long played an important role.

Beyond Santa Fe, outside the city, the surrounding landscape of piñon-covered mountains, dramatic canyons, rolling hills, and hard-edged mesas is quickly traversed by automobile. From the air, or looking at a map, it is easy to parse the Southwest into broad regions defined by expansive river drainages and intervening mountain ranges. But on the ground, on foot, the land reveals a more fine-grained diversity of washes, arroyos, ridges, parched basins, wooded parklands, and verdant box-canyons. The observant can see traces of the countless number of human beings that have walked this land before. Flakes of chert emerging from the sandy soil on the edge of a ridge overlooking the bend of a seasonal stream locate a camp where hunters, thousands of years ago, watched for game seeking water. Low mounds covered with cholla cactus hide the collapsed masonry walls of an Anasazi pueblo. Earth eroding from the mounds spreads carpets of colorful pottery shards underfoot. Hikers today who try to pick their way through this complicated topography inadvertently find themselves walking ancient trails marked by pictographs pecked into rocky outcrops [58]: images of undulating horned serpents, masked dancers, or the mythic humpback flute player, Kokopelli (see p. 84). For all its open ruggedness and "natural" beauty, there is probably not one inch of this country that was not familiar to someone at one time.

Today's Pueblo communities trace their origins to ancestors who left their Underworld homes and emerged upon this terrestrial earth to settle it. Archaeologists believe they can trace the origins of local cultural sequences back nearly nine thousand years (7000 BC), to slightly variant pre-ceramic traditions to the north and south. These early hunting and gathering peoples were few in number but covered a great deal of territory, seeking out seasonally available resources during cyclical rounds of purposeful wandering. Knowledge of corn, beans, and squash, cultigens that had been domesticated in the Mexican highlands by 5000 BC, reached these early peoples sometime during the first millennium BC. But they adapted cautiously, mixing these more risky, labor-intensive foods with the wild resources of the land. Archaeologists can identify the roots of what would, by AD 200, become three of the great agricultural traditions of the Southwest: the Hohokam to the southwest, the Mogollon to the southeast, and the Anasazi to the north. The descendants of the Mogollon and Anasazi today are what are referred to here as "Pueblo peoples." The O'odam, sometimes called the Pima and Papago, of southern Arizona claim descent from the Hohokam.

Painted pottery
In addition to agriculture, knowledge of pottery-making techniques also migrated up from Mexico. When broken bits of distinctive brown pottery appear among the early agriculturalist sites of southern New Mexico and southeast Arizona, archaeologists identify the Mogollon culture, in contrast to nearly identical sites without pottery. Some archaeologists suspect they are actually the same people, some of whom made pottery, some of whom did not. In fact, two different traditions of pottery making entered into the southern Southwest during the third century AD: the Mogollon brown wares built with coils of clay pinched together with fingers and scraping tools, and the Hohokam tradition of southern Arizona where potters thinned coils of clay into vessel walls using a paddle-shaped tool, a technique called "paddle and anvil." By AD 600, knowledge of pottery making had traveled northward and been embraced by early farmers of the Colorado Plateau and the San Juan Basin.

Archaeologists privilege pottery as an archaeological artifact because of its durability in the ground, but also due to the fact that its techniques of manufacture are passed hand-to-hand, generation after generation, and therefore tend to change slowly over time. Abrupt shifts in manufacturing techniques or styles of decoration hint at population movements or other significant cultural events. Modern scientific analysis can identify the component minerals of clay and temper (material mixed into the clay to give it body and strength) so archaeologists can often trace the origins of raw materials to local sources or distant ones, the latter often indicating trade in finished pots. The agricultural societies of the Southwest depended upon pottery. These fragile yet indispensable utensils lasted but a few years before breaking, so there was always a need to make or procure new ones. This more-than-fifteen-hundred-year tradition holds up a mirror to Pueblo societies, reflecting day-to-day and ritual activities, movements from place to place, patterns of trade, and many other details of cultural history. Furthermore, today as yesterday, the creation of pottery remains one of the pre-eminent forms of artistic expression among Pueblo peoples.

When looking at the wares made by the earliest Anasazi potters, working between AD 600 and 800, it is clear that most pottery was intended for the chores of cooking and storage. These vessels tend to be plain undecorated wares fired a dull gray color. Rare but widespread throughout the range of the early Anasazi, archaeologists find serving bowls with designs painted in black mineral paint. The sparse geometric patterns that spiral up their interior walls are clearly drawn from those found on early Anasazi coiled baskets. Other, more rarely encountered designs show simple figures standing hand-to-hand, arranged around the interior wall of the bowl as if dancing in a circle [59]. A meal, of course, is a social occasion when people gather together to share food. The differences between undecorated culinary pottery and painted vessels would seem to lie in the public, perhaps ritual occasions when painted pottery was used.

After AD 800 painted pottery expanded to include a number of new forms: dippers, pitchers or mugs with handles, canteens, and variously shaped jars. Two large and spectacularly painted *ollas* (large storage jars) were preserved in a stone-lined storage recess beneath the floor of a residential room in a late ninth-century pueblo near present-day Red Rock, Arizona [60]. Their carefully prepared paste, creamy white slip, and expansive decoration painted with organic vegetal pigments contrast sharply with contemporary gray wares used for domestic chores. Loops low on the sides and the vessels' constricted necks suggest that they were suspended in a way to facilitate pouring their heavy contents. The appearance of highly decorated storage jars among the inventories of Anasazi households corresponds with a shift from communal storage facilities, shared by the village, to storage rooms attached to individual households, reinforcing an impression that painted pottery was linked to display, hospitality, and ritual.

During subsequent centuries, Anasazi potters perfected the complicated processes and techniques required for large-scale production of exquisitely decorated black-on-white wares. By the twelfth century, potters used large kiln sites near sources of firing fuel yet distant from residences. Specialized artists, perhaps extended kinship groups or dedicated communities, made the pots and supervised these massive and technically challenging firings. Decorated pottery circulated widely through trade, and

59 (opposite top) Painted bowl (La Plata black-on-white). Anasazi culture, Basket Maker III period, c. AD 600–700. This exceptionally early example of Anasazi painted pottery was made in the Cibola region, just north of present-day Zuni Pueblo.

60 (opposite centre and below) Two large storage jars (Kana-a black-on-white). Anasazi culture, Pueblo I period, AD 700–900. These and two other vessels were recovered from an early Anasazi settlement during the period just after the shift from pit house structures to rooms with shared walls built on the ground surface. The jars had been placed in a slab-lined storage room beneath the floor of one of the rooms.

61 Painted bowl (Mimbres black-on-white), from the Mimbres valley, southwestern New Mexico. Mimbres culture, AD 1000–1150. The humpback figure on the left, with a cane in one hand and a rod (perhaps a long flute) in the other, resembles Kokopelli, a mythical figure who appears in Pueblo oral traditions. He and another figure with the hindquarters of a hoofed animal confront an enormous horned fish draped across a conical burden basket.

local potters emulated popular styles and techniques but with their own local variations. When they moved with their communities, they introduced their skills and wares to new regions. Anasazi decorated pottery that survives today reveals a highly organized artistic tradition in which knowledge and skills were passed from one generation to the next, each refining technique while innovating new and dynamic styles.

To the south, Mogollon peoples developed a parallel ceramic tradition, no doubt in dynamic interaction with their Anasazi neighbors. Early Mogollon potters produced reddish-brown wares painted with red geometric designs. By AD 1000, Mogollon artists had perfected a black-on-white technique closely related to Anasazi black-on-whites to the north. Potters slipped deep hemispherical bowls snow white and used a black mineral paint to create tightly constructed geometric patterns executed with great precision. Most remarkable, however, are Mimbres black-on-white bowls with pictorial images painted in the interiors, found almost exclusively in the Mimbres valley of southwestern New Mexico [61]. Fish, horned toads, aquatic birds and insects, human figures engaged in seemingly ritual activities, or strange admixtures of human and animal forms composed in what may represent mythic narratives, grace the interiors of these frankly astonishing vessels. Most of the bowls have been recovered from burials beneath the floors of large Mimbres Valley apartment complexes. Many bowls exhibit signs of use, however, and a few others have been found in other kinds of settings, hinting at ritual uses prior to funerary interment. Unlike other highly decorated wares of the ancient Southwest, Mimbres pictorial bowls were never traded outside the Mimbres valley, suggesting a ritual significance maintained with a purposeful exclusiveness among the Mimbres people.

The Cibola region, comprising the upper reaches of the Little Colorado and Zuni rivers with their sources in the mountainous terrain of the central Arizona and New Mexico borderlands, had always been frontier zone between Mogollon and Anasazi culture. Here, beginning in the eleventh century, potters created an enormously popular series of red-slipped wares, mostly serving bowls, which were traded widely to Anasazi and Mogollon communities to the north and south. Called White Mountain Red Ware, this pottery tradition was enriched considerably by Anasazi potters emigrating southward after 1300 and establishing pueblos and closely linked pottery traditions in the area of the so-called Mogollon Rim, west of present-day Phoenix. The dramatic designs of the Pinedale and Fourmile polychromes, made with red and white slips, black mineral paints, iron oxide glazes, and a fugitive white paint, combine the precise geometric vocabulary of the black-on-white tradition with dramatic curvilinear scrolls and pictorial forms [62]. To the northwest, newly established pueblos

62 Painted jar (Fourmile polychrome), from the Mogollon Rim region of Arizona and New Mexico. Anasazi culture, AD 1325–1400. The stepped designs in black suggest rising thunderclouds with white forks of lightning. The dotted spirals attached to the thunderclouds hint at life-giving water within the clouds. Butterflies grace the neck of the jar.

among the Hopi mesas created widely traded Jeddito and Sikyatki black-on-orange, black-on-yellow, and polychrome wares. The innovative designs and techniques of fifteenth-century potters, and the broad dissemination of their styles through trade, laid the foundation for the Pueblo pottery traditions practiced today.

Architecture and ritual
Up until the eighth century, the earliest Anasazi lived in small villages composed of "pit houses" with separate storage structures. Some villages included one or more good-sized pit houses that were not intended as homes. Their stone benches and a feature resembling a "sipapu," a ritual hole in the floor opening to the Underworld, suggest that these non-domestic constructions are ancestral to the semi-subterranean ritual chambers of the later Pueblo villages called "kivas." Kiva-like structures proliferated at larger villages after AD 800, suggesting that each represented a network of social relationships that bound together several households with ritual obligations. There are six kivas at present-day Zuni Pueblo, for example. Here the word refers both to the architectural structure and to the ritual organization that draws together members from many different Zuni families. The six kiva organizations of the Zuni cooperate with each other to complete a cyclical round of annual ceremonies that ensure the continued success and well-being of the community.

By AD 800, most of the Anasazi had built masonry and adobe houses on the surface of the ground that included both residential spaces and storage rooms. But villagers continued to use pit houses as kivas and positioned them out in front of the small room-complexes as separate ceremonial structures. The scattered villages of the early Anasazi moved often. Villagers searched for choice locations to settle for a few decades or more and then abandoned them to move elsewhere in response to new challenges or opportunities. Settlements did not exist in isolation, but depended upon similarly shifting networks of neighboring villages to which residents looked for trade, assistance, marriage partners, and overall support. It seems clear that the kiva and its communal rituals played a strong role in maintaining these relationships, when hosting visitors, when sharing food, when reinforcing the solidarity of shared spiritual belief.

Chaco Canyon, located among the arid table-lands of northwestern New Mexico, consists of about 10 miles (16 km) of broad bottomlands sheltered within low sandstone cliffs to the

63 Pueblo Bonito, Chaco Canyon, New Mexico, Anasazi culture, built and expanded from AD 850 to 1115. Pueblo Bonito is the largest of the Great Houses of Chaco Canyon and its environs. The large number of kivas, burials, and ritual goods at this perplexing architectural complex has led some archaeologists to believe that Pueblo Bonito functioned less as a domestic residence and more as a ceremonial center.

north and south. It had always been the home of Anasazi farmers but saw a sharp increase in the size, number, and complexity of Anasazi settlements during the tenth and eleventh centuries. Here, Anasazi architects built planned communities of several hundred rooms nestled against the northern cliffs of the canyon, sheltered from the wind and warmed by the southern sun. Pueblo Bonito, which grew to be the largest, was expanded seven times during the tenth and eleventh centuries [63]. The fullest extent of its crescent-shaped plan accommodated as many as forty circular kivas and eight hundred rooms stepped back in multistoried tiers around a central plaza. During the eleventh century, Chaco Canyon accommodated nine such "Great Houses," as archaeologists call them, as well as several lesser communities and hundreds of smaller homesteads. Spillways and canals directed precious water from the surrounding cliffs to well-planned fields. Some 245 miles (405 km) of roads, or rather carefully prepared paths with steps and ramps to tame the rugged terrain, connected Chaco to distant outlying communities, some of them Great Houses themselves. The function of some of the "roads," however, remains unclear, since they do not seem to lead anywhere at all. The developments of Chaco Canyon are unique to Anasazi history, but part of a larger phenomenon of regional

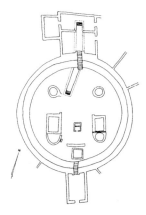

64 Casa Rinconada, New Mexico, Anasazi culture, built during the height of cultural activity at Chaco Canyon, AD 1020–1100. Casa Rinconada is one of a few free-standing and isolated Great Kivas; others were built within Great House complexes. People assembled inside, seated on the benches around the circumference, and participated in elaborate ritual performances.

cohesion fueled, in part, by opportunities to participate in trade and ritual.

Kivas were a fixture of many Anasazi settlements. Ritual activities on a much more massive scale are suggested by the Great Kivas of Chaco Canyon and its outlying communities. The largest of the Great Kivas, Casa Rinconada, stands separately from any of the Great Houses [64]. It is a huge circular chamber, 63 ft 6 in. (19.4 m) in diameter, faced on the interior with plaster over fine masonry veneer. Four thick columns of pine, footed upon sunken sandstone disks, once supported the roof. Stairways descend from ground-level antechambers on both the north and south sides of the kiva, and a low stone shelf or bench encircles the voluminous interior space. Hundreds assembled here to witness and participate in impressive theatrical ceremonies illuminated by a fire burning in an elevated masonry firebox near the middle of the floor. A low masonry wall, or fire screen, to the south of the firebox hid a small sub-floor chamber where ritual specialists might seclude themselves during different episodes of a ceremony. A hidden passageway allowed performers to emerge into the center of the kiva from beneath the floor. Casa Rinconada had been designed, to use art historian J. J. Brody's words, as a "ritual theater" of monumental scale. At least one Great Kiva is found at each of the nine larger Great Houses at Chaco, and others are located among the Chaco outliers. They range in size from 40 to 60 ft (12 to 18 m) in diameter, each oriented north and south, with four interior support posts arranged in a perfect square, a masonry firebox in the center, and stone benches around the sides.

Archaeologists found great quantities of worked turquoise in Chaco Canyon, particularly at Pueblo Bonito and other Great Houses. The Anasazi used turquoise beads and pendants extensively for offerings and other ritual purposes. Archaeological evidence suggests that the Chaco communities procured turquoise mined from distant locations and controlled its dispersal as finished ritual objects (beads, inlays, pendants) during the tenth and eleventh centuries. Archaeologist W. James Judge sees a strong link between the growth of Great Houses, Great Kiva ritualism, and Chaco control of turquoise as a ritual substance. The Great Kiva ceremonies and lure of sacred turquoise brought Anasazi, and perhaps others, from the surrounding regions to Chaco Canyon to participate and contribute in what archaeologists today call "the Chaco phenomenon." The performative nature of Anasazi ritual, the potential for trade in highly crafted ritual objects, and the demanding requirements of Great House and Great Kiva architecture all depended upon the skills and knowledge of Chaco artists and ritual specialists.

Marine shell ornaments and ritual objects, such as beaded necklaces and shell trumpets, confirm Chaco relations with the Hohokam of the Phoenix basin to the south [65]. Hohokam trafficked in marine shell harvested from the Gulf of California and worked into beads and bracelets. Copper bells made in Mexico also passed through Hohokam hands as they made their way by trade to Chaco Canyon and the Mimbres valley. In turn, the Hohokam imported both Anasazi and Mogollon decorated

65 Shell pendant, from the Martinez Hill site, south of Tucson, Arizona. Hohokam culture, AD 900–1100. Hohokam traders acquired marine shell from the Gulf of California, supplying themselves, the Anasazi, and the Mogollon peoples. This half of a bivalve shell is carved as a frog or toad.

66 Casa Grande, Arizona. Hohokam culture, c. AD 1300. This late Hohokam structure, shown here as it appeared more than one hundred years ago, evidently combined some kind of elite residence and temple atop a blocky platform mound.

pottery. The Hohokam flourished during the tenth century with civic institutions related more closely to those to the south in Mexico. Instead of kivas, Hohokam communities built ballcourts. The Mesoamerican ballgame was not simply a sport contest, but a complex expression of community-held cosmological beliefs. Larger Hohokam communities, such as Snaketown with a population of approximately 1000 residents, were organized around central plazas flanked by platform mounds and ballcourts. It is fair to say that the eleventh century saw tremendous growth and innovation among the cultural institutions of the Southwest, and greater complexity among the relationships between distant and yet not so isolated regional systems of the Anasazi, Hohokam, and Mogollon peoples.

By AD 1150, the great experiment at Chaco was largely over. The precarious canyon environment could no longer support the Great Houses, despite their far-ranging contacts. They were abandoned and population growth shifted north, at least temporarily, to the Mesa Verde region. By AD 1300, subtle climatic shifts, resulting in sequential droughts, forced the Anasazi to abandon the Colorado Plateau altogether and move south to the present homeland of Pueblo peoples: the Hopi mesas, the Cibola region of the Little Colorado drainage, and the Rio Grande valley. (Anasazi also settled in the Mogollon Rim region but abandoned it by 1500.) There they merged with Mogollon peoples migrating northward. Among the Hohokam, regional conflict may have resulted in the collapse of inter-regional ballgame ceremonialism and the abandonment of Snaketown. The Hohokam re-organized, following the more characteristically Mesoamerican pattern of control under leading families whose power could be expressed through monumental public works. The massive, four-story adobe "compound" of Casa Grande, with its 4 ft (1.2 m)-thick walls, built during the late thirteenth century by the Hohokam near present-day Florence, Arizona, combines a chiefly residence on a platform mound with the astronomical function of charting the seasons [66].

Kachinas

Many of the late Anasazi towns established during the fourteenth and fifteenth centuries were quite large and built with a different plan from their predecessors to the north in the Colorado Plateau. They included large open plazas and square kivas instead of the older style of round ones [67]. When archaeologists excavated the square kivas of a village site called Kuaua, located on the west bank of the Rio Grande just north of present-day Albuquerque, they found murals painted on the interior walls that depict mysterious masked figures. Similar figures appear in other kiva murals of the fifteenth and sixteenth centuries, like those at the abandoned Hopi town of Awatovi [68], but also as images pecked or painted upon rocky outcrops or incorporated into the imagery of Fourmile and Jeddito pottery of the fifteenth century. Archaeologist E. Charles Adams thinks that these images of masked figures evidence new ritual practices of the fifteenth-century pueblos, and that the innovative square kiva architecture

67 Plaza of Old Oraibi, Third Mesa, northern Arizona. Hopi culture. The vicinity of Old Oraibi has been inhabited by ancestors of the present community since AD 1150. In this photograph of the old town, a kiva entrance is visible in the center of the plaza.

68 Mural fragment from Awatovi, Hopi culture. The Hopi community of Awatovi was established during the 1330s. Excavations sponsored by Harvard University recovered over 200 individual mural paintings from 20 different kivas. Many of the figures painted in the murals can be recognized among the Hopi Kachinas of today. The diving figure wearing a conical cap may be one of the War Twins who appear during ceremonies at Winter Solstice.

and plazas were constructed as the settings in which such rites could be performed. When the Spanish observed masked performers after their arrival in the sixteenth century, they were told that the masked dancers were *Cacinas*, or Kachinas as we spell it today.

Most of the present-day Pueblos perform Kachina ceremonies. The Spanish aggressively suppressed these practices in the interests of subjugating the Pueblos and converting them to Catholicism, so their survival depended upon secrecy and resistance to the outsiders' scrutiny. Only the western Pueblos, the Hopi of northern Arizona, and the Zuni of the Cibola region of western New Mexico, could afford to maintain their Kachina practices openly, since they were distant from the core of the Spanish administration in the Rio Grande valley. Hence, today, the Hopi and Zuni Kachina ceremonies are the best-known to outsiders.

The Kachinas are ancestral spirit beings who visit the pueblos during regularly scheduled intervals of the year to bring rain, agricultural fertility, blessings of continued well-being, and the pleasure of their company to the living generations of Pueblo people. According to Zuni tradition, the Kachinas had agreed to stop visiting in person because they posed a danger to living people, but they asked the members of the Zuni community to impersonate them, replicating their appearance with masks and costume. Every male member of the Zuni community participates in this agreement after they come of age. Each owns a mask made of leather that fits over his head like a helmet. It can be painted and ornamented to represent many different Kachinas. The owner scrapes the mask clean when the ritual is over. The six kiva organizations of the Zuni collaborate to determine each year which of the several different Kachinas should appear and they organize the logistics of performance among the kiva members. There are hundreds of different Kachinas among the Hopi and Zuni; some appear regularly, others rarely, but their appearances and ritual performances are closely tied to the cyclical round of seasons.

The Kachina ceremonies of the Pueblos mobilize sacred knowledge, ritual performance, and artistic skills in service of the community and its broader exterior (including spiritual) relations. Shalako, the arrival of the "couriers of the rain bringers," for example, is an enormously elaborate public festival at Zuni Pueblo

69 Fred Kabotie (Hopi), *Zuni Shalako*, gouache on paper, c. 1928–32. Kabotie shows three of the six giant Shalako Kachinas that arrive at Zuni Pueblo every year in early December. They are accompanied by a pair of guardians, the Salimopia Kachinas, carrying whips.

that requires the sustained efforts of its principal actors and their families for the entire year. It marks the conclusion of the ritual year in early December, just before Winter Solstice when the New Year begins. The dramatic arrival late in the afternoon of the six Shalakos, 9 ft (2.7 m) tall horned birds with halo-like crests of macaw feathers and eagle plumes, begins the night-long event [69]. Within six houses, newly built or refurbished for this purpose, Zuni residents and visitors gather to feast, listen to the chanted intonation of long, memorized prayers, and watch while the giant Shalako dance throughout the night.

Among both the Hopi and Zuni, men carve small dolls of cottonwood root painted or dressed to represent one or another of the Kachinas. Traditionally, these are given to young girls as rewards for exemplary behavior. One such doll, purchased by ethnobotanist Francis Elmore at Zuni Pueblo during the 1930s, represents Saiyataca, also known as "Long Horn," one of the most important of the Kachina priests, who also dances all night during Shalako and ascends to a rooftop at dawn to intone prayers in loud, declarative tones [70]. The doll is dressed and ornamented

70 Kachina doll, made by a Zuni man during the 1920s or 1930s. The doll represents Saiyataca, the Rain Priest of the North, who arrives at Zuni just before the large Shalako Kachinas during the Shalako ceremonies. He leads a group of followers by shaking his deer scapula rattle during each heavy step.

71 Kachina doll, made by a Hopi man during the 1930s. This doll represents one of several Hemis Kachinas who dance together in a long line during the "home coming" ceremonies at the end of the Kachina cycle among the Hopi Pueblos. They distribute fruits of the harvest and other gifts.

with all the details of Saiyataca's appearance: the mask with its characteristic single horn on the figure's right side, "for long life," fringed with black wool; a full-cut cotton shirt; valuable sea shells draped around its neck; a bow and arrows in one hand, and a deer scapula rattle in the other.

Another doll from one of the Hopi pueblos collected by Francis Elmore represents a Hemis Kachina, one of several identically costumed dancers who perform in a line dance during Niman, the Hopi ceremony that celebrates first harvest and the end of the Kachina season in July [71]. The dance takes place outside and proceeds from one plaza to the next throughout the pueblo where residents and visitors can watch. The Kachinas distribute gifts – freshly harvested melons and squash to everyone, bows and arrows to boys, and Kachina dolls to girls. Details of dress and ornament are painted on the Hopi dolls instead of using cloth, yarn, and other materials as with the Zuni dolls. The stepped headdress, or *tablita*, of the Hemis Kachina emulates the terraced formations of rain clouds.

72 Hemis Kachina, carved by Alvin James, Jr. (Hopi) during the 1970s. James and other Hopi artists innovated the "action" Kachina carving, a sculpture that – rather than being a Kachina doll – represents a Kachina dancer. These carvings are intended for galleries, collectors, and the art market.

The two Kachina dolls collected by Francis Elmore were made around the 1930s, when dolls were sold to outsiders. Prior to that time, both Hopi and Zuni people were reluctant to do this. More recently, some Hopi artists, in particular, have specialized in creating Kachina figures for sale at art fairs or galleries. Alvin James, Jr.'s figure, carved in the 1970s [72], is rendered in a far more animated, dance-like pose than the earlier Hemis Kachina doll. James is one of a recent generation of Hopi artists who stress lifelike realism and accuracy of descriptive detail in their work.

The weavers

When the Spanish arrived in the Southwest during the sixteenth century, looking to expand upon their lucrative conquest of Mexico, they found fields of the Rio Grande Pueblos planted with cotton. Little cotton fabric has survived in the archaeological record of the Anasazi, but the few recovered textiles display a number of sophisticated techniques of manufacture: finger weaving (braiding) and the use of back-strap or upright looms [73]. Cotton had been cultivated north of the Mogollon Rim since at least AD 1000, and cotton blankets and other woven articles had been traded widely, like pottery and other valuables. The Spanish requisitioned large numbers of cotton blankets on an annual basis as part of the *encomiendas* system of tribute imposed upon the Pueblos during the seventeenth century, one blanket per household according to the order of 1635, in addition to food, labor, and other resources. Although the Spanish brought European treadle looms for use in workshops established in Santa Fe, Pueblo weavers preferred the traditional upright loom for use within their own communities. More importantly, the Spanish brought domesticated animals such as horses, cattle, and Churro sheep. Pueblo weavers began to spin wool yarn for blankets, in addition to cotton, early in the seventeenth century.

The Navajo, or Dineh as they call themselves, also learned to weave blankets and other types of garments using an upright loom

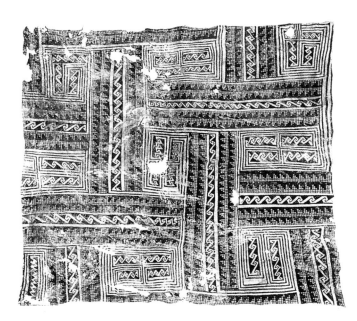

73 Painted cotton blanket. Anasazi culture, c. AD 1250. Hidden House site, central Arizona. The Anasazi clearly had developed elaborate textile arts of loom-woven cotton fiber, but little has survived in the archaeological record.

and yarn spun from cotton and the wool of Churro sheep during the seventeenth century. The Navajo and Apache had established themselves in the Southwest by AD 1500, perhaps earlier. They speak an Athapascan language and "Dineh" is the same name as their closest relations well to the north in western Canada. Originally a hunting-and-gathering people, the *Apache de Nabajò*, as the Spanish called them, did some farming as well. Early Spanish records describe the Navajo as fierce raiders, running off horses and Churro sheep, and taking captives as slaves. But they also traded extensively with the Pueblos and the Spanish. They harbored refugees of the Pueblo Revolt of 1680 when, in a campaign of organized and armed resistance, the Pueblos expelled the newcomers. After the Spanish had returned to the Rio Grande valley with sufficient force in 1693, many Pueblo residents retreated to the northwest, around and beyond the Hopi mesas, where they settled, and in some cases merged, with Navajo. The Navajo synthesized many of the cultural influences offered through these episodes of their history, but the husbandry of Churro sheep as a source for meat and wool and the craft of weaving suited them in particular. While the creation of textiles among the Pueblos was, and still is, a man's activity, weaving fell to women among the Navajo in keeping with their notions about the proper division of labor by gender. During the subsequent centuries and up to the present day, Navajo women have excelled at the arts of weaving.

In addition to providing blankets, dresses, horse blankets and the like for themselves, the Navajo have always created textiles to trade with outsiders. They supplied fine woven wearing blankets (*mantas*) and serapes to the Pueblos and Spanish with thin striped patterns based upon Spanish models dyed with imported indigo blue dyes. Black-and-white banded "chief's blankets," some with stripes of indigo blue, were favored by neighboring Ute, Cheyenne, and other Plains tribes to the north [74]. Elaborate serape-style patterns of the mid-nineteenth century drew from Rio Grande Hispanic and Satillo (northern Mexican) blankets [75]. These could be wrapped around the shoulders as a wearing blanket or slit with a neck hole in the center and worn as a poncho. But Navajo weavers were not mere copyists. Their patterns acknowledge the preferences of fashion while offering startling innovations executed with great intricacy and dexterity. Navajo weavers improvised. They supplemented their tight homespun yarn with yarns unraveled from trade cloth and, later, commercially prepared and dyed yarns. By the 1860s, some

74 Wearing blanket, woven by a Navajo woman, Arizona, *c.* 1850. This kind of striped blanket, known as a "first phase chief's blanket," was a particularly popular trade item among the tribes to the north, particularly the Ute.

75 Serape, woven by a Navajo woman, Arizona, *c.* 1860. With the slit cut down the center, this garment was worn as a poncho or serape. Favored by those of Mexican descent in the Southwest, the design borrows features of Mexican textiles, but remains distinctively Navajo.

blankets included a confusing array of raveled yarns, raveled and respun yarns, and multiple-ply trade yarns, all combined in dazzling and colorful patterns. By 1880, the best quality blankets were woven entirely of imported "Germantown" yarns (named after the Pennsylvania town where the yarn was manufactured), available in an unprecedented variety of colors. Navajo weavers responded to these new yarns with intense "eye-dazzler" patterns displaying shimmering effects of inter-penetrating color contrasts.

The exemplary quality of Navajo textiles should be understood within the context of the multi-cultural environment of textile production in the Southwest after Spanish settlement. The desirability of finely woven textiles created a market for Navajo weavers, offering opportunities beyond the confines of their own communities [76]. Hispanic, Pueblo, and Navajo traditions borrowed freely from one another, weavers motivated by the sheer necessity of supplying blankets, garments, and other categories of textile that were fundamental to social life. And the cultural terrain of the Southwest kept changing, too. After the independence of Mexico in 1821 and the incorporation of New Mexico and Arizona as territories of the United States in 1848, new opportunities for the creators of textiles emerged. Navajo weavers kept abreast of these events, despite the great hardships their people endured. Theirs was an adaptable art, built upon generations of tradition but simultaneously with the flexibility to understand what was required from the changeable nature of their social environment.

Artists, traders, and tourists

For centuries the Rio Grande Pueblos had produced much of the pottery used throughout New Mexico, and they had brought pottery to sell at the Santa Fe market since the seventeenth century. For their own domestic use, they made bowls, large storage jars, and smaller wide-mouthed water jars. The last were fundamental to the daily chore of collecting water for household use. By the 1880s, Tesuque, Cochiti, San Juan, and San Ildefonso pueblos, among others, all within a day's wagon ride of Santa Fe and its curio shops, made special varieties of figurines, miniatures, and innovative and eccentric vessels designed to appeal to the curious visitor and consumer [77]. Enterprising traders also offered these items by mail-order catalogue. When the Santa Fe railroad trains made their regularly scheduled stops at Laguna Pueblo, travelers purchased water jars directly from local potters [78]. The railroad encouraged tourism and, to this end, its food concessionaire and eventual hotelier, Fred Harvey, heavily promoted Southwest Native arts, opening galleries at hotels in Albuquerque

77 Indian pottery, photographed by Ben Wittick, c. 1880. This assortment of figurines made by potters of Cochiti and Tesuque pueblos were probably assembled for this photograph by Santa Fe curio dealer Aaron Gold. The lively and imaginative figures were made to appeal to Santa Fe's tourists.

78 Water jar, made by a woman of Laguna Pueblo, *c.* 1890. The Santa Fe railroad ran right by Laguna Pueblo. The train stopped and travelers could get out and take pictures and buy painted jars, like this one, from Laguna women who came out to meet the train.

79 Painted jar, made by Nampeyo (Tewa-Hopi), *c.* 1900. Ceramic artist Nampeyo studied excavated pottery from ancient Hopi sites and helped create what became known as Sikyatki-revival pottery. For many years Nampeyo was a featured artist-in-residence at Hopi House, an Indian art and craft gallery at the El Tovar hotel on the south rim of the Grand Canyon.

and at the Grand Canyon, and employing artists as demonstrators. The expanded market for Pueblo pottery and other Southwest Native arts encouraged artists and increased their ranks.

Many exceptional artists rose to these opportunities. Nampeyo, a Tewa-Hopi potter born in Hano in 1859, worked with trader Thomas Keam to create an innovative, high-quality style of pottery based upon pieces excavated by archaeologist Jesse Fewkes from nearby ruins [79]. Called Sikyatki-revival, the archaizing sensibility of this pottery quickly made other styles obsolete. Its success in the marketplace meant that new potters were recruited on all three mesas, so that by 1891, nearly half of all Hopi women made painted pottery, and all of it for trade.

Nampeyo's creations stand out, and she is the matriarch of a long line of descendants who, to this day, excel as innovative ceramic artists.

At San Ildefonso Pueblo, several female potters and their husbands collaborated, the women making the pots and the men painting the designs. Probably the best known of such couples were Maria and Julian Martinez who experimented with several different styles of decoration (black-on-red and polychrome painting) until they arrived upon their landmark "signature style" just after World War I. Archaeologist Edgar Hewett, who employed several residents of San Ildefonso during his excavations at nearby Frijoles Canyon (now part of Bandelier National Monument), encouraged Maria and Julian to see if they could reproduce a variety of black pottery he had discovered at the site. Their experiments resulted in the invention of a "black-on-black" style of pottery decoration that contrasts highly polished backgrounds with matte black designs [80]. Julian, who also enjoyed some success as a painter of watercolors and murals, drew from his knowledge of the collections at the Museum of New Mexico, where he was employed from 1909 to 1915. The generation of Maria and Julian Martinez, including Maximiliana Montoya and her husband Crescencio Martinez, Tonita Martinez

80 Jar (black-on-black design), made by Maria and Julian Martinez, c. 1930. This is one of the largest and most ambitious jars made by this ceramic artist couple. Maria built and burnished the jars to their lustrous finish, while Julian was responsible for the painted design, here an undulating horned serpent with lightning bolts and thunderclouds.

Roybal and her husband Juan Cruz Roybal, among others, transformed San Ildefonso as their success became widely recognized and their descendants and others became noted artists as well. San Ildefonso is renowned today for the artists who live and work there.

Navajo weavers, ever responsive to the potential for innovative directions, also worked with traders during the 1880s and 1890s. As the demand for blankets declined, Navajo women made rugs woven from heavier, more durable yarns. Traders discouraged the use of commercial yarns like the colorful Germantown yarns popular during the 1870s and 1880s, thinking that homespun in natural colors appealed more to buyers interested in Indian handicrafts. On the other hand, J. B. Moore of Crystal Trading Post encouraged weavers to emulate the patterns of Oriental carpets with their borders and designs organized around a central escutcheon. Weavers also found success with designs that included pictorial forms drawn from Navajo sand paintings, in which healers would create pictorial images on the ground, using sand mixed with pigment as part of a ritual to cure disease. The designs illustrate salient moments of a chanted narrative that recalls the origins of the Navajo world and the activities of hero twins and other spirit beings. As early as 1900, some Navajo weavers made rugs with images of *yei*, the holy people represented in sand paintings, or *yeibichai*, rows of Navajo dancers who participate in some curing ceremonies.

During the 1850s, Navajo men added silverwork to their inventories of art production. Perhaps the first, a blacksmith named Atsidi Sani evidently learned the basic skills required to transform silver coins into jewelry from a Mexican blacksmith. By the time the Navajo had returned to their homeland in 1869, after imprisonment at Bosque Redondo, the art of making bracelets, pendants, and other ornaments of silver had been established among them. One suspects that the experience of being uprooted and required to abandon land and possessions may have contributed to the desire to convert wealth into portable ornaments. Early Navajo smiths worked silver with simple casting and annealing techniques, adding decorative markings with files and straight chisels. A talented and influential silverworker named Astadi Chon produced the first documented silver headstall for a horse and the first thick, disk-shaped ornaments for belts called "conchas." Later generations introduced the techniques of soldering, mounting stones of turquoise, and the use of decorative stamps inspired by the tools of Mexican leatherworkers. Like weavers, Navajo silversmiths of the late nineteenth century formed alliances with traders who provided silver and stone for the production of jewelry and other categories of objects for sale to tourists. Throughout the twentieth century, styles changed and workmanship became increasingly sophisticated, using large cut or irregular pieces of polished turquoise set in massive bracelets, necklace pendants, concha belts, brooches, and bolo ties [81]. The contemporary jewelry traditions of the Hopi and Zuni Pueblos originated from the instruction of Navajos. Today, Navajo men and women make fine jewelry that may, on one hand, build from the techniques and styles of the past or may, on the other, look to modern and contemporary jewelry design for inspiration.

The artists working in the Southwest during the last decades of the nineteenth century blazed the way for what Native American art would become during the subsequent century. Artists updated media with ancient roots in the Southwest to find success among the buyers of their time. New media, like watercolor painting, will be discussed in the last chapter, which focuses on the twentieth century. While some of this creativity was directed outward, individual communities also strived to protect ritual arts from the commercial concerns of outsiders. The popular appeal of authentic Native American culture, which fueled interest in pots and rugs, resulted as well in the trafficking of sacred objects and artifacts looted from archaeological sites. Native artists of the Southwest today continue to balance ritual and artistic concerns relevant only to local communities against the opportunities and advantages offered by the outside world.

81 Group of bracelets made of silver with turquoise inlays, made by Navajo men between 1900 and 1930. Navajo men started making silver jewelry as early as the 1850s.

Chapter 5   Plains

The prairie grasslands stretch from the arboreal forests of northern Canada to the mesquite shrub savannahs of the Rio Grande. They represent the largest of the indigenous North American vegetation zones, although recent history, in the form of modern agriculture and ranching, has so transformed this vast grassy core of the North American continent that it is difficult to imagine it as it once was. Teeming with native plants and wildlife, this fertile region is thought to have supported as many as two million people – more than ten per cent of the total population of indigenous North America.

The central interior of North America was one of the last regions surveyed by Europe-based outsiders, but what they saw had already been transformed by the deadly epidemics that preceded them. The prosperous agricultural communities that once crowded major river valleys had declined in number to the very few that were visited by early explorers like William Clark and Meriwether Lewis in 1803. Lewis and Clark found two Mandan villages of earth lodges, for example, located on either side of the Missouri River in what is now North Dakota. The survivors of a recent smallpox epidemic who had gathered there said that only forty years earlier there had been a total of nine Mandan villages. Smallpox had been only the most recent of the many pandemics that afflicted the American heartland during the later sixteenth century and that hit agricultural villages particularly hard. Archaeologists count hundreds of agricultural village sites stretching from Iowa to North Dakota along the Missouri River, all of the so-called Middle Missouri tradition dating between AD 800 and 1600. These had been built by the ancestors of the Mandan. After another scourge in the 1830s, only one village would remain.

82 Ghost Dance dress, one of a small group of painted Ghost Dance garments made by Arapaho women (and perhaps male collaborators) of Oklahoma after 1889. The painted designs combine traditional images of Arapaho cosmology, such as the cedar tree on the lower left, with Ghost Dance symbols, such as the crow and white-tailed Western magpie.

The descendants of Spanish horses brought to the Southwest also greeted early white visitors to the plains. Horses had come to the Plains tribes via trade with the Navajo, Apache, and Ute. By 1750, the tribes of the Plains kept large herds and they had become part of the very fabric of Plains Indian culture. The image of the equestrian Plains Indians roaming freely over the sparsely inhabited grasslands, as witnessed and documented by the testimony of explorers, fur trappers, military men, and Native elders interviewed by anthropologists, tends to dominate consideration of Plains Indian culture and art. As significant as horses had become, the traditions of Plains culture had grown from the land itself and its unique environment. The horse had simply been pressed into service to benefit life-ways that had evolved over thousands of years.

Pictures on stone
At Head-Smashed-In Buffalo Jump in southern Alberta, generation after generation of hunters drove herds of buffalo over a well-concealed cliff to their deaths. The name "Head-Smashed-In" does not refer to the fate of the buffalo. The Blackfeet gave the site that name to recall a tragic incident when a curious child attempted to watch the dramatic hunt by standing on a ledge along the face of the cliff as the buffalo fell over from above. He misjudged his position, however, and when the dead and dying buffalo piled up, their bodies eventually crushed him. Archaeologists have excavated through some 30 ft (9 m) of butchered buffalo remains at the base of the cliff, representing over five thousand years of hunting. Early Archaic "Bitterroot" points found at the earliest levels date to 3500 BC and correspond to those found at the Mummy Cave site in Wyoming. Pelican Lake people later used the site, beginning in about 900 BC. They were followed by the Avonlea tradition (perhaps Athapascan speakers), and they used the jump sometime after AD 100. People of the Old Woman tradition followed, in about AD 850, and we know that they were the ancestors of the present-day Blackfeet. As this site-based scenario suggests, the history of the plains is rich in movement and migration, but the traditions defined by archaeological study did not simply disappear. Research linked with linguistic studies and accounting for oral traditions can now probe the deep roots of historically known Plains cultures.

Ancient artists left images pecked or painted on exposed rock in many different locations throughout the northwest plains. Pictographic art can be linked to specific traditions and ethnic

84 Pictographs at the Writing-On-Stone site, southern Alberta. Men of the Blackfeet and other tribes have visited this site for hundreds of years, leaving pictographic records of their battle honors inscribed on the rocks. This scene shows warriors, several with large shields, engaged in combat.

groups only tenuously. Pictographs of the "Early Hunting Tradition," as described by James Keyser, feature elaborate representations of big-game hunting, in which hunters with the help of dogs drive elk and other large game into traps. Some of these are located within the narrow canyons used for game drives among the southern Black Hills of South Dakota. These sites and others in Wyoming correspond to the territories of the Pelican Lake tradition mentioned above and believed by archaeologist Karl Schlesier to be ancestral to the present-day Kiowa. But any relationship between the Pelican Lake peoples and Early Hunting Tradition pictographs must remain very tentative for the time being.

Another series of widely dispersed rock images shows warriors holding large shields that cover most of their bodies [83]. A painting on rock within the Valley of the Shields in southeastern Montana shows three standing warriors with circular shields painted evocatively in white, purple, red, green, and orange. Each of the shields is painted with a different design. Schlesier links early shield-bearing figures to Athapascan peoples who would later become known as the Kiowa Apache. A radiocarbon sample from the site has produced a date of about AD 1100.

83 Shield-Bearing Warrior pictographs (from Keyser and Klassen), from various sites in Montana and Wyoming. The three figures together, fourth from the bottom, are from the Valley of the Shields site, also known variously as Valley of the Chiefs or Weatherman Draw, in Montana.

The rugged sandstone bluffs north of the Milk River in southern Alberta are scribed with thousands of pictographic images, a location known today as Writing-On-Stone [84]. Some show shield-bearing figures locked in combat. These commemorate battle honors.

Characteristically, the artists pared down the imagery to the essentials of identity (portrayed through individualistic shield designs), weaponry, and action – who struck whom and with what. Combat images showing mounted warriors date sometime after 1730 or so, when the local Blackfeet and Shoshone began to acquire horses in abundance. In some instances, mounted warriors with small shields ride down warriors on foot with large shields and strike them with lances. Archaeologists estimate that most of the pictographs at Writing-On-Stone date within the last five hundred years, but some could even be over a thousand years old, like the shield-bearing figures at the Valley of the Shields. Clearly, artists frequented the site to add pictographs throughout the last millennia. Many of the older pictographs have simply eroded away.

Gifts of spirit beings

The enormous shields carried by warriors in pictographs became obsolete relics of warfare on foot. Warriors on horseback carried smaller, more maneuverable shields. David Thompson, a trader for the Hudson's Bay Company, heard a story of pre-horse combat from an elderly Cree man named Saukamappee with whom he spent the winter in 1787–88. Saukamappee had participated in an expedition with his Blackfeet allies against a tribe he called the Snake (perhaps the Shoshone). Hundreds of warriors faced each other, but after chanting their war songs, they sat down on the ground with their large shields covering them. Some were so large they covered two men. Then both sides let loose arrows, but after a day of such fighting, both sides retired with no one killed. Years later, the two sides faced each other again, the Snake with horses and the Blackfeet and Cree with flintlock guns. The guns prevailed in this instance (although the Snake evidently dismounted their horses and faced their enemies on foot). New weapons required new tactics, but the shield persisted. Its protective powers were not dependent upon size or physical strength alone.

Shields and their designs were gifts from powerful spirit beings intended to aid and protect worthy men in combat. Men acquired the rights to make and use shields as a result of visions sought through isolated fasting. When prayers were successful, spirit beings came to fasting men and showed them sacred objects, such as shields, and instructed them about their powers. Bull Lodge, for example, a well-known Gros Ventre warrior and spiritual leader, experienced a vision in which an old man showed him

85 Shield belonging to Little Rock, a distinguished Cheyenne warrior, mid-1800s. The painted design shows the Thunderbird hovering in the center of the sky, flanked by the crescent moon above and the constellation Pleiades below, accompanied by four additional birds, and encompassed by the horizon of the earth painted around the outer edge of the circular shield.

86 Shield painted by No Two Horns (Hunkpapa Lakota), later 1800s. This rendering of the Thunderbird, by No Two Horns, a well-known warrior and artist, shows its wings extended and radiating power.

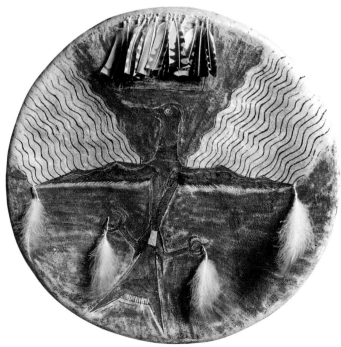

a shield and then pointed to a party of enemy warriors. "He advanced on the charging warriors, holding the shield before him, and he began to sway back and forth, left and right." As Bull Lodge observed, "This [old] man's party was not losing any warriors, and they were killing many of the opposing party." A shield provided spiritual protection well beyond its physical properties. In another vision, Bull Lodge saw himself shaking his shield after battle and the spent bullets of his enemies fell from it and rattled on the ground like rain.

The design painted on a shield showed the identity of the owner's spiritual protector. Bull Lodge's gifts came from the Thunder Beings or Thunderbird. Bull Lodge had been a young boy when the Thunderers first showed him his shield. It was "painted half red and half dark blue. A painted rainbow went all around the edge. In the center, a black bird was painted and from each side of the bird's head, green streaks of lightning ending at the rainbow's inside rim." The shield Bull Lodge made after this vision consisted of two circles of stiff buffalo hide glued together. He painted the image he saw on a supple deerskin cover that fit over the rawhide core. The cover is now lost but several men of different tribes had also received such gifts from Thunder Beings, as evidenced by the designs on their shield covers. The shield that belonged to Little Rock, a Cheyenne, shows the Thunderbird hovering in the dome of the sky, flanked by the crescent moon above and the constellation Pleiades below, accompanied by four smaller birds, all encompassed by the encircling horizon [85]. No Two Horns, a prominent and accomplished Hunkpapa Lakota, also possessed a shield painted with the image of the Thunderbird, its outstretched wings radiating waves of thunder [86]. Depending upon the source of the vision, other shields might be painted with images of buffalo, grizzly bears, or a variety of other powerful creatures.

The powers of the cosmos also found expression on painted garments worn by adherents of the Ghost Dance during the late 1880s and 1890s. Inspired by the visions of Paiute prophet Wovoka, the Ghost Dance promised a return to traditional life with plenty of buffalo and no whites. An Arapaho Ghost Dance dress is painted with crows which acted as messengers from the ancestors, white-tailed magpies who were Wovoka's guardian spirits, and the turtle and cedar tree drawn from the Arapaho stories of origin [82]. Similar garments made by the Lakota were believed to have had the ability to stop bullets.

Histories on hide and paper

The accomplishments of successful combat found expression as pictographs in places like Writing-On-Stone, but also as drawings on items of clothing such as shirts and robes. Garments might combine episodes from several different events, crowding their surfaces with biographical detail. A buffalo robe in the Musée de l'Homme collection, dating perhaps to the eighteenth century, seems to tell the story of a series of encounters, or perhaps a single, long, running fight, between warriors on horseback with painted shields and enemies predominantly on foot, many with guns and red shot pouches [87]. Dotted lines show the paths of the mounted warriors, past seven enemies on the upper right, for example, until the warrior with a red and green shield dismounts his black horse to kill an eighth. A sword drawn on the top of the enemy's head indicates the blow, or *coup*, struck against him. Individual encounters of shield-bearing horsemen against groups of enemies are similarly indicated throughout the composition. Generally speaking, friends are shown on the right, enemies to the left.

87 Pictographic robe made of buffalo hide, painted during the late 1700s by an unknown artist. This exceptionally early depiction of Plains combat shows mounted warriors attacking enemies on foot. Several individual actions are indicated, perhaps different episodes of a single large fight.

By the mid-nineteenth century, men also used paper, often bound in books, with pens or pencils to notate their war honors. They procured notebooks, ledgers, or other kinds of bound paper either through trade or by seizing them during armed conflict. One such book, inscribed with an introductory note by the commanding officer of Fort Dodge, Kansas, in 1868, evidently belonged to an Arapaho chief named Little Shield, who was a signatory of the Fort Laramie Treaty later that same year [88]. Art historian Janet Berlo speculates that the inscription was intended to introduce Little Shield to members of the Peace Commission sent by President Ulysses S. Grant to implement his peace policy after years of warfare on the plains. The ruled pages of the book are filled with images of Little Shield's personal exploits accompanied by penciled annotations. One shows his victory over a Pawnee on foot armed with a rifle. Little Shield shot him while galloping on horseback, as indicated by the rifle that touches the Pawnee's bowed head. Although drawn with pencil and colored ink on paper, the pictorial language used by the artist to portray the event relates closely to similar scenes on the older media of painted garments and pictographic inscriptions.

No Two Horns, the Hunkpapa mentioned earlier, also led an eventful life, as reflected in the number of art works he produced late in his life while living on the Standing Rock reservation in North Dakota before his death in 1942. He had participated in

88 Page from a book of drawings by Little Shield (Arapaho), probably made during the 1860s. This drawing shows Little Shield's defeat of a Pawnee warrior armed with a rifle. Note that the artist shows the result of the encounter by drawing his rifle so it touches the enemy's head.

89 Drawing by No Two Horns, showing an event during the Battle of the Little Big Horn when his beloved blue roan was shot from beneath him. No Two Horns identifies himself with his shield portrayed above his head (see fig. 86).

90 Horse stick, carved by No Two Horns and carried by him during the Grass Dance to honor his horse killed in battle (see fig. 89). The horse sustained seven wounds before it fell.

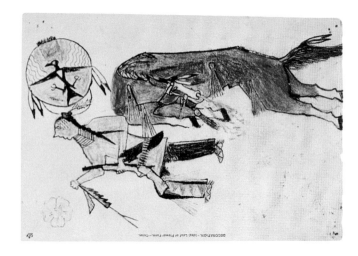

several successful encounters against the Crow and distinguished himself at the Battle of the Little Big Horn in 1876. At the Custer fight, his horse was fatally wounded and one of several of his drawings now preserved at the State Historical Society of North Dakota honors the horse by recalling its heroic death [89]. The blue roan twists in agony as No Two Horns tumbles forward, his distinctive shield poised over his head. No Two Horns also carved several wooden dance wands representing this horse and its mortal wounds [90]. The "horse stick" was intended to honor the horse when carried during the Grass Dance, a popular ritual performance throughout the plains during the 1880, which celebrated men's accomplishments in battles past. Other dance wands or clubs from Standing Rock are carved with images of their traditional Crow enemies, distinguished by their heavily greased, upright bangs and red face paint, and are intended to recall victorious actions against them.

The owners of tipis, the buffalo skin and later canvas lodges of Plains peoples, sometimes painted them with expressions of their visionary experiences, or more rarely, scenes of battle. In the year 1845, the Cheyenne chief Sleeping Bear gave a painted tipi to the Kiowa leader Little Bluff as a token of friendship and alliance. The gift consisted of the right to reproduce the tipi, painted with images of war honors, and subsequent copies descend down through the lineage of Little Bluff to this day. The painted design of the tipi is divided into two equal parts. Diagonal black and yellow stripes on one side refer to war expeditions led by Sleeping Bear and Little Bluff. One of Little Bluff's contemporaries, a fiercesome warrior named Heart Eater, added the twelve war axes stacked vertically down the center of the design. The battle scenes on the left changed with every version of the tipi, commemorating the accomplishments of each generation of owners. Notable events so recorded include the occasion when the Comanche Head Pendant, hidden behind breastworks, single-handedly held off Mexican troops, or when the Kiowa war chief Big Bow and his wife Black Bear escaped Mexican soldiers after being wounded. Ohettoint, the grandson of Little Bluff and one of the Fort Marion prisoners (see below) painted a model of the tipi. This lineage of Kiowa warriors and artists also produced James Silverhorn and Stephen Mopope (see p. 197).

The pictographs, paintings, and drawings produced by men of the plains provided visual testimony to the notable events in their lives. As the broader outside world closed around them during the later nineteenth century, this documentary practice sometimes reflected new and unfamiliar experiences. In 1875, seventy-two Cheyenne, Kiowa, and Comanche (and one Caddo) were rounded up by military authorities and sent east to be imprisoned at Fort Marion in St. Augustine, Florida. All were well-

91 Drawing by Zotom, a Kiowa and one of seventy-one southern Plains men (and one woman) imprisoned at Fort Marion, St. Augustine, Florida, in 1875. Here Zotom shows the newly arrived prisoners gathered on the parapet of the fort looking out toward the bay.

known warriors selected for incarceration because of their accomplishments in battle. Zotom, a Kiowa born in 1853, had participated in raids throughout Texas and Mexico, and had been identified at an attack upon a party of buffalo hunters at Adobe Walls in the Texas panhandle during the spring of 1874. At Fort Marion, he was one of several men who produced drawings for sale to visitors. Most of the drawings avoid overt references to incidents of combat, perhaps at the behest of the jailors or, more simply, because potential buyers might have found such images distasteful. Instead, the Fort Marion drawings tend to generalize, with images of the hunt, dances, and ceremonies. Notable among Zotom's drawings, however, are those that catalogue his experiences after capture: the long journey to prison by train; the hunt for and killing of the Cheyenne chief Grey Beard after he had thrown himself off the moving train in an attempt to escape; the prisoners gathered on the parapet of the imposing stone fort the day of their arrival [91]. In the last-named picture, the perspectival rendering of Fort Marion's architecture, the topographical setting of the bay with its headlands and lighthouses, ships receding in the distance, and the vantage point, distant from the scene to impose compositional order, all seem derived from study of photographs. The novel experiences and means of Zotom's expression, however, remain no less authentic than those of the many artists who inscribed images on the cliffs at Writing-On-Stone centuries before.

Pipes and carvers
Pipestone National Monument protects a shallow stone quarry located in present-day southwestern Minnesota where pipe carvers have been extracting a red pipestone called catlinite for over five hundred years. Quarrying through as much as 4 to 12 ft (1.2 to 3.6 m) of hard quartzite exposes a layer of red catlinite suitable for carving but nowadays rarely more than a few inches thick (nineteenth-century accounts describe strata as thick as 18 in., or 46 cm). Carvers of the Oneota archaeological tradition, ancestral to the Iowa and Winnebago, removed stone from the site for pipes and pendants. The sixteenth-century Iroquois, whose trade interests expanded across the Great Lakes at that time, were great consumers of catlinite. In 1676, Father Louis Andre, a Jesuit missionary visiting the Winnebago villages of Green Bay, Wisconsin, witnessed the arrival of a party of Iowa with buffalo hides and red stone pipes to trade. The Dakota, or Eastern Sioux, expanding westward from the Minnesota forests, controlled the territory around the site by the eighteenth century,

although quarrying parties from throughout the region apparently found access without much difficulty. Arriving parties camped, fasted, and prayed in preparation before removing stone. The admonishment, current today, to remove only as much as needed may account for the lack of evidence of any broad trade in the raw material. Instead, pipes produced in a plethora of tribally based styles – Pawnee, Dakota, Ojibwa – seem to have been carved by individuals or small parties who went to the trouble of procuring their own stone. Joseph Nicollet, a geologist who visited the site in 1838, avoided a party of Sauk and Fox, camped with some Eastern Sioux, and was told to beware of more parties from "the nations of the Missouri" who visited regularly during that time of year.

Pipes made of red catlinite preserved today testify to the great skill and artistry of individual pipe carvers. Three can be attributed to an unusually gifted Dakota master whose name we do not know but who was active during the 1830s and 1840s. The most elaborate of the three pipes has a drum-shaped bowl perched in the back of a small dog [92]. The artist used inlaid lead to create the radial pattern on the bowl and the buffalo leg design on the horizontal shank. The tableau carved on top of the shank is most remarkable. A band chief, identified by the peace medal he wears around his neck, offers a glass of brandy across a table to a diminutive man, perhaps a member of his band. All three pipes attributed to this carver include related imagery: chiefs with cups or casks of brandy. Although there were many who condemned the use of alcohol in the fur trade, and still do today, it was part and parcel of the business in Minnesota during the 1830s. In fact the distribution of alcohol maintained a formal structure. Trade

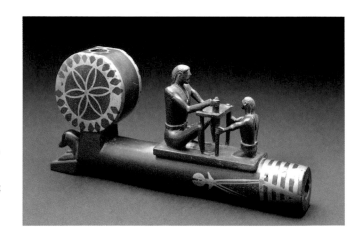

92 Pipe bowl, carved by an unknown Eastern Sioux man during the 1830s or 1840s. This is one of three very elaborate pipe bowls attributed to this artist's hand. All three include the signature-like pattern representing a buffalo leg, complete with hoof, inlaid in lead on the shank of the pipe.

"captains," the band chiefs who led fur-hunting parties, customarily met with the trader first, before a general exchange of goods for furs. The band chief received the alcohol, often in barrels, which he then distributed to his followers to drink in acknowledgment of their allegiance. The image of the band chief who controls trade alcohol is a symbol referring to his authority, made clear by the differential scale of the chief and his follower as carved on the pipe bowl.

Smoking pipes and tobacco play a role in almost every dimension of Plains social and religious life. In addition to the thousands of pipes owned and used by individuals, many religious rituals required them and included episodes of ritualized tobacco smoking. Smoking tobacco as part of a ceremony acknowledges and animates the greater spiritual and cosmological context of all human endeavors. Today, some people of Native ancestry express discomfort with the fact that smoking pipes are sometimes displayed in museums as works of art or sculpture.

Porcupine quills and glass beads
While working among the Cheyenne, conservationist and ethnographer George Bird Grinnell met an elderly member of the Cheyenne Quilling Society named Picking Bones Woman. The origin of quillwork, she told him, came from a young man who had discovered that his wife and son were really buffalo. Out of love, the young man had followed his family to their buffalo home. When he returned, he gave to the women of his community what he had learned during his time among his buffalo family: the knowledge of how to prepare buffalo hide robes and decorate them with porcupine quills.

Plains communities placed high value upon the industry and skills required of women to prepare hides for clothing, lodging, and other necessary items. The techniques of decoration, with porcupine quill and later glass bead appliqué, emphasize the aesthetic value of such work above and beyond utilitarian necessity. The creation of finely decorated items, particularly those intended for ritual use, represented the highest status of feminine achievement. Cheyenne women recognized successive grades within their Quilling Society linked to the production and decoration of different categories of objects: 1) moccasins; 2) baby cradles; 3) circular ornaments (rosettes) for tipis; 4) robes and backrests. Similarly, among the Lakota, young women honored by the puberty ceremony known as Isnati Awicalowampi were thereafter called Buffalo Women and accepted an honored role

93 Cradle decorated with quillwork, c. 1880, very likely made by a woman whose name was recorded as Fire Wood, one of the Northern Arapaho sacred workbag keepers active at the Wind River reservation, Wyoming.

among their communities which included the expectation that they would produce fine quillwork and beadwork. These young Lakota women underwent lengthy training under the guidance of elders until they had mastered the techniques of arts production prior to marriage.

Cedar Woman, an Arapaho elder who spoke to anthropologist Alfred Kroeber during his fieldwork a century ago, was the keeper of one of seven sacred workbags that held incense, paint, and implements for sewing. These had been passed down from generation to generation. Only women with exemplary skills and proven industriousness might be considered for this honor. As another woman explained to Kroeber, if someone who is inexperienced attempts to embroider robes with quills, she is doomed to failure. Excellence can be accomplished only through prayer, instruction by example, and the appropriate ritual preparation through elders. The seven sacred workbags represented the collective knowledge, skill, and experience of untold generations of Arapaho women. Their keepers ensured the continuity of practice through example and instruction. They worked with the other women on collective projects and at least one workbag keeper was required for the creation of a decorated tipi or buffalo robe.

A group of exquisite baby carriers decorated with porcupine quills (at least fifteen are known today) were produced under the supervision of sacred workbag keepers of the Northern Arapaho who live now on the Wind River reservation in Wyoming. Cleaver Warden, who worked as an ethnographic informant at Wind River, recorded in his notebook of 1904–5 that an elderly workbag keeper named Fire Wood had made sixty baby carriers during her lifetime. Her workbag had come from her mother, Bird Woman. All the surviving baby carriers are remarkably consistent in design and in the high quality of their workmanship [93]. Customarily, the sponsor of the baby carrier, often the mother's sister, assembled and hosted a feast for a group of experienced women to work with her to make all the component parts. The circular porcupine quill rosette placed on the top of the baby carrier represents the baby's head, but may be reused later as a tipi ornament. The design and decoration of the baby carrier, stretched upon a frame, is said to resemble that of a tipi and symbolizes the wish that the baby should grow into adulthood and own one.

The fastidious and exacting quality of Cheyenne and Arapaho ornament (the peoples are closely related) may in fact stem from their more collective approach to the production of certain tradition-bound objects. On the other hand, the traditions of women's art on the plains permitted inspired creativity as well. A single master quillworker, or at best a close circle, is responsible for a small but spectacular group of quill-decorated objects made during the mid-nineteenth century. Best known among them is a shirt presented to 2nd Lt. Charles G. Sawtail by Brule Lakota Chief Spotted Tail at Fort Laramie, Wyoming, in 1855 [94]: hence art historians speculate that the maker was Brule too. The broad shoulder and sleeve strips and the neck flap are embroidered with a technique that resembles checkerwork weaving, a startling innovation in Plains quillwork that is found nowhere else.

By the time early European visitors began to acquire the decorated hides and garments that are found in museum collections today, Plains hide-workers were already decorating their work with glass beads made in Venice, combined with porcupine quills and other materials. A dress tailored in an early style that combines many different kinds of trade goods was brought back to Washington by Meriwether Lewis and William Clark after their expedition of 1803–4 and presented to future First Lady Dolly Madison. The dress illustrated here may be that one, or, alternatively, it may have been deposited in Charles Willson Peale's Museum in Philadelphia by a different source in

94 Shirt presented by Lakota Chief Spotted Tail to 2nd Lt. Charles G. Sawtail at Fort Laramie, Wyoming, in 1855. The shirt was made by an unknown woman who employed a rare and distinctive technique of quillwork embroidery to decorate the large shoulder and sleeve strips of the shirt.

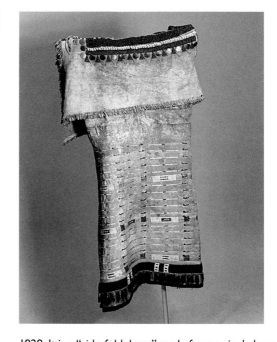

95 Side-fold dress collected during the early decades of the nineteenth century in the Upper Missouri river region. Its decoration employs a number of exotic trade materials: glass beads, wool cloth, cowrie shells, and tin pendants.

96 (opposite above) Knife case, made by a Cheyenne woman and collected in 1866 by one of the work party who built Fort C. F. Smith on the Bozeman Trail, connecting Fort Laramie to Montana. Note the distinctive "lanes," or parallel rows, of bead appliqué that result from the technique of "parallel stitch."

97 (opposite centre right) Knife case, made by a Crow woman living on the Crow reservation, Montana, during the 1890s. The geometric designs relate to those used by women for painted parfleches (see fig. 98).

98 (opposite below left) Parfleche, a buffalo rawhide container, made and painted by a Crow woman of Montana, c. 1880.

1828. It is a "side-fold dress" made from a single large elk hide cut to wrap around the body and sewn with a single seam on the left side [95]. The body of the dress is delicately embroidered with horizontal bands of dyed porcupine quills, a pattern that resembles the treatment of buffalo robes. Bands of large blue and white glass beads frame the ornament on the dress with heavy horizontal borders along the lower hem and just below the neck. In addition, the decoration incorporates brass buttons, cowrie shells imported from the South China Sea, "tinkler" pendants cut from imported tin, and tufts of red wool yarn unraveled from cloth milled in Britain. The large glass beads are a type known today as "pony beads." They came in a restricted range of colors, predominantly blue and white as here, but also more rarely red, black, and yellow. The use of pony beads characterizes glass bead ornament on the plains until about 1850.

By the 1860s, Plains women had a broad range of different colored, smaller sized "seed-beads" to choose from. Color preferences, traditions of technique for application, and choices about design, form, and structure among women of different communities developed into far more strongly articulated "tribal styles" during the 1860s and 1870s. Parallel stitch favored by Cheyenne women, for example, with beads applied within parallel lanes, derived from the techniques of porcupine quill appliqué but

enlivened by patterns of alternating colors within the lanes [96]. Crow women of Wyoming and Montana, on the other hand, developed their own particular "Crow stitch" technique [97], which was better suited to the tightly nested triangles and oblong shapes that characterize "parfleche" painting [98]. The parfleche was a storage container made of folded rawhide and painted with colorful geometric patterns. Women applied color to the rawhide

surfaces with cut sections of buffalo rib, their ends ground to expose the absorbent, sponge-like marrow that could be dipped in pigment and used like a modern-day ink marker. Crow beadwork appliqué after the 1860s is clearly related to the designs of parfleche painting, not quillwork. Throughout the Plains region, the geometric design traditions of both quillwork and parfleche painting informed the emergent art of glass bead appliqué as it grew in popularity during the later nineteenth century. Beadwork grew to become the dominant medium for the decoration of Plains garments, bags, pouches, horse and tipi ornaments, and several other categories of objects.

Plains cultures extolled the virtues of women's industriousness, care, and skill in making things, partly because the things themselves represented such great value, culturally, economically, and spiritually. For example, the Oglala band of Lakota conferred the title *Ongloge Un*, or "shirt-wearer," upon four able men who were delegated to oversee the general welfare of the people. When a newly elected *Ongloge Un* received his resplendent garment, made with considerable care and ceremony, he was told, "Though you now wear the shirt, be a big-hearted man.... This shirt here means you have been chosen as a big heart; you are always to help your friends...."

Generosity lies at the center of Lakota cultural values. Women worked hard to make many different kinds of decorated items for "give-aways," events at which social relations were acknowledged and reinforced through the formal distribution of gifts. Give-aways became an extremely important feature of reservation life among the Lakota. Prominent families, designated as sponsors when the tribe presented them with a symbolic penny (*máza 'ala*, literally "red iron"), spent the entire year assembling, commissioning, and manufacturing goods for give-aways scheduled for the Fourth of July. Government policy discouraged ceremonies at any other time of the year. Lakota give-aways of the reservation period, particularly the period between 1880 and World War I, inspired the production of enormous quantities of beaded items, many decorated with images of Fourth of July American flags. The Fourth of July celebrations, their attendant ceremonies and give-aways, and the material and performance arts required for their success all contributed to the support of Lakota ethnic identity at a time when it was under a great deal of coercive threat from the outside world.

Clearly, mothers, aunts, and grandmothers who had been prominent artists of their own generations had nurtured talented women who led the proliferation of Lakota beadwork at the beginning of the new century. The requirements of dances and give-aways, and opportunities to sell at fairs or at Wild West shows which employed several generations of Lakota men, and even sales through mail-order catalogues, all produced great demand for the skills and talents of bead-workers [99]. Today, most beadwork produced on the Lakota reservations goes to powwow dancers, whose elaborate and meticulously made regalia provides a real advantage in competitive dancing. The growth and proliferation of powwow dancing after the 1950s throughout "Indian Country" (a perceptual space that encompasses all Native communities) reaffirm the importance of decorated regalia as a symbol of Native cultural identity and vitality, providing the occasion and a performative structure for its display. Less obvious, perhaps, in the highly structured spectacle of contemporary powwow dancing, are the efforts of artists who, by creating contemporary regalia, reshape the traditional roles of Native arts in ways that can flourish in the world today.

99 Beadwork display of Joseph and Edith Claymore (Lakota), both of Standing Rock reservation, North and South Dakota, c, 1900–1910, photographed by Frank Fiske. The elaborately beaded suitcases and satchels were created by Edith.

Chapter 6   Far West

The varied topographies of the Pacific edge of central North America, now the state of California, offered a variety of opportunities for Native societies. To the north, communities settled along salmon rivers. The Great Central Valley, sheltered by the Cascade and Sierra Nevada ranges to the east and the Klamath and Coastal ranges to the west, fed its residents with seed grasses, acorns from several species of oak, and a nurturing habitat for game animals. The abundant marine life of the southern coast nurtured littoral communities. On the eastern side of the Pacific cordillera, the environment transitions abruptly to the more challengingly arid ecology of the Great Basin. Life-ways geared to these local habitats were already established as long as three thousand years ago. Where possible, large language groups sprawled across several environmental zones, coastal, inland, and riverine, and established networks of exchange, trade, and mutual dependency during times of need. Social rituals of gathering for feasts, trade, funerals, or for periodic ceremonies to "renew the world," knit dispersed communities together in far-flung networks of multi-faceted relationships.

The West Coast is the site of a long and complex ethnic history, as evidenced by the great diversity of languages found there. Over sixty different, mutually unintelligible languages are spoken in the region. Evidently, however, as different language groups joined together within the West's distinctive topography, traditions of cultural and artistic practice tended to merge. The northern Klamath Valley provides a good example. Most archaeologists and linguists agree that the Karuk, the original inhabitants of the valley, were joined by the Wiyot around AD 900 and then later by the Yurok after AD 1300. By the time of European

100 Pictographs representing big horn sheep from the Little Petroglyph Canyon, Coso mountains, Inyo County, California. The images were created by hunters between 550 BC and AD 950.

contact, these three linguistic groups had grown so close that it is virtually impossible to distinguish the differences between Karuk, Wiyot, and Yurok twined baskets.

Paint and stone

Artistic traces of ancient life in California include dozens of spectacular rock art sites, including the oldest well-dated pictograph in North America, a herringbone pattern painted in Tecolate Cave in the Mojave Desert radiocarbon-dated about 7300 BC. Few sites date to more than two thousand years ago, however. Out of a broad range of diverse images and sites, we can select three fairly distinctive traditions for consideration.

Up in the Coso mountains of Inyo County, hunters of big horn sheep pecked their images into prominently exposed rocks [100]. The hunters emphasized the broad, meaty bodies of the animals, rendering them as bulky crescent shapes with spindly legs, small heads, and gracefully curved horns. Pictographs of hunters with bows and arrows and stocky figures with squared bodies also appear, but the images of the big horns predominate. Obsidian hydration dates taken from projectile points and butchering tools provide dates for the pictographs that range between 550 BC and AD 950. Evidently the big horn population collapsed due to over-hunting in around AD 950, providing a logical terminal date for the images. Archaeologists speculate that the larger part of the big horn pictographs date from the centuries just before, as the big horns became more scarce and hunters sought to increase their numbers through the ritualistic creation of pictographic game racing along the canyon walls of their habitat.

Well to the south, in the arid lands adjacent to the Colorado River, ancient ritualists scraped the desert floor to create monumental geoglyphs, or ground drawings. The Blythe geoglyphs, discovered by an aviator in the 1930s, are probably the best known [101]. A giant figure, arms outstretched, measures over 60 ft (18 m) in length and is accompanied by a four-legged creature that resembles a mountain lion. In all, Blythe includes ten different drawings in three groups, all within 1,000 ft (300 m) of one another. Hundreds of additional drawings dot the broad desert region on both sides of the Colorado, from Nevada to the Gulf of California, in addition to trails and dance circles pounded hard by impressions of human feet. The local Yuman people locate their origin stories at these sites and oral traditions tell of rituals of pilgrimages to pay homage to the powers of creation. Dates for geoglyph sites range from as old as 900 BC to AD 1200.

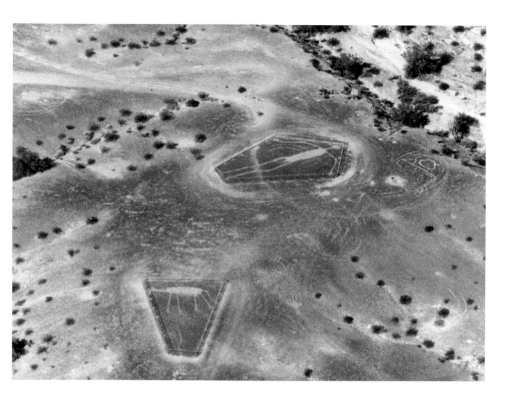

101 Blythe geoglyphs, or ground drawings, near Blythe, California, just above the Colorado River. The human figure in the upper portion of the photograph measures over 60 ft (18 m) in length. Oral traditions of the Yuman tribes claim these and other large ground drawings in their vicinity as pilgrimage sites.

A loose-knit tradition of painted and pecked imagery hidden away under overhanging ledges and rock shelters found along the length of interior California stems from practices that evidently persisted into the nineteenth century. Some of the most elaborate were made by Chumash people at sites located within coastal mountain ranges of southern California. Painted Cave, for example, now preserved as a state park, is located in the canyon country just above present-day Santa Barbara. Inside, spread over the walls and the ceiling, artists applied a bold palette of mineral pigments to create a dizzying array of overlapping shapes: serrated pinwheels, boldly striped figures, and segmented bands of color [102]. At Painted Rock, an isolated, horseshoe-shaped rock on the Carrizo Plain across the Sierra Madres at the southern end of California's Great Central Valley, Chumash paintings range across the interior walls.

There are dozens of similarly painted sites attributed to the Chumash and the southern Yokuts in southern California. The oral traditions of the Chumash recall that these sites had been created by religious specialists known as 'alchuklash. It has become customary to speak of such people as "shamans." The word "shaman" comes from the Evenk language of northeastern Siberia. There, a shaman is a kind of spiritual practitioner who mediates between society and the invisible world of spirits. Divination of the future, travel to the spirit world, and alliances with spirit helpers characterize the supernatural abilities described by the broad use of the term when discussing religious practices of Native North Americans. Through close observation of the sky and the movement of the sun, moon, planets, and stars, the 'alchuklash divined whether the coming year would bring abundance or hunger. He gathered power from these celestial bodies and enlisted the aid of spirit helpers. He also sought out secluded sites, rock shelters, and enclosures as portals to the spirit world, accumulating power there and performing rituals to influence the cosmos for the benefit of his community. The paintings he made are simultaneously renderings of visionary experiences, acknowledgments of his spirit helpers, and part of his ritual practice. The dots, concentric circles, and pinwheels found in many Chumash paintings represent celestial bodies. The strange human and animal combinations show the transformation of the shaman when immersed in the spirit world. Rattlesnakes, frogs, and other creatures portray his spirit helpers.

102 Painted Cave, in Painted Cave State Historical Park, near Santa Barbara, California. The paintings are the result of repeated visits by Chumash shamans over a period perhaps as long as 1,000 years. Some of the images may represent astronomical events, such as the complete solar eclipse of 24 November 1677.

103 Tubular pipe, made of steatite and decorated with shell beads inlaid in asphalt, found on San Nicholas Island, off-shore southern California, home of the Gabrielino culture, AD 1400–1600.

People of the southern coast also worked in stone, notably a fine gray steatite quarried by the Gabrielino inhabitants of Santa Catalina Island off the coast of present-day Los Angeles. Chumash living on the mainland and islands of the Santa Barbara Channel carved large, nearly globular bowls of steatite, thin-walled and often decorated with tiny marine shell beads set in gummy black asphalt applied to the surface. When broken, fragments of these functioned as fry pans. Similar techniques of stone carving and ornament with shell beads are visible in enigmatic effigies of whales and other creatures. A tubular stone pipe recovered from a Gabrielino site on San Nicholas Island, west of Santa Catalina, is carved with the head of a seal-like creature, with inset shell for eyes and a collar of shell beads clustered at the center of the tube [103]. As is the case for rock paintings, religious practitioners or shamans very likely used such effigy pipes, but little is known today about tobacco ritualism on the pre-contact southern California coast.

Baskets

Nowhere else in North America did basket making play such an integral role in Native life as in the Far West. Some students of material culture attribute the importance of baskets to the techniques required to process acorns into palatable food. Such practices are shared among almost all the California peoples: collecting, milling, leaching acorn flour, storing, cooking. Baskets are also used for collecting grass seeds, for trapping birds and fish, and as conveyances for everything from infants to firewood. Some of the baskets were designed and made principally for utilitarian use, but others were crafted with fine design and meticulous technique. For women, making fine baskets was an extension of their gendered tasks of wild food gathering and preparation. While weaving required great technical skill and meticulous labor, basket makers also had to possess essential knowledge of the surrounding environment in order to establish where weaving materials could be found and when it was best to collect them. Once assembled, plant materials required lengthy and careful

104 Large feast basket, woven by a Miwok woman during the late 1800s. Miwok village chiefs might own several baskets like this one and use them to serve food while hosting feasts.

105 Large baskets filled with acorn mush, photographed at a Southern Maidu feast conducted sometime between 1900 and 1910.

preparation before they were ready for use. Such skills and technical virtuosity created considerable social value for baskets, which could be expressed in many different ways.

Large coiled basketry bowls made with small, tight stitches were used for cooking. Liquid expanded the coils to make them watertight and heated rocks placed inside boiled the contents. Samuel A. Barrett, an anthropologist at the Milwaukee Public Museum, collected a particularly large and fine basketry cooking bowl of a type, he was told, which customarily belonged to Miwok chiefs for use when hosting feasts [104]. The Southern Miwok inhabited the hills and mountains of the Sierra Nevada range where chiefs and their families presided over communities with modestly sized territories [106]. A chief's responsibilities included managing relations with neighbors. Hosting inter-village feasts was one of the most effective means of maintaining goodwill. The chief's cooking baskets filled with steaming acorn mush, accompanied by displays of gifts, greeted the guests [105]. To serve, several men were required to carry the baskets filled with heavy liquid by means of a rope tied around the middle. Women used smaller baskets to dole out generous servings. The host might offer a large cooking basket as a gift to a chiefly guest, acknowledging their mutual status and binding their communities together in friendship. On another occasion, a chief might present a large cooking basket to his successor at the time of his marriage. Customarily, a chief's baskets were cremated with him at the time of his death.

Gifts of fine baskets accompanied nearly all the significant events of social life among the Pomo of central California. Parents suspended miniature baskets on their baby carriers to delight their infants. A family presented their daughter with a beautiful "washing" basket on the occasion of her first menstrual confinement. While it had no utilitarian purpose, with its fine ornament of quail's plumes, it resembled in miniature the kind of basket used for bathing infants, and thus expressed the hope for grandchildren. The family of a prospective groom received baskets as gifts from the betrothed bride's family. They signified the industriousness, skill, and wealth the bride brought to the match.

106 Callipene and Lena Brown (Southern Miwok), photographed by D. H. Wulzen in Yosemite Valley, June 1901. Callipene, born around 1813, was a prominent leader among the Miwok of Yosemite Valley and a highly regarded basket weaver. Lena Brown may have been her granddaughter.

107 "Treasure" basket, made by a Pomo woman, and decorated with red woodpecker feathers and shell beads. Customarily presented as honored gifts, or consumed by fire during funerals, this basket was collected in 1837 and taken to Berlin.

108 Jump Dance basket, made by a Hupa woman, 19th century. Men carried these baskets and other valuables while performing in the Jump Dance (see fig. 110). They are intended to represent large horn "purses" (see fig. 109) stuffed with shell money.

109 Horn purse, made of antler, and carved and engraved by a Yurok man. These cylindrical containers kept safe long strings of shell beads, sometimes referred to as "shell money." They closed with a thin strip of antler (missing here) bound over the narrow opening. This one was purchased for the Brooklyn Museum in 1905.

110 Photograph of Hupa participants in a "Jump Dance" conducted in Klamath Valley during the 1890s. The Jump Dance is an opportunity for men to display wealth, as represented by their headdresses decorated with red woodpecker scalps, their heavy necklaces of shell beads, and the baskets that represent enlarged purses, as if filled with shell money (see figs 108 and 109).

Friends and relations exchanged small "treasure" baskets, ornamented with the colorful feathers of birds or cut shell beads representing wealth, as gifts during ritual and social occasions [107]. Small shallow "feather" baskets had no other purpose than their ostentatious display. Designed for suspension so that their glittering pendants of marine shell could dangle freely, the underside of a *tapica* or "red basket" is entirely covered with a mosaic of red woodpecker feathers supplemented with black topknot plumes from quails. Mourners suspended such jewel-like baskets from scaffolds erected over funeral pyres as expressions of love and respect for the dead.

In perhaps the most overt instance of using baskets as an expression of wealth, Hupa women of the Klamath Valley region made twined basket "purses" [108], resembling, in enlarged form, the carved antler "wallets" used to store valuable marine shell beads (sometimes called "shell money") [109]. These served no other purpose than to symbolize wealth when carried by men performing the ostentatious "Jump Dance" [110]. Draped with shell necklaces and wearing broad headbands decorated with bright red woodpecker scalps, these men competed against one another with song, dance, and the display of sumptuous valuables.

Baskets and the marketplace
Native communities of California supported the refined skills and artistry of basket makers by converting their creations into objects of profound social value. This was accomplished through their use and display during social and religious rituals, their exchange as a means of creating and reinforcing binding relationships, and ultimately, their consumption by fire during funerary ceremonies as expressions of mourning for the dead.

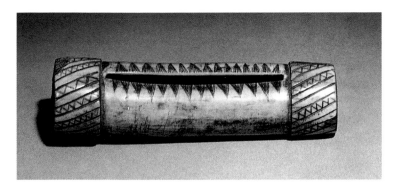

After the arrival of European intruders – first the Spanish, then their Mexican descendants, and finally Anglo-Americans from the east – basket makers found their talents increasingly redirected to the more sumptuary and commodity-based value systems of the outsiders. Initially, Spanish missions pressed basket makers into the sumptuary trade, commissioning presentation pieces and sewing baskets for use by the Spanish elite. A century later, white Americans sought out California baskets as unique American "collectibles." Many California basket weavers, whose communities suffered depredations on every front, responded to these challenges and opportunities with remarkable energy and creativity.

Although Spanish explorer Juan Rodríguez visited Santa Catalina and the Santa Barbara Channel Islands during his cruise up the California coast in 1542, Spanish colonization of California was postponed until the "sacred expedition" of 1769, which established an initial mission at the site of present-day San Diego. San Diego de Alcalá and the twenty additional missions established subsequently through 1823, forcibly gathered together the inhabitants of surrounding communities to live in captivity and labor at the *reducción*, or mission site. There are few more brutal histories of European subjugation of Native peoples than the events that followed the creation of the Spanish missions (including the administration of the colony by Mexico and the subsequent Anglos). The Chumash, the most populous southern California language group at the time of contact, suffered a precipitous decline. The Spanish established five missions among them and by 1804 all the Chumash had been forced into residency. The missions pressed into service the traditional artistic skills of their neophytes, including the production of precious coiled baskets. Like many of the peoples of the west coast, Chumash weavers produced a variety of basket types, both twined and coiled, for storage, transport, processing food, and other tasks. "Treasure" baskets, fastidiously sewn with minute coils and subtle decoration, had been exchanged as gifts and used to store valuables. Chumash basket weavers converted these into sewing baskets for the Spanish, sometimes including inscriptions or dedications worked into the design. A broad-brimmed hat, now in the collection of the British Museum, seems to have been adapted from the traditional Chumash hemispherical cap for use by Spanish Fathers [111]. Perhaps most remarkable are a set of broad, coiled basketry bowls and trays that incorporate emblems from Spanish coins into their designs. One, now at the Phoebe A.

111 Coiled basketry hat made for a Catholic priest by a Chumash neophyte, perhaps of the Spanish Mission of Santa Barbara, where the explorer George Vancouver collected it during the winter of 1792/1793.

112 Basket decorated with the 18th-century coat of arms of the kings of Spain, derived from Mexican-minted Spanish coins. The baptism of a twenty-one-year-old Chumash woman as Ana Maria Marta was recorded in 1788, and she very likely made the basket.

Hearst Museum of Anthropology, is inscribed "Ana Maria Marta, neophyte of the Mission of the Seraphic Doctor San Buenaventura made me…" [112]. Lillian Smith, who looked into mission records, thinks that this Ana Maria Marta, also known as Lapulimeu, had been baptized with that name on 5 June 1788. Evidently, the basket had been sent to Mexico as a gift from the Mission Fathers at San Buenaventura. Small collections of "treasure" baskets assembled by visitors to California ports hint at a mission-based cottage industry of luxury Chumash baskets. Such collections include the assortment brought back to Spain by explorer Alejandro Malaspina after his expedition of 1791, as well as a collection of *tabaqueras*, small globular baskets with lids for pipe tobacco, brought to Boston by trader William Alden Gale between 1810 and 1835. Even today, Chumash baskets of this period are among the most highly prized and valued among collectors.

Mid-nineteenth-century California became a difficult, often hostile environment for Native peoples. After decades of disease, land loss, and slavery, families found income from basket making most welcome. By-and-large, mid-century Anglo immigrants bought baskets locally for practical and decorative purposes. But by the 1880s, as art historian Marvin Cohodas observes, collecting Indian baskets had become a consumer "craze" fueled by tourism and an increasing interest in Native American arts and crafts as a distinctively American interior décor.

Traders, collectors, museum curators, amateur ethnologists, enthusiast writers, and a growing consumerism that privileged the natural, homemade, and distinctive American character of American Indian art combined together to create an unprecedented market demand for Western Native-made baskets. Several individual artists stood out in this environment. Louisa Keyser (c. 1855–1925), who would become one of the most accomplished and widely known basketry artists from the West, had worked as a laundress for Carson City storeowners Abe and Amy Cohn before they discovered her talent. Keyser developed an ambitious and innovative variety of basket, a large spherical form the Cohns called a *degikup*, which was inspired, in part, by the popularity of Pomo and Maidu baskets among collectors [113]. The tightly coiled baskets are masterfully

113 *Degikup*, or spherical basket, decorated with a pattern known as "beacon lights," made by Louisa Keyser (Washo), also known as "Dat so la lee." She started working on the basket on 1 July 1904 and completed it on 6 September 1905, according to records kept by trader Amy Cohn.

114 "Trinket" basket, made by Elizabeth Hickox around 1914. Hickox's mother was Wiyot and her husband's mother was Hupa, but the couple were raised in the Karuk territories of the Lower Klamath river valley, where they remained. The trinket basket, a form at which Hickox excelled, was developed for the curio trade.

conceived with understated designs carefully modulated to their swelling, rotund shapes. The Cohns invented a fictitious persona for Keyser. They gave her the name "Dat so la lee," and proclaimed she was a Washo princess. Keyser made baskets sold by the Cohns for thirty years (1895–1925) for little more than room and board, although the baskets sold for enormous sums compared to prices earned by other contemporary basket weavers.

Elizabeth Hickox (1872–1947) was the single greatest practitioner of Klamath Valley basket weaving, and her work is noted for its innovations and distinction. Elizabeth was the daughter of Polly Conrad Steve, a Wiyot born around 1848, and Charles Conrad, a miner from Kentucky who abducted Polly when she was eighteen (it was quite common for white immigrants to abduct Native women as "country wives" and housekeepers at this time). Elizabeth herself married a mixed-blood man, Luther Hickox, who with his brothers had inherited a modest goldmine operation near the Karuk settlement of Ossipuk. Elizabeth, her mother, and her daughter Louise all contributed to their family's relative affluence by weaving baskets. Elizabeth and Louise specialized in finely woven "trinket" baskets with knob-shaped lids [114]. Their refinement of materials and meticulous care resulted in unprecedented quality. Some of

Elizabeth's baskets boast as many as eight hundred stitches per square inch. Her baskets achieved broader recognition through the efforts of Grace Nicholson of Pasadena, a dealer who procured baskets for the most prominent collectors and museum collections of her day.

Louisa Keyser and Elizabeth Hickox are just two of hundreds of Western basket weavers who plied their skill and received modest cash reward during the basket "craze" of the first decades of the twentieth century. Women supplemented traditional designs with innovative animal or human figures, labored on massive over-sized baskets [115] or more quickly produced miniatures. They sold their creations through traders and dealers, or at local fairs and "Indian days." Local patrons established standards and awarded prizes. Eventually the market dwindled, but many families continued to nurture basket-weaving skills and imparted their knowledge to succeeding generations. One of the biggest threats to Western basket weaving today is the environmental crisis that threatens the habitat of traditional materials.

115 Large coiled basket, made by Carrie Bethel (Mono Lake Paiute), 1930s. Bethel worked on this basket for four years and it is the biggest she ever made. Large, elaborately decorated baskets that were finely made attracted purchasers and big prices.

Chapter 7　Northwest Coast

Every year, as they have for thousands of years, hundreds of millions of salmon traverse some thousand miles of the Fraser River, juveniles swimming seaward to the Pacific, mature fish near the end of their lives swimming inland to spawn. The massive river, winding its way from the Eastern Canadian Rockies to the Pacific Coast near modern-day Vancouver, is just one aspect of the great ecological ferment of the North Pacific coast. The rugged seashore, dense old-growth forests, and rivers that descend from the formidable approaches to the Canadian Rockies all support abundant wildlife. But for the coast- and river-dwelling people of the region, the ebb and flow of the salmon's life cycle must have resembled great breaths and exhalations of life-giving oxygen. For many, the annual predictability of salmon runs provided stability and security; its failure meant famine. Even today, many Northwest Coast Native communities measure their vitality in terms of the salmon fishery. In addition to salmon, Northwest Coast societies diversified with off-shore fishing, whaling, foraging for mollusks, and pursuit of other resources. Some archaeologists theorize that the environmental setting of the North Pacific Coast, where natural abundance supported community expansion but always under the threat of over-extension and collapse, contributed to growth of the complex and closely intertwining social relations so characteristic of Northwest Coast Native cultures. Societies banded together in inter-related villages under lineage chiefs and nurtured relations with neighbors while ensuring the security of their own defense (or the success of any necessary aggression on their part). Architecture, sculpture, regalia, and their creation, display, and exchange, play a pivotal role in the complex and competitive mechanizations of Northwest Coast chiefdoms.

The roots of Northwest Coast art

Many of the distinctive aspects of recent Northwest Coast art and culture emerged in the archaeological record during a span of time between 500 BC and AD 500. Innovative cultural attributes of this period that seem to presage the characteristic aspects of more recent Northwest Coast Native societies appear at the Marpole site, a large village nestled on the mainland side of the Fraser river delta's north arm, sheltered from Georgia Sound by Sea Island (now the location of Vancouver International Airport). Marpole can be linked to similar village sites along the southern British Columbia coast, from the lower Fraser through the southern Straits of Georgia inhabited during the same period. Archaeologists group these sites together as belonging to the Marpole phase (400 BC–AD 400), inhabited by ancestors of the modern Coast Salish. The Marpole site includes the remains of several large houses built of upright support posts of cedar and covered with split planking, some of the earliest of such houses detected by archaeologists on the Northwest Coast. They

116 Miniature pestle, carved of antler in the form of a great blue heron, 400 BC–AD 400. Marpole site, Fraser river delta region, southern British Columbia. This is one of the more elaborate antler carvings recovered from the Marpole site.

117 Club, made of whale bone, c. 500 BC. Boardwalk site, near Prince Rupert, British Columbia. Note the small animal head visible in the figure's headdress. The club was buried with a cache of weapons and copper bracelets.

resemble in many ways the large winter houses built by historic Northwest Coast peoples centuries later. Stone mauls, hand-hammers, wedges for splitting off the massive cedar planks necessary for house construction, and other tools found at the site testify to the woodworking skills of Marpole village residents.

Among the many artifacts recovered from the site were a number of effigies carved of bone and elk antler: "pins," clasps or toggles carved as bird heads, fragments of human figurines, and a remarkable pestle of antler with a handle carved as a delicately rendered heron [116]. Three so-called "seated human effigy bowls" of stone also came from the site. Over one hundred and fifty of these bowls, each slightly different, have been found on the southern coast and in the interior within the Fraser and Thompson river valleys. The figures, their mouths often parted as if in song, sit with a bowl in their lap. This bowl is frequently carved with the faces of animals or monsters, and in some examples rattlesnakes hang down the backs of the seated figures or are draped across their foreheads. Wilson Duff, a pioneer of Northwest Coast art scholarship, reasoned plausibly that since the most elaborate of these had been found upriver, the form and the cultural practices associated with the seated figure effigy bowls had most likely originated there. The Fraser valley has always been a conduit for trade and cultural exchange between riverine and coastal people. Although there is no general agreement about the significance of the seated human effigy bowls, they hint at sacred technologies and use by religious practitioners, individuals whose social value and power was enhanced by the ownership of such objects and the knowledge of how to use them.

To the north, excavations in the vicinity of Prince Rupert near the mouth of the Skeena River (the homeland of the modern Tsimshian people) reveal a great deal about the foundations of the cultural traditions of the northern coast. In the wooden carving of a bird that evidently functioned as a bucket handle from the Lachane site (520 BC–AD 320), art historians recognize features of the "form-line tradition," a style of painting and carving developed with great sophistication by the modern Tlingit, Tsimshian, and Haida peoples. Some of the most intriguing and perplexing among the Prince Rupert artifacts, however, evidently functioned as weapons of war. A warrior's cache of weapons at the Boardwalk site included a paddle-shaped hand club made of whale bone, a human head wearing an animal crest headdress carved on its handle [117]. This style of club is a widely dispersed type. A very

closely related example was found in the vicinity of Puget Sound in Washington State, hundreds of miles to the south of the Boardwalk site. The Nuu-chah-nulth of Vancouver's west coast and Washington State's Olympic Peninsula employed similar clubs, the handle carved with the head of a hooked beak bird. One of these was found at the eighteenth-century Ozette site, which will be discussed shortly, and another was brought home by botanist Archibald Menzies who accompanied Captain George Vancouver aboard the *Discovery* during his explorations of the Georgian Sound between 1792 and 1794 [118]. Clearly, this type of weapon had retained its high esteem over thousands of years.

Some traditions of imagery and their associated ideas did not survive to recent times. The strange and complex forms visible among the thirty-five stone clubs of the Hagwilget cache discovered on the Skeena River in 1898 have no counterpart among the myriad effigy figures rendered by more recent Northwest Coast artists. Their ribbed shafts, phallic handles, and strange animal shapes are each unique creations but clearly related as a set [119]. Others of the general type appeared elsewhere in the Skeena River area, but only one from a datable context. On that basis, it is plausible to believe that the type can be dated to about 500 BC. But there is little trace of their esoteric imagery or stylistic conventions in more recent Northwest Coast art.

The scant archaeological discoveries of these few artfully created objects testify to continuities of tradition thousands of years old. One can only imagine, however, the artistic richness of objects that have not survived in archaeological contexts, those made of ephemeral materials such as wood, hide, and basketry. A broader picture is revealed as the result of a catastrophic and tragic mudslide which suddenly buried a Makah village now known as the Ozette site on the Olympic Peninsula sometime around 1750. The encasing mud sealed the portion of the village it had destroyed and preserved the ruins without substantial decay. Archaeological excavations beginning in 1970 recovered 55,000

118 *Chitoolth*, or club, made of whale bone, collected among the Nuu-chah-nulth, or Nootka, of Vancouver Island by a member of the 1792–94 expedition led by George Vancouver.

119 One of thirty-five stone clubs found together, known as the Hagwilget cache, at an old village site on the Skeena River in 1898. Other, similar clubs have been found in the area since, but only one in a datable archaeological context, 500 BC–AD 1.

120 Oil dish, carved of wood recovered from the Ozette site, a Makah village on the tip of the Olympic Peninsula (Cape Flattery), buried by a mudslide sometime around 1750. Archaeologists have recovered more than 55,000 individual artifacts from the site.

artifacts and 40,000 fragments of at least four houses, thus providing a nearly all-encompassing view of the community's material culture. Many astounding sculptural objects of carved wood came from the site, including a well-preserved serving bowl in the form of a reclining figure [120]. The style and concept of the Ozette bowl closely resemble that of a similar vessel collected by Captain James Cook at Yuquat, a Nuu-chah-nulth community on the west coast of Vancouver Island. The Makah and Nuu-chah-nulth are essentially the same people, speaking the same language. Makah elders helped archaeologists identify many artifacts recovered during the excavations at Ozette.

Crests and their display
On the Northwest Coast, images created by artists stand in testimony to claims of ancestry and to the material and social rights of family groups. Anthropologists call this kind of image a "crest," and the concept pertains equally to the Tlingit, Tsimshian, and Haida peoples of the northern coast. But a crest is more than just an image. A crest is composed essentially of three things: a proper name, usually referring to an animal or spirit creature; a story or history that explains a family's relationship to that creature; and an object, such as a crest hat, a decorated robe, or a house post, which displays an image of the animal or spirit being and by doing so evokes the story. Crests belong to families, but the concept of family among the people of the northern Northwest Coast is very broad. The most basic family group is the household, an extended matrilineal family that takes residence collectively in a large winter house. Households that trace back ancestral relations between each

other (biological or fictive) are bound together as clans. And every clan belongs to a particular exogamous grouping (Raven or Wolf among the Tlingit, Raven or Eagle among the Haida, and Raven, Wolf, Eagle or Killer Whale among the Tsimshian, although customarily only two are operative within any one community). Exogamous means simply that marriage partners always come from the opposite group. Crests and the stories they tell may belong to the household, the clan, or these larger exogamous groupings. The stories tell of strange encounters between spirit animals and ancestral family members of the ancient past or refer back further to culture heroes, like Raven, who helped shape the world.

Crests, however, must be understood in the context of how they are presented and seen. Each generation must claim the stories and names from the past, by family right, but also by public acknowledgment. This is done at a ceremony called a potlatch, a feast, where others are invited to witness the claiming of names, the telling of stories, and the display of objects with images of animals and spirit beings recalled from the ancestral past. A potlatch is organized when a family member wishes to claim a name, after the death of a senior chief, for example, when a maternal nephew takes the name left vacant by the passing of his uncle, the senior chief. One of the most impressive displays of crests for such an occasion would be the commissioning and raising of a totem pole, a vertical sculpture that utilizes a substantial portion of a whole monumental red cedar. The word "totem" is a misnomer here. The term comes from the Algonquian word "dodem," meaning spirit. Crest creatures are not "totems" even in the anthropological sense of the word. These monumental carvings are more accurately referred to as "memorial poles," since a memorial potlatch to commemorate a deceased chief is the most common reason for their creation.

In 1888, the senior chief of the Wixha household of the Wolf clan in the village of Gitanyow (formerly known as Kitwancool), a Gitksan Tsimshian community located on the Upper Skeena River, raised a pair of memorial poles in front of his impressive cedar plank house in honor of his nephew, who had been killed as a young man by the colonial police [121]. The memorial poles had in fact been intended for a deceased senior chief, but the purpose of the potlatch shifted in response to the tragic death of the beloved nephew. The principal image of the pole on the left is a monstrous bird known as Mountain Eagle. Long ago, so the

121 Two memorial poles at the Gitksan Tsimshian village of Gitanyow (formerly known as Kitwancool), Upper Skeena River, British Columbia, carved by an artist identified by ethnographer Marius Barbeau as Haesem-hliyawn. The poles were commissioned and erected in 1888 by the senior chief of the Wixha household of the Wolf clan. The major crest displayed on the pole on the left is Mountain Eagle (the large bird toward the top) and on the right is Split Person (the figure standing at the top).

ancestral stories say, Mountain Eagle had kidnapped a young woman of Wixha ancestry and made her his mate. But the monster craved human flesh, and it ate all their half-bird, half-human children. The woman escaped and returned to her family, and her story became part of the family's history to be commemorated by the display of crests. The figure standing below Mountain Eagle on the memorial pole is Sharp Nose, whose blade-like nose split human victims like salmon, until a young hero of the Wolf clan killed him. On the second pole, to the right, the most significant crest is Split Person, who stands at the top with two small figures on his head. In the crest stories, Split Person has two heads, one trunk, and one stomach.

The massive winter houses, made of cedar posts and split cedar planks, can also bear crests of the resident family. The interior of the Whale House of Klukwan, a Tlingit community of southern Alaska, whose residents belonged to the Ganaxteidi clan of the Ravens, was installed with an elaborate interior screen, or

122 Interior of the Whale House at the Chilkat Tlingit village of Klukwan, Alaska. Several crests of the Ganaxteidi clan of the Ravens are visible: the Rain Screen that serves as a partition visible in the back, the Woodworm interior house post on the left, and the Raven interior house post on the right. The house posts were carved by Kadjis-du-axtc, according to ethnographer Louis Shotridge, sometime before 1834.

partition, which separated the quarters of the resident chief from the rest of the house [122]. Known as the Rain Screen, it is linked by art historian Aldona Jonaitis to the origin story of how Raven brought rain to the earth. The image shows the massive head of Raven, flanked by feathers and its outstretched hands. The crouching figures that range across the border at the top and sides represent splashing raindrops. The interior house post that frames the screen to the left shows a figure holding a woodworm, or grub, recognized by its segmented body. The carving refers to a story about a monstrous woodworm that consumed entire houses before it was killed. The opposite house post shows Raven again, but now in human form. This carving refers to another episode in a cycle of Raven stories having to do with the origins of the world. In this particular story, Raven catches a salmon and tricks other animals that have gathered and asked Raven to share. Promising a barbecue, Raven sends them away on fool's errands so he can eat the fish himself.

At potlatches, crests can also be displayed on large conical hats worn by chiefs. The Sea Lion House of the L'uknax ádi Ravens of the Tlingit community of Sitka possessed a crest hat carved with the image of Raven [123]. Called the "Raven Barbecuing Hat" it recalls the same story of Raven and the salmon and how he tricked the other animals. During the mid-nineteenth century, the Ganaxteidi Ravens of Klukwan disputed the right of the Sea Lion House Ravens to display the hat, claiming the story was theirs. They took the hat and, by so doing, provoked war. Peace was restored eventually, and the hat returned, but this incident illustrates the dynamic nature of crests and their deployment in potlatches. Family ancestry, and the importance attached to it, must be claimed and defended. Monumental works in cedar,

123 Raven Barbecuing Hat, Sea Lion House of the L'uknax ádi Ravens of the Tlingit village of Sitka, Alaska, early 19th century. The hat references an episode of the Raven cycle of crest stories in which Raven organized a barbecue to fool the other animals and keep a salmon he had caught to himself.

memorial poles, interior screens and house posts, and the treasures owned by the family, such as crest hats, give claims palpable reality. Their display at large public feasts establishes their legitimacy. By accepting the abundant food and gifts distributed at potlatches, the guests acknowledge their hosts' ancestral greatness.

The name of the man who carved the Wixha house memorial poles at Gitanyow was Haesem-hliyawn, who was one of the best-known carvers of his generation (active c. 1840–1880). The master Tlingit carver commissioned to make the Woodworm and Raven posts of the Whale house at Klukwan some time before 1834 was recorded by Tlingit ethnologist Louis Shotridge as Kadjis-du-axtc (c. 1760–1850) from the village of Wrangell. We know little more about these two men, but a couple of pertinent aspects of their identities are fairly certain. They were very likely chiefs themselves, or at least high-ranking in their clans, and they belonged to the marriage group opposite to those who commissioned the work. By custom, these matrilineal households commissioned crest carvings from their in-law's families, in other words from the same group as the fathers of the household's children. The rules of exogamy locked northern Northwest Coast societies together through intermarriage, and the respective roles of families linked this way were strictly defined. When a memorial pole was to be erected, or a house built, the household would not perform the labor of creating the crests themselves. They paid their in-laws to do it, as they performed the same chores for them on the occasion of their potlatches. The in-laws were often also the principal guests at the event and were "paid" in gifts to witness and acknowledge the household's claims.

Once crest objects have been created, households never relinquish their rights over them. In 1958, the title holder of Chief Wixha at Gitanyow signed an agreement with the Museum of Anthropology at the University of British Columbia. The museum would remove and care for the Wixha memorial poles and, in return, would supply modern reproductions, which remain on display in the community today. The Klukwan villagers had a more difficult time retaining their rights over the contents of the Whale House. A landmark court decision in 1974 returned the interior house posts and Rain Screen to the community after they had been improperly sold (so the court ruled) to an art dealer. Today, they are on display for visitors to the community house at Chilkat.

Not all objects carved and painted with images of animals bear crests, however. Crests are most commonly deployed on

124 Bentwood chest, attributed to a carver of the Nisga'a Tsimshian, Nass river region, British Columbia, active in the 1800s. Many of the chests thought to have been produced by carvers of this region traveled through trade to other communities. This chest was collected among the Haida of the Queen Charlotte Islands.

memorial poles, houses (interior posts, partition screens, and paintings on the exterior facade), wooden serving dishes used at potlatches, crest hats, and other kinds of regalia, such as formal garments. The images that appear on large storage chests and smaller boxes are not crests, but abstract images of more generic animals that are often difficult to identify [124]. The artists employed a series of conventions to create the images, a tradition of artistic practice that stems back at least to the time of the Lachane site bucket handle (500 BC), the earliest known object where the tradition can be recognized. Bill Holm, an artist and art historian, calls it the "form-line tradition." Designs begin with a strong organizing "form-line" which outlines the component parts of the image. On the rain screen described above, or on the conventional design of a wooden storage chest, the form-line inscribes the broad dimensions of the animal's head and its diminutive body. Spaces within the form-line are filled in with a series of standard elements: "ovoids" that serve as eyes or locate the shoulder and hip joints; "U"s that often suggest feathers or fins; and anatomical details like hands and claws that sometimes provide clues to the creature's identity. Form-line designs can be painted, carved in shallow relief, or often both. The form-line tradition is a conservative discipline and master artists rarely transgressed the rules. Within the system, however, they found

125 Chief's seat, carved by Captain Richard Carpenter, or Du'k!wayella, of the Heiltsuk town of Bella Bella in British Columbia, before 1900. Carpenter's distinctive style of "form-line" carving has permitted the attribution of several additional works to his hand.

great opportunities for their skills and creativity. By observing carefully how form-line designs were created, art historians have been able to recognize the hands of individual masters even when their names are no longer known. The attributes of a design carved and painted on an elaborate settee, or chief's seat, signed by a Heiltsuk master artist named Richard Carpenter (Du'k!wayella 1841–1931) [125], helped identify several chests and boxes that can now be attributed to his hand: narrow, calligraphic form-lines leave large open spaces for secondary and tertiary design elements. Boxes and chests made by Carpenter and other Heiltsuk artists were traded widely. Many boxes also come from Haida artists of the Queen Charlotte Islands, or the Tsimshian who neighbor the Heiltsuk to the north. Chiefs acquired them to store household treasures or to give away at potlatches.

Tlingit women from the Chilkat River region wove form-line designs into the patterns of mountain goat wool blankets with warps of cedar bark [126]. The images are not crests. Women copied the designs from pattern boards painted by male artists [127]. Like boxes, mountain goat horn spoons, and food vessels, Chilkat blankets, as they are called, traveled far from the community of their manufacture through trade. Chiefs of the southern communities coveted them particularly for the "chief's dance," a demonstration of power in which a chief hosting a potlatch danced with a Chilkat blanket, a frontlet headdress, and a raven rattle to summon masked dancers representing powerful spirit beings into the dance house (see below).

126 Robe, woven by a Chilkat
Tlingit woman of southern Alaska
around 1890. The techniques and
skills of weaving robes of mountain
goat wool and cedar bark were
once far more widespread in
southern Alaska and British
Columbia, but due to epidemics
and population decline, women of
the Chilkat Tlingit became the sole
carriers of the tradition during the
later 19th century.

127 Pattern board, a hand-hewn
cedar plank with a design for a
Chilkat robe painted on it by a
Chilkat Tlingit man of southern
Alaska around 1890. Chilkat
women derived their designs for
woven robes from painted pattern
boards like this one, which appears
to have been the model for the
robe illustrated above (fig. 126).

The art of the Tlingit shaman

As mentioned earlier, the word "shaman" comes from the Evenk language of northeastern Siberia. There, a shaman is a kind of spiritual practitioner who mediates between society and the invisible world of spirits. He or she does so by falling into a trance, leaving the body, and journeying to the spirit world. Shamanistic practice crossed the Bering Straits, and this very special category of mostly men and some women can be found among the Yupik and Inuit (Eskimo), and, to varying degrees, the Native peoples of the Northwest Coast. The shaman played a powerful role in Tlingit society and the objects required for Tlingit shamanistic practice provided a particularly rich opportunity for the sculptural skills of Tlingit artists.

In many cases the role of the Tlingit shaman was hereditary, but the spirit helpers of a deceased shaman selected the initiate from descendants within the same family. A shaman was often identified as a child if he or she resembled a shaman in the family's past or had some other physical particularity. The shaman relied upon these spirit helpers, known as *yek*, to locate lost items, identify thieves, exorcise disease-causing spells among the sick, expose the malevolent practices of witches, spy upon the enemy's camp, and combat the powers of shaman adversaries. All animals possess spirits and a shaman hoped to accumulate as many as possible to assist him. But some were more powerful than others. The land otter was most important. Mountain goats, frogs, octopuses, mice (the master thieves to detect thieves) also figured prominently. Aldona Jonaitis, who studied the identities of Tlingit *yek*, proposed that the most powerful were able to transgress realms of habitat – the amphibious freedom of frogs and land otters for example – as a metaphor of the ability of a shaman to pass freely from this world to the next. Others confounded conventional categories of identity, such as the exotic and difficult-to-classify octopus and mountain goat.

A shaman required a collection of objects in order to practice – among the most important, a set of at least four masks. A more powerful shaman might have eight or nine. These represented his *yek* and summoned them to participate during a shaman's performance. A mask owned by Kowee, a shaman and also a Raven hereditary chief of the Auk Tlingit, is carved with a human-like face surmounted by the head of a land otter and flanked by three mountain goats on either side [128]. A frog emerges from the mouth like a tongue. A shaman collected and preserved the tongues of powerful spirit animals as attributes of their power, so

images of tongues figure prominently in Tlingit shamanistic art. Reputedly, this mask had belonged to two generations of shamans prior to Chief Kowee, who died around 1850.

A shaman also possessed a rattle customarily in the form of an oystercatcher, a shore bird that inhabited the liminal ground between land and sea. A shaman's rattle from Hoonah is carved with an image of a reclining shaman on an oystercatcher's back, positioned between a pair of octopus tentacles, his feet on the head of a land otter, and a frog on his breast who offers his tongue [129]. When performing, the shaman wore a special headdress (some consisted of a crown of goat horns), a painted hide apron, and a necklace of bone, walrus ivory, or whale tooth charms carved as spirit helpers. These objects were never kept in a house but were secluded away in a box, sometimes kept on the roof but more often outside the village on isolated platforms, structures, or in caves. When a shaman died, his body and

128 Mask, owned by an Auk Tlingit chief and shaman of southern Alaska, known as Kowee, who died around 1850. The large land otter poised over the forehead, the mountain goats framing the face, and the frog emerging from the mouth are all the shaman's guardian spirits.

129 Shaman's rattle from the Tlingit town of Hoonah, southern Alaska, carved during the early to mid-1800s.

130 Guardian figure erected at a shaman's grave site near the Tlingit town of Yakutat, southern Alaska, estimated to have been carved between 1820 and 1840.

131 (opposite) Dagger or fighting knife called Ixti'ku gwal'aa, or "emaciated shaman dagger," made, according to oral tradition, by a woman named Saayeina'aat, of the L'uknax ádi Ravens of the Chilkat Tlingit town of Yandeist'akyeé during the 1700s.

equipment were similarly isolated in a grave house distant from the community. Wooden figures representing shamans and powerful spirits were arranged around the grave house to guard against intruders [130].

A shaman could make his own equipment or could ask others to do so. The quality of the carving on many Tlingit shaman masks suggests that they had been commissioned from the best carvers, but some shaman among the Tlingit may have been fine carvers too. Unlike with crest objects, the shaman approached carvers from his own matrilineal relations, preferably a brother or matrilineal cousin. Other categories of objects made by Tlingit artists, but not used by a shaman, employed images of *yek*, clearly in an effort to improve their spiritual efficacy. As Aldona Jonaitis has pointed out, for example, hooks for catching halibut, a risky offshore enterprise in a small canoe, were sometimes carved with images of the octopus, land otter, and mountain goat. Shamanistic images also improved weapons of war, such as massive protective helmets, bone-crushing clubs, and stabbing daggers. An extraordinary dagger forged of iron, once a treasure of the Tluqwaxadi clan of Klukwan, is named Ixti'ku gwal'aa, "emaciated shaman dagger" or "shaman's thrust" [131]. The hilt of the dagger shows the shaman's face, the details of eyes, mouth, and ears fashioned of separate pieces of iron and copper and riveted to the underlying hand-forged iron. According to family tradition, this dagger was made by a female ancestress of the clan from a meteor that had fallen upriver from the village. There are several accounts of pre-contact ironworking along the northern West Coast, most often referring to logs (possibly masts) washed up on-shore studded with iron spikes and nails.

The ways of the mask

In 1884 the Canadian Indian Act was amended to read, in part, "Every Indian or other person who engages in or assists in celebrating the Indian festival known as the 'Potlatch' ... is guilty of a misdemeanor and shall be liable for imprisonment...." The law was addressed principally to the Kwakiutl (or Kwakwaka'wakw, meaning those who speak the Kwak'wala language) who lived along the north end of Vancouver Island and the adjacent mainland. Ironically, Franz Boas, the first anthropologist to study potlatch practices carefully, arrived to work among the Kwakiutl two years later. The Kwakiutl chief who greeted him on 6 October 1886 warned, "We want to know whether you have come to stop our dances and feasts, as the missionaries and agents who live among our neighbors try to do. If you come to forbid us dance, be gone. If not, you will be welcome among us." The Kwakiutl largely ignored the prohibition until authorities began to enforce it aggressively after 1920. In one notorious instance, the participants of a 1922 potlatch were prosecuted, but some were given suspended sentences if they agreed to give up their masks and potlatch goods. The agent then sold them to eastern museums. The potlatch amendment was deleted from the Indian Act in 1951, and the Kwakiutl have worked hard to get the masks they surrendered in 1922 back. Despite the government's efforts, the Kwakiutl potlatch had never disappeared.

The government prohibition against potlatches and Franz Boas's anthropological interest in them stemmed from a confluence of events that resulted in an unprecedented expansion of potlatch ceremonies during the late nineteenth century. The beginnings of white settlement in Kwakiutl territory, marked by the founding of the town of Fort Rupert in 1849, resulted in increased wealth for the Kwakiutl from trade and labor though in addition to a drastic decline in the size of their communities due to devastating diseases. Colonial rule repressed intra-village conflict, expanding the potential for potlatch partners. Potlatches of the past had been comparatively few, but now socially aspirant Kwakiutl families gathered new-found wealth to give away as potlatch gifts and aggressively claimed vacant titles in an inflationary spiral of increasingly extravagant and frequent ceremonies. Government agents and frustrated missionaries reacted against such behavior as profligate and un-Christian, and politicked for regulation. Local officials remained steadfastly unimpressed with the performative aspects of Kwakiutl ritual. During potlatches, Kwakiutl chiefs staged elaborate dramatic narratives in which masked dancers impersonated powerful supernatural beings. The masks created by Kwakiutl carvers for these performances are astounding creations, showing fantastic creatures whose features come to life with hinged jaws and movable eyes, or which split in two to reveal another face inside, all controlled by strings and other mechanical contrivances. The growth of potlatch ceremonialism during the second half of the nineteenth century ushered in a golden age of Kwakiutl sculptural arts. It was after the young Boas had encountered a collection of Kwakiutl masks assembled in Berlin in 1885 by ethnographic impresario Adrian Jacobsen, that he arranged to travel to British Columbia to undertake fieldwork the next year.

The Kwakiutl conducted potlatches to memorialize the dead, to mark the union of families through marriage, to bestow names or titles upon family members, or to wipe away the shame of a humiliating event. Large potlatches involving guests from several villages often combined a number of these functions. Among the most prominent of the several masked performances that might be staged, high-ranking families initiated their youth into the hamatsa, or Cannibal Society, a privilege that stemmed from an ancestral encounter with deadly cannibal spirits. Customarily, a chief gave the Cannibal Dance to his son-in-law for the benefit of future grandsons, so rights to the dance were disseminated widely. Hamatsa initiations, like most masked dances, took place in winter, since that was when cannibal spirits journeyed south from the North End of the World and frequented Kwakiutl villages. Boas called these seasonal ritual events "the Winter Ceremonial." The dramatic performance enacts the kidnapping of the initiate by cannibal spirits and his return transformed into a cannibal himself, crazed by hunger for human flesh. Chiefs of the family cure the dancer, purging the cannibal spirit from his body. The performance culminates in the appearance of cannibal spirits represented by dancers wearing masks of enormous cannibal birds, their beaks snapping voraciously as they dance.

Born in the village of Tigwaxsti, Willie Seaweed (1873–1967) is probably the best-known Kwakiutl carver of dramatic masks for the Cannibal Dance: Gwaxaml the Cannibal Raven; Huxwhukw the Cannibal Crane; Galukwaml the Crooked Beak. The name "Seaweed" actually comes from Willie's chiefly title, Siwidi, meaning "paddled to," the highest-ranking position of the Nakwaxda'xw Kwakiutl who live in the vicinity of the Queen Charlotte Strait. Willie inherited the title and also the name Hilamas from his father, who himself was a well-known carver. Hilamas the elder had fathered another carver from a previous marriage named Johnny Davis (Lalakanxid). Artists among the Kwakiutl often came from high-ranking families but customarily did not make masks for their own potlatches. They provided this service to other chiefly families for payment, and hired out the work necessary for the display of their own chiefly privileges. A Crooked Beak mask carved by Willie Seaweed during a period of prolific activity in the 1940s exemplifies the hyperbolic drama of the Cannibal performance [132]. The prerequisite hook of the upper beak arches high above flaring red nostrils, balanced by the hyper-extended scroll of the lower jaw. These exaggerated appendixes maximize the hinged movement of the broad jaws, as

132 (opposite) Hamatsa mask, carved by Willie Seaweed, a Nakwaxda'xw Kwakiutl of Queen Charlotte Strait, British Columbia, during the 1940s. The mask appeared in potlatches up through the 1970s.

the dancer lifts his head vertically upright and audibly snaps the lower jaw open and shut while emitting the piercing cry of this human-devouring bird. Seaweed made the mask for Sam Weber and it was used in Cannibal Dances up until the 1970s.

Before assembled guests at Kwakiutl potlatches, chiefs paraded their ancestral bonds to countless mythic beings depicted by masked dancers. Each dance is tied to the narrative of its acquisition: an ancestral hero or heroine who traveled far from home and encountered marvelous or perhaps potentially deadly creatures, but returned with their treasures in the form of masks and dances. For the most powerful and prestigious dances, like the Cannibal Dance, the ancient spirits return and kidnap members of the family, but they are restored to the community by the powers of the chiefs. For others, the chief dances with a raven rattle and frontlet headdress in a manner that impersonates a shaman and calls spirit beings into the dance house before the assembled guests. Some presentations, like Kumugwe' (Chief of the Sea), Bak'was (Chief of the Animals), or Atlakam (forest spirits), employ dozens of masks and spirit characterizations, each with its own distinctive identity and appearance [133].

133 (right) Bullhead mask, carved before 1901 for the Dance of the Undersea Kingdom, a dance prerogative of Gwawa'enuxw Kwakiutl of Hopetown, British Columbia. Here the mechanical transformation mask is fully open, revealing the last of its three faces.

The chiefs of the Nuu-chah-nulth also conducted Winter Ceremonial dances, but here spirit wolves instead of cannibals kidnapped the high-born initiates. During the ceremonies of their cure and restoration to society, the chiefly sponsors staged masked dances with representations of powerful spirits. To the north, Tsimshian chiefs hosting potlatches demonstrated their control over *halait* or "spirit power" by putting on masked performances. Haida chiefs claimed to have acquired the rights to present masked dances from their mainland neighbors. The masks created for these events represent the height of the Northwest Coast carver's art. The prestige of their sponsors depended so much upon the success of the artists' creations that humiliation, even death, followed should they fail. The social aspirations of a family's future depended upon plausible and forceful ties to the ancestral past and the spiritual powers that ancestors had obtained. There are few other places in the world where the productivity of artists has played such an integral role in the conduct of society.

Northwest Coast artists and the outside world

The precious objects procured by early explorers during the late eighteenth century – masks, heirloom weapons, and other treasures – may have been offered as diplomatic exchanges to these peculiar strangers with their awe-inspiring ships. But soon Northwest artists began to see the outsiders as a lucrative new outlet for their skills and creativity. The Queen Charlotte Islands, home to the Haida people, was heavily harvested of sea otters between 1805 and 1830 and became a prime provisioning spot for the northern Pacific whaling fleet. Visitors to the Queen Charlottes soon began to acquire small elaborate smoking pipes made of argillite, a jet-black clay stone from a quarry site known as Slatechuck Mountain. These are really effigies of pipes, because they cannot be used for smoking. Early pipes offer fantastic menageries of crest-like animals, although artists avoided specific crest images. Argillite carvers soon began to incorporate into their carvings images of sailing captains, fragments of sailing ships, and other motifs familiar to their ship-bound visitors [134]. Miniature memorial poles, house models, and boxes followed, along with small, free-standing sculptures, typically representing a shaman or illustrating a common story (the "bear mother" was a favorite). Haida artists clearly looked to the market for inspiration, experimenting with different subjects and focusing on those they found to be most popular among buyers.

134 Two sailors of argillite with ivory inlay, made by a Haida carver of the Queen Charlotte Islands, British Columbia, some time, it is estimated, around 1845. Haida carvers began making argillite (black slate) carvings for "otherworldly" visitors, like these American or British sailors, around 1830. Here the artist has captured the clothing and quizzical body language of the potential purchasers of his work.

It would not, however, be accurate to describe arg[illite] carvings as simply tourist-art curios. There is good evide[nce] the best Haida carvers, those high-born individuals custom[arily] approached for major crest commissions, also carved argillite for sale. Art historian Robin Wright recognizes the hand of Squiltcange, an early nineteenth-century artist mentioned by Charles Edenshaw, on a set of mortuary posts at the Haida village site of Kiusta and also on some extraordinarily refined argillite carvings. (Excavations at Kiusta confirm that argillite was carved there.) Wright also thinks that Albert Edenshaw (c. 1812–1894), one of the most prominent chiefs of the nineteenth-century Haida, carved argillite as a young man while living in Kiusta. Without question, Charles Edenshaw (c. 1829–1920), Albert's maternal nephew, and heir to his name and title, is recognized today as one of the most accomplished masters of argillite carving on the Northwest Coast. One of his more elaborate works is an impressive miniature chest of argillite that stands upon four diminutive frog feet [135]. Edenshaw combines a masterful interpretation of form-line relief on its sides with a free-standing figure perched on the lid. The composition on the lid illustrates a well-known Haida story of the first human beings, brought forth from a clam shell by Raven into the world. Raven in human form and dressed as a Haida chief stands on the clam shell, the faces of the first humans at his feet, peering up at him from the edge of the giant clam.

135 Model chest of argillite, carved by Charles Edenshaw (Haida), c. 1900–10. This masterful carving combines the form and design of a traditional bentwood chest (see fig. 124) with a figural rendering on the lid of an episode of the Raven cycle of stories. Raven, in the form of a Haida chief, looks on as the first human beings emerge from a clam shell.

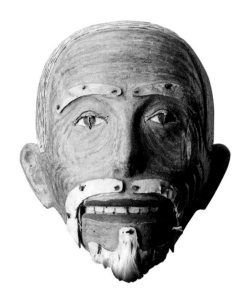

Simeon *sdiihldaa* (c. 1799–1889), an Eagle chief at Masset, is remembered as a maker of canoes and carver of memorial poles, frontlet headdresses, and argillite models, but is known today particularly for his human face masks [136]. Their distinctive round faces and clear-eyed expressions are unmistakable, although it has taken Bill Holm and Robin Wright considerable effort to restore this man's name to his body of work. His masks of white men may have been used in humorous performances that made fun of the outsiders' rude habits. Some masks were evidently sold directly to collectors.

136 Mask, carved by Simeon *sdiihldaa* (Haida) from the town of Masset, Queen Charlotte Islands, British Columbia, active until just before his death in 1889. This mask is clearly intended to represent a white man, with his facial hair and narrow nose.

137 "Killer Whale Leaping," a gold box made by Bill Reid (Haida), 1971. Trained as a jeweler, Reid enjoyed great success and recognition late in his life for his work based upon the study of the old Haida masters.

More modern Haida artists pay homage to these past masters. Bill Reid (1920–1998) trained as a jeweler in Toronto and worked for the most part in silver and gold, but he completed a number of monumental commissions late in his life. His gold box of 1971 builds from the tradition of Haida feast dishes, but here in miniature [137]. A vibrant killer whale leaps up over the mirror-like finish of the top as if suspended weightlessly. Robert Davidson has also created a substantial corpus of work, prints on paper [138], masks, and bronze sculpture, through his meditative introspections of form-line structure. Although contemporary Northwest Coast artists participate in exhibitions and sell works through galleries, by and large they remain deeply involved with potlatches and other aspects of traditional social life as it has persisted to this day as a vibrant part of community life.

138 *Raven Stealing the Moon*,
Robert Davidson (Haida),
silkscreen print on paper, 1977.
In addition to making prints,
Davidson is also an accomplished
carver of masks.

Chapter 8   Arctic and Subarctic

North of the Arctic Circle the cycle of night and day slows from a planetary to a solar rhythm, a pace not governed by the quick spinning of the earth on its axis but by the more leisurely journey of the earth around the sun. Along the northern Alaskan and Canadian coast, the sun dips below the horizon for the last time in early November, beginning the long Arctic night, not to rise again in a new dawn until February. As the winter approaches, "freeze-up" locks open water into impermeable ice. Living things that have not fled south move to a more somnambulant tempo, awaiting spring. Seabirds begin to reappear in April, ushering in a parade of returning migratory animals throughout the succeeding months: nesting birds, spawning fish, whales through the Bering Straits to the west and into Baffin Bay in the east, and caribou to their calving grounds across the tundra to the north.

Four thousand years ago, human societies rose to the challenges of this unique environment by evolving life-ways and technologies suited to the grand ebb and flow of Arctic life. Archaeologists have found earlier sites, but sustained evidence of a purposeful colonization of the Arctic coast seems to have begun by approximately 2500 BC. It is clear from these first, earliest settlements that human life here depended upon the ability to make things, carefully crafted tools that helped transform the peculiarities of environment into useful resources. Peoples of the Arctic Small Tool Tradition (2200–1000 BC) depended upon their skills to locate local sources of suitable stone and create small and delicate stone tools: chipped blades, burins, micro-blades, and scrapers. These fundamental processing and fabricating tools hint at inventories of additional tools, weapons, and conveyances of wood, bone, antler, and ivory.

Art of hunting

In the central Arctic of Canada's northern Quebec and Northwest Territories, Dorset culture emerged from the "Pre-Dorset" variant of the Arctic Small Tool Tradition by 800 BC. Dorset people built sizeable semi-subterranean houses excavated into the tundra, with upper walls of piled earth and roofs of animal hide. Oil rendered from sea mammal blubber and burned in soapstone lamps made living throughout the Arctic winter in such houses possible. Compared with later residents of this region, the Dorset possessed a rather limited hunting technology. On the other hand, they committed a great deal of skill and craft to the task of creating images. They carved small pendants and figures of wood, antler, and walrus ivory: images of animals, human dolls with articulated arms and legs, and startlingly lifelike miniature masks. For the challenging, risk-laden lives of Dorset people, these pendants and amulets may have represented a spiritual technology, a means to influence the world around them. Several pendants depict the polar bear, man's most fearsome predatory competitor in the central Arctic. Often the animal rendered in these amulets seems unbound by gravity, legs trailing behind and forepaws hanging limply, as if the creature is flying or floating through space [139]. Are such images spirit polar bears that act as hunters' helpers? Did the amulets offer protection against these dangerous animals? Or do they recognize those who had killed polar bears, at considerable risk, by representing their flaccid, lifeless bodies? Such questions remain difficult to answer. Dorset art, however, with its keen observations of animals, suggests an ideology that perceived few boundaries between the activities of human beings and of other creatures of the environment.

To the west, after 1000 BC, life in the Bering Straits region focused increasingly on the ample maritime resources – walrus,

139 Figure of polar bear carved from walrus ivory, recovered from a Dorset culture site in the Igloolik area, just south of Baffin Island, Nunavut Province, dating to the Middle Dorset period, AD 100–1000. This is one of many small Dorset charms that show polar bears as if flying or floating.

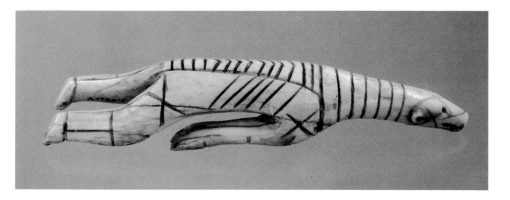

whales, and seals – with a growing inventory of tools, utensils, and hunting technologies. Distinctively decorated implements and hunting weapons characterize the Okvik and Old Bering Sea traditions (AD 1–700) rooted in the Chukchi peninsula of Siberia but spread across the Bering Strait to St. Lawrence Island and some isolated locations on mainland Alaska. Okvik and Old Bering Sea hunters employed a specialized and well-crafted variety of heavy harpoon for hunting large sea mammals. A toggle head fitted with a stone blade detached from the harpoon when thrust through the heavy hide of a walrus. A line bound to the toggle head dragged an inflated bladder float to tire the wounded animal until it could be killed with lances. Hunters carved the toggle head and a heavy foreshaft for their harpoons from walrus ivory and engraved them with fine web-works of linear design. They also bound an ivory counter weight, or "winged object," to the butt end of the harpoon for balance. An Okvik winged object excavated from St. Lawrence Island is stained nearly black from dark graphite that percolates through local groundwater [140]. Characteristic Okvik patterns enliven its surfaces: fine lines, stippled dashes, and concentric circles. Okvik and three variants of Old Bering Sea styles of engraving (Old Bering I, II, and III) can be distinguished, their subtle differences representing regional styles or gradual changes over time. Although it is possible to discern broad stylistic patterns, each object is unique, a product made by or for the hand of an individual hunter. Such careful attention to the creation and decoration of hunting weapons

140 Winged object, a counterweight for a harpoon, carved of walrus ivory and engraved with designs in the Okvik style, recovered from St. Lawrence Island, Bering Straits, dating to 300–1 BC. This is one of several different functioning parts of an innovative harpoon design that made colonization of the Bering Straits region possible.

141 Box to store slate lance points for whaling, owned and probably made by an Inuit *umialik*, or whaling chief. His "kit" of whaling paraphernalia was found on Sledge Island, just offshore Norton Sound, Alaska, in 1912.

reflects respect and deference for the hunter's dangerous yet potentially magnanimous quarry. The hunting rituals of later Arctic peoples are replete with gestures of respect and gratitude toward hunted animals, offered with the hope that the *inua*, or spirit of the quarry, would continue to give up its body and flesh for the use and nourishment of human beings.

The receding pack ice of springtime provided opportunities to hunt whales with techniques first explored by the Old Whaling culture of Cape Krusenstern, Alaska, as early as 1400 BC. Okvik, Old Bering Sea, and especially later Punuk and Birnirk peoples of the Bering Straits region (AD 300–1000) refined whaling as a collective, community endeavor. Point Barrow, on the northern tip of Alaska, supported a large Birnirk whaling community. Thule culture, growing out of Birnirk and Punuk roots, brought whaling traditions with it as Thule peoples expanded their range east as far as western Greenland by AD 1000. The descendants of these traditions, such as the Inuit-Inupiaq (Central Eskimo) residents of Point Barrow, continue to hunt whales today. Hunters pursued migratory whales in the leads or channels that developed during the spring between firm shore ice and slushy young offshore ice. Success depended upon highly regarded senior men, whaling captains, or *umialik*, who possessed experience, knowledge, and powerful spiritual abilities. The *umialik* presided over a close group of kinsmen who, after lengthy ritual preparation, camped on the edge of the pack ice close to the opening leads waiting for whales to come by. In such close quarters, skin boats could be launched

142 Whale plaque intended to hang on the bow of an *umiak*, or skin boat, when whaling. This is part of an elaborate whaler's kit found on Sledge Island, Alaska, in 1912 (see also fig. 141).

and a whale harpooned quickly. An unknown whaling chief who lived in the vicinity of Sledge Island, on Norton Sound, owned an elaborate assortment of weapons and charms to ensure success while whaling. He kept sharp yet delicate slate blades for harpoons and lances inside a wooden box carved like a bowhead whale [141]. There the blades became familiar with the locations of vital organs and their deadliness improved. A box in the shape of a whale's head, the most precious part of the animal, stored whetstones for the sharpening blades. The *umialik* also owned a wooden plaque carved with the image of a whale to hang on the bow of his *umiak*, or skin boat, while hunting [142]. The underside of the plaque is encrusted with glistening chunks of iron pyrite and polished, brightly colored stones. Such charms honored the whale so it might swim close and allow itself to be caught. This whaler's kit, found on Sledge Island, also included floats carved as human-like whale spirits, stone-tipped lances, and additional charms.

Hunters all depended upon spiritual assistance: the spiritual powers to find animals, draw them close, and convince them to give their bodies. Neglect or carelessness of spiritual requisites for successful hunting meant failure, hunger, and eventually starvation.

When hunters created their inventory of weapons and implements, they did not focus just upon their functional utility. They created objects to evoke beneficial spirits, identify with other powerful predators, flatter their quarries with intimate knowledge of their anatomies, and rehearse successful kills by demonstrations of control over the bodies of their prey. For example, hunters who sought seals and walrus using kayaks in the waters of Norton Sound, Alaska, wore hunting hats of wood, with an extended visor in front to shade the eyes and charms carved of walrus ivory attached to its surface. The ivory wings and heads of seagulls attached to the hat aided the hunter's ability to soar over the waves in his kayak and locate prey. On the hat illustrated here, the gull wings and heads attached to either side of the hat crowd together three walrus heads in a vertical row down the center, their heads carved as if emerging from the water [143]. Hunters in kayaks customarily hunted these large and dangerous animals in groups, surrounding them and herding them together so that the hunters could collaborate during the kill.

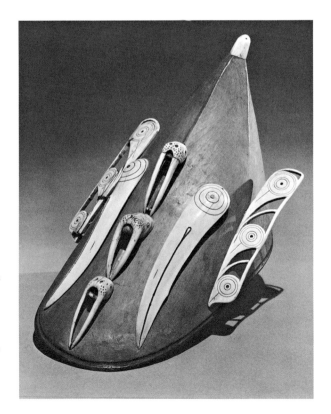

143 Hunter's hat owned by an Inuit man of Norton Sound, Alaska, before 1886. Wearing this hat while hunting walrus from a kayak assisted the hunter, not only by shading his eyes from the sun, but also by encouraging him to emulate the seagulls, represented by ivory charms on the hat, which herd walrus together where they can be harpooned.

144 Funerary mask, made of walrus ivory and found at the Ipiutak site, near Point Hope, Alaska. Several remarkable walrus ivory carvings were discovered during excavations at the site, which has been dated AD 1–800, including at least one other mask like this one.

Masks and shamanism

At the Ipiutak site, located on the beach ridges of Point Hope in northern Alaska, 125 miles (200 km) north of the Arctic Circle, collections of engraved walrus ivory objects were interred with the dead, including at least two masks pieced together from sections of engraved walrus ivory bound by lashings [144]. Ipiutak is a large village site of some six hundred houses (not all inhabited at the same time) dating from AD 1 to 800. The masks and other charm-like objects found accompanying burials at Ipiutak hint at the ritual practices of shamanism [145]. Arctic shamans interceded for humans in the world of animal spirits to ensure good relations with game animals. They also cured the sick by retrieving their straying souls and they restored fertility to women. An elaborate shaman's burial at the Ekven site, an Old Bering Sea village and cemetery on the Siberian mainland, included a large collection of shamanistic objects: a mask and drum, ivory ornaments that would have been attached to special garments, plus a number of elaborately decorated hunting weapons and women's utensils. Interestingly, amidst tools and weapons associated with both genders, the shaman buried at Ekven was a woman.

Masks and their collective rituals derived from the interior lives of Arctic peoples, both intellectually and physically, as the long, less active months of winter took people inside to perform rituals and enjoy social events. Throughout the Arctic, late fall and the early months of winter are devoted to festivals and feasting. Supplies have been laid in, game has retreated to winter ranges, and life turns inward toward family and the community. Stories – told, sung, and dramatically enacted – fill the long hours of winter festivals, recounting the adventures of animal heroes, the mystic journeys of shamans, and notable events of the past. Some performances use masks. A set of wooden masks with broad faces and a variety of small attachments accompanied carefully prepared

145 Carving of a baby walrus, made of walrus ivory and found at the Ipiutak site, near Point Hope, Alaska. This and other small carvings found at the site, dated AD 1–800, may have been attached to a shaman's garment, functioning as a charm.

bodies of men, women, and children in a cave on Unga Island, part of the Aleutian chain [146]. Archaeologists have not determined their age, but these masks may have been featured during winter festivals like those observed among the Aleuts by Russian traders during the eighteenth century. Extended Aleut families hosted neighbors in their large communal houses, offering feasts, songs, dancing, and masked performances that represented shamans' spirits.

146 Fragment of a wooden mask found in Delarof Harbor, Unga Island, one of the Aleutian Islands, Alaska.

147 Masked dancers performing in the Cu'pik town of Qissunaq, near Hooper Bay, Alaska, 1946. Note the kneeling posture of the main dancer in front, and the two women who are dancing in unison. The men on the right are singing, accompanied by a large hand drum.

Among the Yupik who live along the central and southern Alaskan coast and the Kuskokwim River, a shaman is called an *angalkuq*, and he or she (usually he) directs most masked performances. The *angalkuq* possesses far-reaching powers to influence the attitudes of game animals. Falling into a trance and leaving his body, the *angalkuq* can travel to the moon to seek out the master of land animals or journey to the bottom of the ocean to find the mother of sea creatures if game is scarce. He is the intercessor between human beings and animals, and the masked performances he orchestrates are like prayers for ongoing good relations [147]. In the communal men's house, or *qasgiq*, the best carvers made masks under the shaman's instruction. They most often appeared in pairs, worn by two energetic dancers selected by the *angalkuq*, who stood by and offered his audience detailed commentary. One mask of a pair collected from the village of Napaskiak represents "the hole through which the muskrat emerges from his den" [148]. The circular framework is the muskrat den and the face with welcoming arms is the hole. The white disks are bubbles from the breath of the muskrat which signal its presence inside the den. The spirit represented by the mask provides plenty of muskrats in the spring when hunters can pull them out of their dens and use their skins for clothing.

The carvers
In 1983, 73-year-old Yupik carver Nick Charles recalled that he had grown up sleeping in the *qasgiq* with his father, uncles, brothers, and cousins. There he learned to carve by watching the older men. "I learned from my dad. The only way the men worked

148 Dance mask from the town of Napaskiak on the Kuskokwim River, Alaska, carved by a Yupik man, perhaps around 1900. The mask represents a muskrat's den with the muskrat inside. The white disks are bubbles that reveal to a hunter the presence of a muskrat.

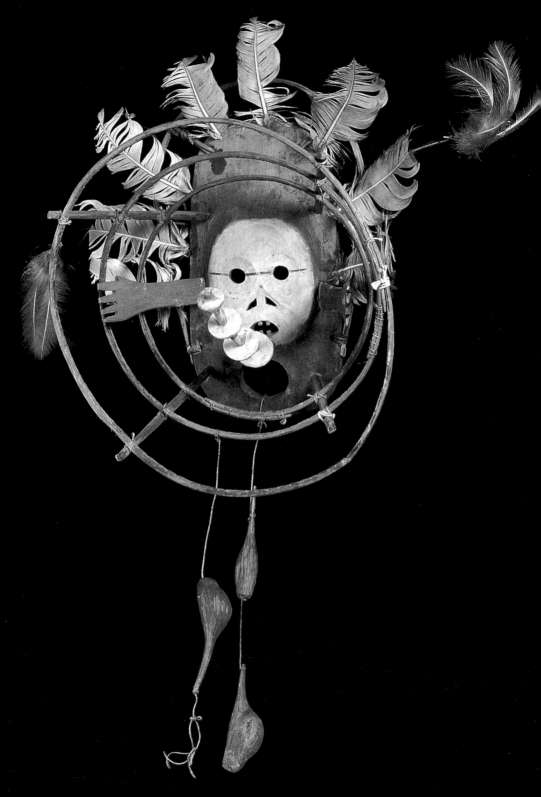

was on the wood. Making fishtraps, splitting wood, making sleds, making kayaks." The long winters of *qasgiq* life, of drowsy sweat baths, stories, and constant, patient whittling and carving while seated on a floor strewn with woodchips, have characterized the lives of Arctic men for more than a thousand years. Men collected driftwood (particularly roots), whale bone, and walrus ivory in anticipation of the long winter months when there would be time to make and repair the equipment needed for the coming seasons. The *angalkuq* might ask those who worked with wood best to make masks for upcoming festivals. There was no secrecy about it: the other men watched progress with interest. Carvers responded to the instructions of the *angalkuq* but felt free to combine longstanding representational conventions with their own imaginative interpretations.

Men also carved for pleasure. Edward William Nelson, who was sent to Alaska by the Smithsonian in 1877, noted that "men appeared to delight in occupying their leisure time in making carvings" and that "many little images are made as toys for children." The men carved dolls, miniature kayaks, sleds, dogs, game animals, bears, and other things that children used to rehearse grown-up lives in play. Images told stories. To illustrate stories told to entertain one another, young girls drew pictures in the snow with "story knives" made of ivory and carved by their fathers and uncles [149]. Men themselves engraved many of their own implements with narrative tableaux of stick figures engaged in hunting walrus, paddling in kayaks, and even trading with the whites in their sailing ships [150].

White visitors became more common on the Alaskan Arctic coast during the late nineteenth century, mostly whalers and missionaries at first. Arctic men discovered they could earn cash by selling ivory carvings. Images of walrus, caribou, and polar bear made good souvenirs, as did categories of objects more familiar to whites: cribbage boards, paper knives, and ship models. One of the most successful and accomplished of the carvers and engravers of ivory for sale was named Angokwazhuk, better known as Happy Jack. Born in 1870, Angokwazhuk was raised in a community on the coast of Cape Nome. He lost his toes from frostbite when stranded on the ice while hunting as a young man, but shortly thereafter in 1892 he managed to secure work on a whaling vessel. There he made his first cribbage boards and learned scrimshaw techniques from sailors. When the gold rush community of Nome erupted during the winter of 1898 to 1899, Angokwazhuk settled there to peddle his carvings as Happy Jack.

149 "Story knife," carved of walrus ivory by a Yupik man who lived in the town of Kongiganak, Kuskokwim Bay, Alaska, before the period between 1877 and 1881 when it was collected by Edward William Nelson for the Smithsonian Institution. Men carved story knives for children, who used them to draw pictures in the snow to illustrate tales told to their friends.

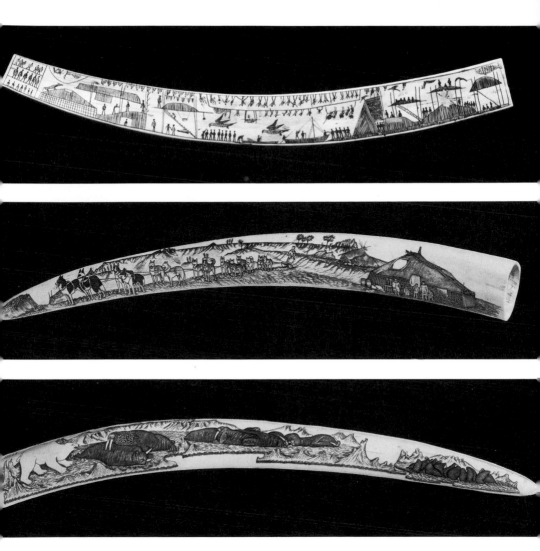

150 (top) Walrus tusk, engraved by a Yupik or Inuit man during the 1890s. The narrative quality of Alaskan Native art is illustrated here with this crowded scene of trade and transport engraved on the ivory.

151 (centre and below) Walrus tusk, engraved by Happy Jack, or Angokwazhuk (Inuit), while in Nome, Alaska, during the early decades of the 20th century.

His engraving technique surpassed any of the circle of carvers that gathered in Nome during the first decades of the twentieth century. He specialized in reproducing portraits from photographs juxtaposed on walrus tusks with slumbering walrus, herds of caribou, and dog-sled teams [151].

Carvers on Little Diomede, King, and St. Lawrence Islands and adjacent areas still carve walrus ivory for sale today, although there are concerns about dwindling opportunities. Recognizing the limitations for economic development in the north, Canada launched an initiative to establish artist cooperatives among the Canadian Inuit during the 1950s. Canadian Inuit artists specialized

152 "Migration," a carving of soapstone and other materials, created by Joe Talirunili, an Inuit resident of Povungnituk, on Hudson Bay, Quebec, around 1975. Talirunili is one of many Inuit artists who began to produce soapstone sculpture through Native-run cooperatives established in the 1950s.

in carving local stone and making lithographic prints from drawings. Their subjects stem from the narrative tradition: stories of life and the humans and spirit beings that animate it. Sculptor Joe Talirunili (1899–1976), for example, grew up in the region of Povungnituk Bay (Puvirnituq), near the northeast shore of Hudson Bay in Arctic Quebec. James Houston, the principal organizer of the government's cooperative program, first visited the area in 1949 under the auspices of the Canadian Crafts Guild to collect Inuit arts and crafts there. The present community of some 1,200 Inuit was established around a Hudson Bay post in the 1950s and the Povungnituk artists' cooperative soon followed in 1960. Making stone sculpture attracted Joe Talirunili since he had been disabled by a hunting accident when a young man. His *Migration* of c. 1975 is one of many carvings he made representing an *umiak* crowded with paddlers [152]. The subject stems characteristically from a story of life experience. As a child, Talirunili survived an accident in a similarly crowded boat when it capsized and forty people drowned.

Women working hides
"We used it all," explained Inuit woman Lucie Kownak in 1981. "I don't think we ever used to leave any part of the caribou behind." Arctic peoples hunted caribou for food, but also for their hides, tendons, antler, and bone. Life would not be possible in the

harsh Arctic climate without warm clothing made from the hides of caribou, seal, and other animals. The hollow, insulating hairs of caribou hides made these skins best for parkas and trousers. In many parts of Alaska and the Canadian Arctic, it was possible for Inuit to travel inland during late summer and fall to hunt caribou. Skins taken during this season were best for clothing. Later in the fall the hides became too heavy with winter fur. In spring, the caribou molted and their hides tended to be full of holes from insect bites. Women performed the tasks of hide preparation, pattern cutting, and sewing. As Emily Nipishna Alerk of Baker Lake explained to curator Judy Hall: "I use a scraper to soften and stretch the skin at the same time. Then I use another scraper to take off the inner surface of the skin.... If the skin is too hard, I chew on it to make it softer.... It would take five caribou skins for the coat, mitts, pants, and boots. You would use two caribou skins for the outer coat and if you had a shirt inside you would use another one. So you would catch about four caribou to do the inner and outer coat."

Winter wear required an inner parka (Emily calls it a shirt) with the hair worn inside and an outer parka with the hair worn outside so it would shed snow and ice. Caribou hide clothing had to be remade every season since the insulating hairs grew brittle and broke off after a year of wear. In the west, men who hunted on the water wore waterproof garments sewn together from strips made of walrus and seal intestine. Along the Alaskan coast women also used fish, bird, and muskrat skins. The survival of the family depended upon well-made and durable protective clothing and the task of making and remaking garments never ended. Women learned the necessary skills and techniques at an early age and often worked together to fulfill their responsibilities. Without proper clothing, the community could not hunt or travel. Everything depended upon them.

Garments also functioned as an expressive medium, communicating a great deal about identity and worldview. Subtle differences in tailored features distinguished fashions of different communities: the size and shape of a woman's hood (amaut), for example, or the length and breadth of the extended and fringed "tail" on the back of the parka. Different kinds of parkas distinguished gender and age: details of cut, for example, identified women as unmarried, married with children, or past child-bearing age. Men's garments among the Canadian Inuit emphasized their roles as hunters and their close relations with the caribou. As well as the long broad tail in the back, close-fitting hunting parkas included caribou ears on the hood. Stooped over, with the tail swinging between the legs, hunters could approach caribou herds by imitating their movements. To the west, in Alaska, women sewed in insets of white belly fur from the caribou on the shoulders of their parkas to imitate walrus tusks. Ideally, every individual owned everyday wear, but also special, more highly decorated parkas for dances and other social events. When traders began to visit the west coast of Hudson Bay during the eighteenth century, women gained access to glass beads for the decoration of clothing. Formal parkas decorated with glass beads became far more common after 1860 or so [153]. Women added cloth panels decorated with beads to chest, cuffs, and hood [154]. The cloth and beads themselves represented wealth, and, combined with the artistry of women's needlework, made a powerful statement about the prestige, skills, and industriousness of the family.

Garments and ornament of the Subarctic hunters
Alexander Mackenzie, the fur trader and explorer, when writing of his journeys throughout northern Canada between 1789 and 1793, commented of the Chipewyan, "There are no people more

153 A Caribou Inuit woman named Attirak, from Baker Lake, photographed *c.* 1920 wearing a parka decorated with glass beads.

180

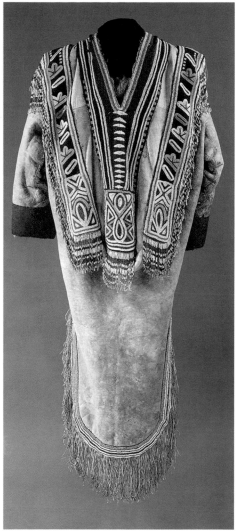

154 A parka made by a Caribou Inuit woman living in the vicinity of Churchill, Manitoba, on Hudson Bay, in 1938. This parka is a dress garment, intended for social events.

attentive to the comforts of their dress, or less anxious respecting its exterior appearance." The Chipewyan, or Denesúliné, as they call themselves, are one of several Athapascan-speaking groups who inhabit the forest-tundra fringe of the western Subarctic. Collectively, they speak of themselves as the "Dene," meaning "the people." Like the Inuit, Dene women made the clothing necessary for living in this demanding environment: winter and summer garments of caribou skins and moose hide. Tanning hides demanded long hours of physical labor and Dene women within a

155 Summer outfit made by a Gwich'in Athapascan woman who lived near the Arctic Red River region, Northwest Territories. Since this garment shows no sign of wear, it may have been intended as a kind of model of early nineteenth-century style clothing made in the 1880s for visitors and traders.

family group often worked together to prepare the several hides necessary for even a single set of garments. A summer outfit made by a woman of the Gwich'in Athapascans, or the Arctic Red River band near the mouth of the Mackenzie River at the Arctic Sea, reveals something of the quality of work and fineness of detail that Alexander Mackenzie referred to [155]. Made of caribou skin, the distinctive cut of the tunic, long with pointed lower edges at front and back, offered snug-fitting protection from the wind with great freedom of movement. Porcupine quills decorate the chest and shoulders. The soft-soled boots are combined with trousers. These, together with the hood and mittens, protected the wearer from biting insects. The garments, so well-made and lavishly decorated, expressed the strong Dene values attached to industriousness, consummate skill, aesthetic sensibility, and love for the family member for whom the outfit was intended.

To the east, across the full span of the continent, Naskapi women also fashioned winter and summer hunting coats from the skins of caribou [156]. The Naskapi of Labrador are the easternmost of the many Cree-speaking groups that range across Canada's Subarctic, the "Woods Cree" being the Dene's most immediate neighbors to the east and south. Like the Dene, Cree-speakers harvested the resources of the land, with an emphasis on big game, in small mobile groups. With the exceptions of changes in technology (the bow and arrow, and later the gun), this way of living had changed little over thousands of years. When Frank Speck, the Columbia-trained anthropologist, was working in the northern Quebec-Labrador Peninsula between 1909 and the early 1920s, he learned that the designs painted on Naskapi hunting coats were intended to honor the caribou. As he explained, "Animals prefer to be killed by hunters whose clothing is decorated with designs." The double curves, lozenge, and myriad other curvilinear forms are arranged in repetitive patterns across the back, skirt, sleeves, and collar. Like the engravings on Okvik and Old Bering Sea hunting equipment, their thoughtful, aesthetically refined patterning is intended to honor the spirits of hunted animals. With the Inuit, Dene, and Naskapi, we see how the garments fashioned from the skins of animals brought home by hunters are closely intertwined with the delicate spiritual relationships between hunter and prey.

It is curious, then, to discover that the cut of Naskapi hunting coats had adapted to European conventions of fashion by the eighteenth century. Particularly noteworthy is the fact that, while both Dene and Inuit patterns are "pullovers" which eliminate any

156 Hunter's coat, made by a Naskapi Cree woman of the Labrador Peninsula, Quebec, before 1825. The designs painted on the coat were intended to help men with the task of hunting moose.

157 (right) Pouch, made by a
Swampy Cree woman of Hudson
Bay, Manitoba, before 1840.

158 (below left) "Octopus pouch,"
so named for the pendant tabs on
the bottom, made by a Metis
woman of the Red River region,
Manitoba, c. 1840.

159 (below right) "Fire-bag," made
by a Cree or Metis-Cree woman
of the Lake Winnipeg region,
Manitoba, during the 1850s.

160 Man's jacket, made very likely by a Gwich'in Athapascan woman of the Arctic Red River region, Northwest Territories, before 1911, when a young man was photographed wearing it.

161 Pair of *mukluks*, made by Mary Agnes Bonnetrouge, a Slavey Athapascan woman living in Fort Providence, Northwest Territories, in 1985.

drafty fastenings, the Naskapi coat is cut so it opens in the front. Responding, perhaps, to the impracticality of this arrangement during certain seasons, Naskapi women sewed the fronts of winter coats shut. A single tunic-like garment, collected from the Gulf of St. Lawrence before 1656 in the collection of John Tradescant (see p. 56), may represent the pre-European fashion in the eastern Subarctic. The patterns of the Naskapi coats from the eighteenth century derived from French *capotes*, short woolen overcoats with hoods worn by traders, fur trade *engagés* and, to an increasing degree, northern Native peoples after the seventeenth century. The fur trade played a powerful role in transforming the life and arts of Subarctic peoples.

Many of the workers who circulated through the posts and forts of the fur trade network were Metis, a term used to describe the descendants from the unions of European men (French, Scots, English) and Native women (Ojibwa and Cree). A strong sense of ethnic identity was reflected in distinctive items of Metis dress: *capotes* or, alternatively, knee-length coats and shorter jackets made of hide with collars, cuffs, and other details drawn from military uniforms; half leggings pulled up just over the knee; finger-woven garters; sashes; and lavish use of floral style decoration in porcupine quills and glass beads [159]. Images of flowers for decoration contrasted with the curvilinear patterns of Naskapi painting and the geometric patterns customarily employed for porcupine quill ornament among the Woods Cree [157]. A distinctive, quite naturalistic style of floral embroidery developed in the Red River region, south of Lake Winnipeg, where Metis settled in buffalo-hunting communities after 1800 [158]. Many spoke French patois and had been raised as Catholics. The Order of the Grey Nuns, established in Montreal during the 1750s but extremely active in the Winnipeg and Red River region after 1840, played a significant role in the refinement of floral style image and technique for the decoration of clothing. The Grey Nuns taught silk thread embroidery with floral images in mission schools. Red River Metis families dispersed throughout the northwest after their unsuccessful rebellions of 1870 and 1885. The dispossession of the Red River Metis and the expansion of residential mission schools throughout the Canadian northwest after the 1860s had a profound impact on the decorative arts of the Woodlands Cree and Dene.

During the nineteenth century, fur traders established a series of posts along the Mackenzie River through the heart of Dene territory. At first the Dene had little use for European clothing, although they admired the qualities and convenience of wool (of only the best quality, traders complained), and reportedly extolled glass beads over almost any other trade item. But the flashy appearance of Metis fur-trade workers and training in the arts of floral embroidery at residential schools worked to transform Dene aesthetic sensibilities. Contrast the summer outfit collected at Arctic Red River, near the polar sea, discussed earlier, with a summer jacket worn by a Dene man at Arctic Red River in 1911 (he was photographed wearing it) [160]. The short jacket of moose hide is decorated with panels of black wool cloth on the front, shoulders, and cuffs, edged with ermine fur and embroidered with images of flower blossoms, leaves, and stems using colorful glass beads. Dene women continue to ply their skills in hide working and sewing today. In 1985 Mary Agnes Bonnetrouge (a name revealing Metis connections), living at Fort Providence, west of Great Slavey Lake, created a strong expression of contemporary Dene values of design and workmanship in the *mukluks* (footwear) she made for art historian Kate Duncan and museum curator Barbara Hail for the collection of the Haffenreffer Museum of Anthropology in Rhode Island [161].

Chapter 9

Artists of the Modern and Contemporary World

The historical events of contact, conquest, resistance, and "survivance," to return to some of the themes that opened this book, brought together from opposite sides of the Atlantic very different cultural values linked to making things – the things, for the sake of convenience, we will call art. There are the very different aesthetic values linked to objects themselves and then the different aesthetic values laden within the cultural activities in which objects played a role. In some instances, the culture of conquest actively repressed local artistic practices, seeing in them values in conflict with their own "civilizing" agenda. Missionary repression of Yupik masked dances, the patronizing Canadian potlatch law of 1884, and the US administrative policies committed to eliminating "Indian Dances" in the United States are all cases in point. In each instance, however, after long struggle, many communities successfully reconfigured such practices for the present while also changing the outsiders' perceptions. Consider the revival of Yupik masked dancing in Alaska, for example, the open expression of Kwakiutl potlatching today, and the phenomenal growth of the modern powwow since the 1950s. In other instances, as we have seen, artists converted the things they made within their local communities – pottery, baskets, and walrus ivory carvings, to name a few – into objects that had commodity value among the outsiders. In so doing, the artists engaged in a kind of dialogue with the outside consumers, educating them, on the one hand, to the values of their craft, and adapting themselves, on the other hand, to the demands of the marketplace.

But there is another history. In addition to resistance and adaptation, what of those artists who actively engaged the artistic

162 Photograph of Zacharie Vincent painting a self-portrait during the 1870s or 1880s. Vincent referred to himself as the last Wendat (Huron) full-blood and painted self-portraits (see fig. 163), which he sold at his home community of Jeune Lorette, just outside Montreal.

values of the outsiders in their own terms, appropriating them, challenging them, and, in some cases, transforming them? Art and art making is a highly charged activity within modern Euro-American societies. Its definitions, philosophies, and practices lie at the heart of how civilization, as Euro-American societies conceive it, defines itself. A cultivated aesthetic sensibility represents a peak cultural value among Euro-Americans, especially among those who command wealth and social power. At the same time, Euro-American traditions of art also value transgressive qualities, artists who break barriers, those whose expressive power derives from their individuality, vision, and "genius," and, within limits, those who wield art as social critique. We have not yet sufficiently addressed those of Native American ancestry who seized the identity of artist in these Euro-American terms, nor examined their reasons for doing so and their accomplishments when they were successful.

Painted images and auto-ethnography
Prior to the twentieth century, few Native men or women worked in the conventionally understood fine arts media of painting and sculpture. One, Zacharie Vincent (1815–1896), a Wendat or Huron of Lorette, painted portraits of himself and his family with oils on canvas [162]. His ancestors descended from Huron converted to Catholicism by Jesuits during the early seventeenth century. In the face of Iroquois aggression, they had fled from their homeland east of Georgian Bay and in 1697 established the settlement of Jeune Lorette (New Lorette) 8 miles (13 km) from Montreal. We encountered them earlier (see p. 61), because many in the community supported themselves by making and selling things: snow shoes, canoes, and bags and moccasins decorated with moose hair embroidery. The picturesque village with its wooden church situated near the falls of the Saint Charles River became a tourist destination in the nineteenth century, with excursions bringing visitors from Montreal. The visual charm of the town and the exotic appearance of its residents when they appeared in full formal dress inspired several Canadian artists. There are many paintings, lithographic prints, and photographs of the village and its inhabitants, and these were marketed presumably to tourist visitors as well as a larger audience receptive to sentimental images of American Indians. Vincent himself, when twenty-three years old, sat for one of Canada's foremost nineteenth-century portraitists, Antoine Sébastien Plamondon (1804–1895). Titled *Le dernier des Hurons*

163 Self-portrait of Zacharie Vincent, oil on canvas, mid-19th century. Vincent appropriated for himself the iconic image of the "Vanishing Indian," as developed earlier in the nineteenth century by non-Indian painters such as George Catlin. Vincent shows himself draped in trade silver, wearing a feather headdress with a silver head band, and holding a smoking pipe and pipe tomahawk, all symbols of his Indian identity.

(*The Last of the Hurons*) the picture won a medal from Quebec's Société littéraire et historique in 1838. Plamondon was a resident of Ancienne Lorette, the older settlement adjacent to Jeune Lorette, and it is tempting to think that perhaps Vincent learned some technique from his older neighbor. His paintings certainly evidence some training.

The several self-portraits Vincent produced throughout his life trace his likeness through advancing years [163]. He customarily presented himself draped in trade silver and wampum, holding smoking pipes or tomahawks (sometimes both), and often wearing a silver headdress with three feather plumes. The notion that Vincent was the "last of the Huron" was evidently not Plamondon's idea, since Vincent himself claimed he was the last Wendat full-blood. His self-portraits join a genre of images that includes paintings by Charles Bird King and George Catlin, the more broadly disseminated color lithographs of McKenney and Hall, and even the much later photographs of Edward Curtis. In all these images, a nostalgic portrayal of Indians wearing and holding iconic symbols of their identities – feather headdresses, pipes, and beads – combines with the sentimental implication that such identities will soon pass into history. The difference here, however, is that Vincent re-claims this much-conventionalized image of the "vanishing Indian" for himself, as both its image and author.

Although fine arts training was not part of the curriculum of most early American Indian education, sometimes access to fine arts media was enough. Harriet Gilstrap, who taught at the Shawnee boarding school at Tecumseh, Oklahoma, during the last decade of the nineteenth century, remembered Earnest Spybuck as a student because he was always drawing pictures. Spybuck (Shawnee, 1883–1949) had been born on the Potawatomi and Absentee Shawnee reservation near present-day Oklahoma City. He later told anthropologist M. R. Harrington that, when a child, he had drawn pictures with a stick in the mud, saying, "Mother Earth taught me to draw." Harrington hired Spybuck in 1910 to produce a series of watercolors for the Museum of the American Indian, Heye Foundation (now the National Museum of the American Indian), illustrating the dances and ceremonies of the Shawnee and other Oklahoma tribes. His *War Dance and Gathering Scene* is one of three that show different episodes of the same event [164]. Spybuck's snapshot captures a single moment, his powers of observation piling detail after detail into this busy, congested image. He shows the wagons, carriages, tents, and pets of the visitors and participants strewn throughout the wooded camping areas surrounding the dance ground. Some spectators chat and exchange handshakes. Others sit together in clumps and watch the performance attentively. The dance itself takes place in the upper left of the picture, the singers and dancers crowded beneath a leaf-covered arbor. The three singers are seated on the left, the figure with a red shirt playing a water drum held between his knees. A group of shirtless men, the principal warriors, wearing roaches and eagle feathers, dance in place in front of the singers. More men dance behind them and a group of well-dressed women stand to the right of the arbor watching.

It is instructive to compare Spybuck's image with an ethnographic description of a War Dance prepared by anthropologist James Howard documenting a ceremony he observed in August 1970. One is struck first by how closely the image and the description correspond, despite the fact that sixty years separated the two events. Furthermore, both Howard and Spybuck engaged their full powers of description, one literary, the

164 Earnest Spybuck (Shawnee), *War Dance and Gathering Scene*, watercolor on paper, c. 1910. This is one of several watercolors commissioned from Spybuck by anthropologist Mark Raymond Harrington for the Museum of the American Indian, now the National Museum of the American Indian.

other pictorial. Of the episode depicted by Spybuck, Howard writes: "The singers faced east and the dancers arranged themselves in a rough crescent formation facing them. Each warrior danced as an individual unit, improvising to the music.... Rapid alternations of toe and heel served to ring the knee and ankle bells. Now and then a dancer would swoop low and then quickly rise to full height." Howard even tells us the women visible in Spybuck's picture standing to the right are "bouncing on their heels." This is ethnography, the deployment of descriptive media to record and document cultural practices. Howard, like a good reporter, places himself at the scene. His text describes his arrival, where he camped, and to whom he spoke. Spybuck may have similarly located himself within his picture as participant-observer. There is a good chance that the man in the lower right of the picture, shaking hands with the man wearing a red bandana (perhaps Harrington), is a self-portrait.

The term "auto-ethnography," as used by professor of comparative literature Mary Louise Pratt, applies to both Vincent's and Spybuck's paintings. In her discussions of colonial literature, Pratt uses auto-ethnography to "refer to instances in which colonized subjects undertake to represent themselves in ways that *engage with* [emphasis hers] the colonizer's own terms."

She was referring to literature, but the same notion can apply to visual arts. The sentimentalizing image of the vanishing Indian and ethnographic description are both strategies Euro-Americans used to shape, for their own purposes, the identities of Native Americans. Vincent and Spybuck engaged these visual strategies self-consciously and by doing so reclaimed the ability to re-cast representations of identity for purposes best suited to them.

The ways in which people thought about Indians and representations of such thought in speech, literature, and images had real consequences for Native people and still do today. Patronizing attitudes toward Native Americans at the beginning of the twentieth century informed public policy. The Allotment Act of 1887 seriously compromised any remaining Native land holdings, thus destroying traditional economies based upon resources of the land. Some religious ceremonies were banned outright while others faced serious opposition from reservation administrators. American Indian education used boarding schools to separate Native children from their language, families, and communities. Many of those in positions of power thought of Native societies as living fossils of an obsolete stage of social progress and saw no value in local or tribal traditions, practices, or language in the modern world. Their goal was total assimilation, the last chapter of conquest, couched in language that described "raising" Indians to the level of white people. On the other hand, this era also marks the appearance of growing ranks of Native writers, ethnographic informants, and visual artists who worked to construct an alternative view using the language, media, and rhetorical strategies of the outsiders to do so. Their message resonated with a growing number of Americans who, for reasons of their own, also questioned the wisdom of effacing American Indian culture altogether.

165 Fred Kabotie (Hopi), *Mixed Kachina Dance*, pencil and watercolor on paper, c. 1919. When they were shown in New York City in 1920, paintings like this one reminded art critics of Egyptian reliefs or friezes on ancient Greek pottery.

166 Crescencio Martinez (San Ildefonso), *Buffalo Dancers*, watercolor on paper, c. 1916. Martinez was one of the earliest Pueblo artists who painted watercolor images of dances, and a generation older than most of the others, but he died in 1918 before the more widespread recognition enjoyed by the younger Pueblo watercolorists.

Artists, patronage, and teaching American Indian art
On 14 March 1920, "Art Notes" in the Sunday *New York Times* included a brief notice that the annual exhibition of the Society of Independent Artists at the Waldorf-Astoria hotel featured an exhibition of watercolors painted by American Indian artists from the Southwest pueblos. The pictures in the exhibition portrayed colorful Kachina dances and animal dances. The artists painted detailed portrayals of single dancers or densely grouped processions arranged across the expanse of a blank background. Walter Pach, the art critic for the *Times*, compared the compositions to those of ancient Egyptian reliefs and Greek vase painting.

Fred Kabotie (Hopi, 1900–1986), then only twenty years old, was among the several artists of roughly the same age included in the Waldorf-Astoria exhibition. Raised in the Hopi community of Shungopovi on Second Mesa, Kabotie had been sent to the Santa Fe Indian School in 1915. There, he and a small group of young men, among them Otis Polelonema (Hopi, 1902–1981) and Velino Shije Herrera (Zia, 1902–1973), had received instruction in watercolor technique from Elizabeth DeHuff, the wife of the school superintendent. Kabotie painted images of Hopi dances, he said later, because they reminded him of home [165].

Alfonso Roybal (also known as Awa Tsireh, San Ildefonso, 1898–1955), another artist shown at the Waldorf-Astoria exhibition, had learned basic drawing and watercolor techniques at the San Ildefonso Day School under the instruction of teacher Esther B. Hoyt and her successor in 1909, Elizabeth Richards. Alfonso, however, came from a family of artists. His relations included maternal uncle Crescencio Martinez and wife Maximiliana, his uncle's in-laws Julian and Maria Martinez (see p. 103), and maternal aunt, Tonita Martinez (later Roybal) and her first husband Alfredo Montoya. All three couples made and sold pottery for the Santa Fe market. The men painted designs on pottery and, at least by 1910, they also painted watercolors on paper. Edgar Lee Hewett, an anthropologist and the Director of the Museum of New Mexico, had employed the three men during archaeological excavations on the nearby Pajarito Plateau and encouraged them to paint images of ceremonies and dances. Here, too, like anthropologist M. R. Harrington and artist Earnest Spybuck, Hewett sponsored the artistically talented San Ildefonso residents to engage in a kind of visual auto-ethnography.

Hewett credited Crescencio Martinez (San Ildefonso, c. 1879–1918) as "the first artist of record" of the San Ildefonso group and presumably the originator of the technique and style emulated by younger painters. His *Buffalo Dancers* of c. 1916, with its three figures portrayed in stately motion, exemplifies the flat coloring and extraordinary emphasis of texture and detail visible in the body painting, textiles, and headdresses [166]. The simply rendered figures become mere armatures for the distinctive regalia of these animal spirit impersonations. Unlike Spybuck, Martinez effaces all references to specific time, place, and incident, creating instead an image of idealized ritual. As more artists joined the ranks of American Indian painters during the 1920s and 1930s, they too would tend to frame their images of American Indian life in terms of the ideal and timeless, rather than the specific and historic.

Patronage shaped the formative years of these artists. Artists and writers, the wealthy and the influential, had gathered in Santa Fe and Taos during the years after World War I, driven by disenchantment with modern urban life too influenced (in their view) by the rancid and decaying culture of Europe. They saw in Pueblo culture something uniquely American that could stand as a foundation for an independent American culture and art. Artists like John Sloan, Robert Henri, and John Marin who had begun their careers in New York City joined the artist colony in Santa Fe and shifted their attention to American Indian subjects and the distinctive New Mexican landscape. Alarmed by the then-commonplace administrative policies that condemned American Indian ceremonies and plotted to undermine land rights, this expatriate *intelligentsia* organized to "save the Indians," as artist Maurice Stearne urged his wife, heiress Mabel Dodge Stearne (later Mabel Dodge Luhan), in a letter of 1916. She, John Sloan, Amelia Elizabeth White, Edgar Lee Hewett, and others became powerful patrons and promoters of the Pueblo artists. The paintings, "rhythm of movement and color summoned to express in the utmost brilliancy, the vibrant faith of a people," in the words of anthropologist Hewett, made a powerful argument about the value of preserving American Indian culture by revealing the beauty of its cultural practices.

Another group of artists painting watercolor images of traditional dances emerged from classes taught by Susan Peters beginning in 1916 at the Kiowa Agency in Anadarko, Oklahoma. The so-called "Kiowa Five" included Stephen Mopope (Kiowa, 1898–1974) and Monroe Tsatoke (Kiowa, 1904–1937), whose subjects ranged from contemporary powwow dancing to illustrations of esoteric ritual, but all rendered in a flat, stark, but colorful style of figures in movement set against a blank page. Between 1926 and 1929, the five Kiowa artists were supported by full scholarships and stipends at the University of Oklahoma and, like the Pueblo artists, their work was shown domestically and abroad. These artists saw their style growing out of "ledgerbook" paintings of earlier generations of Oklahoma artists such as James Silverhorn (Kiowa, 1861–1941), Mopope's uncle. Silverhorn's father was one of the keepers of the Kiowa Winter Count pictorial calendar, and his older brother, Ohettoint (Kiowa, 1852–1934) had been a very active artist when imprisoned at Fort Marion (see p. 116). Ohettoint returned to Oklahoma in 1880 and both he and Silverhorn worked as informants and produced pictures for ethnologist James Mooney. A group of drawings

168 Stephen Mopope (Kiowa), *The Procession*, watercolor on board, undated. Mopope and other artists of his generation were inspired by the older "ledgerbook" artists, such as his uncle, James Silverhorn (see fig. 167).

169 Dick West (Cheyenne), *Cheyenne Sun Dance, The Third Day*, watercolor on paper, 1949. Through his work and teaching at Bacone College, Dr. Walter Richard West brought "traditional American Indian painting" into the mid-twentieth century.

167 James Silverhorn (Kiowa), *Preparing for a War Expedition*, pencil and crayon on paper, c. 1887. This early work of Silverhorn illustrates his strong draftsmanship and vibrant sense of color.

purchased by a local military officer no later than 1887 exemplify Silverhorn's distinctive stylizations of "ledgerbook art" with his emphasis on graceful outline, strong localized color, and rhythmic patterning. The first of the series, titled *Preparing for a War Expedition*, shows a warrior with a trailing eagle feather headdress astride a golden-maned mount [167]. Silverhorn's nephew Stephen Mopope's undated watercolor painting, *The Procession*, shows similar interest in the panoply of Plains regalia, as riders parade before rows of standing spectators [168].

The Oklahoma and Southwest painters of the 1920s created the foundation of what would become institutionalized in the 1930s as "traditional" American Indian painting. Their success and promising indications of expanding tourist markets for artists working in traditional media, particularly in the Southwest, led some to believe that American Indian art could become a mainstay of a modern American Indian economy. Ideas like these led directly to the creation in 1932 of a formal program of arts instruction at the Santa Fe Indian School known as the Studio School, followed in 1935 by the Indian arts program at Bacone Junior College in Muskogee, and also in 1935, the creation of the Indian Arts and Crafts Board as part of a reformed Bureau of Indian Affairs under the Roosevelt administration.

Dorothy Dunn, who established the Studio program in classes she conducted between 1932 and 1937, imposed upon her students the styles developed by the Pueblo and Oklahoma watercolorists. Opaque watercolor technique, flat colors with little or no shading, a descriptive, illustrator's style of drawing, and subject matter that rarely strayed from idealized and romanticizing scenes of ceremony, dance, and mythology characterize the Studio style. Despite what seems in retrospect a very narrow curriculum, the Studio became a magnet for talent, attracting students who would become the foremost Native American artists of their generation. In Oklahoma, Acee Blue Eagle (Creek, Pawnee, 1907–1959), one of the most outgoing and charismatic of the Oklahoma artists, was appointed the first director of the arts program at Bacone Junior College, followed capably by Woody Crumbo (Potawatomi, 1912–1989), who had attended Dorothy Dunn's Studio classes, and Walter Richard (Dick) West (Cheyenne, 1912–1996), a Bacone graduate who directed the program until 1972.

West's *Cheyenne Sun Dance, The Third Day*, executed in 1949 during his tenure at Bacone, exemplifies the core aspects of traditional American Indian painting of the mid-twentieth century [169]. It builds upon the mandate of scrupulous auto-ethnography in its almost diagrammatic portrayal of one of the most sacred moments of the Sun Dance when devout supplicants endure the ordeal of piercing. The dancer in the center is suspended by his pectorals from the central pole of the Sun Dance lodge while heavy buffalo skulls hang from piercings in his back. Sun Dance piercing had been outlawed for decades before West was born and yet his picture summons up this Cheyenne ritual from tribal memory in the most solemn, sentimental, and idealized terms.

Perhaps the most prominent and successful of the Studio School students, Allan Houser (Warm Springs Chiricahua Apache, 1914–1994), through a long and productive life, negotiated for himself an artistic identity that at once accommodated the Studio School agenda while at the same time embracing twentieth-century modernity. Although trained as a Studio-style watercolorist, he turned increasingly to sculpture after the 1940s. He looked to Henry Moore, Brancusi, and Jean Arp for inspiration, but his imagery often remained rooted in Studio traditionalism. The monumental bronzes and marbles of his later years vacillate between idealized Native figures, timeless and immemorial, and abstractions with figural references that look more to Formalist and Surrealist sculpture [170].

The American Indian Fine Arts Movement, as it came to be called, fitted within a narrow pocket of the American art scene for artists and patrons alike. Institutional support, the schools and museums, reinforced the value of "traditional" subject matter and style, which at the same time tended to isolate and marginalize American Indian painters from the many other trends in American art at mid-century. The Annual Indian art exhibitions at the Philbrook Institute of Art in Tulsa, Oklahoma, initiated in 1947 and continued through 1972, featured most of the best artists of the day and also provided a sounding board for deeply felt controversies about traditional versus progressive styles among the participating artists. The juried exhibition and museum purchase competition reinforced a rather limiting artistic agenda intended to "document the records of Indian life and culture through traditional expression of the Indians, and to stimulate the renaissance of this unique expression by the encouragement of Indian artists." But even with this kind of institutional support it was a struggle making a living. Fred Kabotie supported himself by teaching art classes at Oraibi High School from 1937 to 1959. The most successful artists taught rather than making art full-time. Allan Houser, who retired from art making briefly after the war, reflected on his personal experience in 1959 when he lamented, "How can the Indian live by art?" During the 1950s, with the

170 Allan Houser (Warm Springs Chiricahua Apache), *Drama on the Plains*, alabaster, 1977. Trained in watercoloring at the Studio in Santa Fe, Houser later turned his attention to monumental sculpture. He is probably the most widely recognized and celebrated artist of Native ancestry of the twentieth century.

172 (opposite above) George Morrison (Grand Portage Ojibwa), *Red Rock Crevices. Soft Light. Lake Superior Landscape*, acrylic and ink on canvas board, 1987.

173 (opposite below left) Fritz Scholder (Luiseño), *Santana, Kiowa*, oil on canvas, c. 1968

174 (opposite below right) T. C. Cannon (Caddo/Kiowa), *Self-Portrait in the Studio*, oil on canvas, 1975.

171 Oscar Howe (Yanktonai Sioux), *Ghost Dance*, casein on paper, 1960.

United States government pursuing a policy of reservation "termination," it seemed as if few in America cared much about American Indians or American Indian art.

Indian art and the artist individual

> *I've always been an individual and have done exactly what I wanted to do. I've painted only for myself and never for others. I think this is the only way one can approach what is a very strange role of being a painter.* Fritz Scholder

Being any kind of artist in the United States up through the 1940s and 1950s was not particularly easy. Critics, patrons, collectors, museum curators, and other elements of the visual arts establishment waffled in their enthusiasm for European modernism, American regionalism, urban-based social realism, or nostalgia for conservative academicism of the past. Modernism and abstraction were controversial issues even within the most advanced artistic circles. In this light, the bold initiative of young George Morrison (Ojibwa, 1919–2000) seems particularly

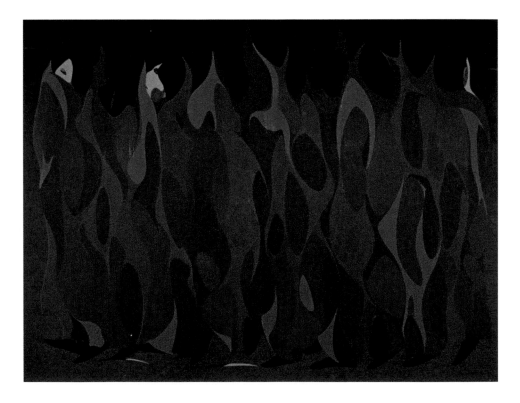

remarkable (see p. 24). Having grown up in the small and remote Ojibwa community of Grand Portage, Morrison left Minnesota in 1946 to pursue and master cutting-edge Abstract Expressionism in New York City [172]. The now legendary rebellion of Yankton artist Oscar Howe (1915–1983) against the strictures of the Philbrook Annual – his abstract pictures were rejected by the 1958 jury – was fueled by his fierce conviction that the rules of entry could not tell *him* what traditional American Indian art was supposed to look like. He insisted that his abstractions of traditional subjects, such as *Ghost Dance* of 1960, were not based on study of European Cubism. His means of expression drew from a very personal visual vocabulary, he claimed, and his own understanding of Sioux spirituality [171].

This kind of path to artistic self-expression while maintaining a sense of cultural tradition can be seen in the career of Joe Herrera (San Ildefonso, b. 1923), son of Tonita Pena, the potter and first generation San Ildefonso watercolorist. Herrera studied at the Studio School beginning in 1940 and mastered the illustrative Studio style, but returned to the MFA program at the University of New Mexico between 1950 and 1953. There, like non-Indian students, he was drawn to Cubism, Kandinsky, and Paul Klee. The result was works such as *Eagles and Rabbit* of 1953 where abstract forms drawn from Anasazi pictographs, kiva murals, and pottery designs are combined in a kind of synthetic Cubism. Herrera's self-conscious appropriation of modernist pictorial language with his own sense of traditional form and content paralleled the thinking of several artists at the end of the 1950s who wished to break what felt like constraints over the practices of American Indian artists.

This, precisely, became the lifelong agenda of Lloyd Kiva New (1916–2002), an Oklahoma Cherokee with a wide-ranging education and a strong entrepreneurial spirit. As a textile artist, teacher, and successful businessman, New played a pivotal role in the Rockefeller-funded New Directions in Southwest Indian Art conference held in Tucson in 1959 and drew together Joe Herrera, jeweler Charles Loloma (Hopi, 1921–1991), and painter Fritz Scholder (Luiseño, b. 1937), among others, as faculty in the subsequent Southwestern Indian Art Project at the University of Arizona from 1960 to 1962. The arts education curricula developed there over two subsequent summers would be moved pretty much wholesale (with many of the faculty) to the reorganized Santa Fe Indian School which opened as the Institute of American Indian Art (IAIA) in 1962. New's vision for contemporary Indian art remained remarkably consistent throughout his career, which included the directorship of IAIA from 1967 to 1972. "The Institute assumes that the future of Indian art lies in the Indian's ability to evolve, adjust, and adapt to the demands of the present, and not on the ability to remanipulate the past."

Painter Fritz Scholder, who served on the IAIA faculty from 1964 to 1969, had studied with Oscar Howe at Wisconsin State College and pop artist Wayne Thiebaud at Sacramento City College before completing his MFA at the University of Arizona in 1964. He and precocious IAIA students T. C. Cannon (Caddo, Kiowa, 1946–1978) and Bill Soza (Cahuilla Apache, b. 1949) began in 1965 to deconstruct the generations of "Indian painting" that had preceded them. Scholder's portrait of *Set-t'ainte*, or White Bear, reconfigures the iconic bust portrait of the American Indian (compare with Zacharie Vincent's self-portrait [163]) in startling new terms with bright Pop colors and broad Expressionistic brushwork [173]. The image is no idealized American Indian, but drawn directly from the Will Soule photograph of the great Kiowa leader who threw himself out of a prison window to his death on 11 October 1878, rather than face life imprisonment. The historic specificity of the image together with the heroic and tragic resonance of its subject, when combined with the aggressive edginess of Scholder's technique, establish a stance of ironic confrontation. Scholder's images are an abrupt departure from the safe and distant nostalgia of earlier generations of pictures. Irony, always present in the historic relations between Native Americans and the culture of conquest, steps to the foreground in the art of the 1960s, paralleling the rise of Native political activism.

T. C. Cannon, a student at IAIA from 1964 to 1966 and possessing an abundance of raw talent, skillfully built upon his Anadarko roots, his images often paying deference to the subjects and colorist sensibilities of his Oklahoma forebears. In his *Self-Portrait in Studio* of 1975, Cannon sits relaxed within his own space, gazing at the viewer with brushes in hand ready to paint, an historic Navajo blanket beneath his feet, a mask from West Africa hanging on the wall to the left, and an expansive Santa Fe vista visible through the windows behind him [174]. He claims for himself the standpoint of observer of the world and consumer of its cultural riches, reversing the habitual role of American Indians as observed and consumed. This powerful definition of self cannot be confined within any conventional identity of American Indian.

> For the first time, a generation of articulate and well-educated
> Indian artists have a positive Indian identity to which they may
> relate. Their new solidarity focuses on their art, an art that is Indian
> in a whole new way. Lloyd Oxendine

These optimistic words come from a special issue of *Art in America*
devoted to "The American Indian" published in 1972. With
hindsight, the statement accurately reflected the situation in two
ways, although this was perhaps only partially understood by the
author. First, "an art that is Indian in a whole new way" stems from
the fact that Native artists of 1972 and thereafter determined
their own artistic identities as Native people, not the government,
the schools, the critics, the patrons, or anyone else. Secondly, the
number of Native American artists *was* growing, and they were
indeed "articulate and well-educated" and often worldly. And they
established a sense of solidarity, by and large, but not tied to any
specific artistic program of content or style. Any collective
identity lay in the "situation" of being an American Indian artist,
to paraphrase critic Charlotte Townsend-Gault. The eclecticism
of American art of the 1970s and thereafter, generally speaking,
offered an open field for exploring many different artistic
strategies. Artists explored their own voices based upon their
own unique outlook and experiences.

Some became committed to the ways in which their art
reflected the values and experiences of their communities. Norval
Morriseau (Ojibwa, b. 1931) had been raised in a small Ontario
community within a family that practiced the traditional Ojibwa
religion of Midewiwin. His decision to reinterpret Midewiwin
images as drawings on paper was initially considered controversial
within the larger Ojibwa community, but not by Toronto artist/
dealer Jack Pollock, who converted Morriseau to the use of
acrylic paint and organized an extremely successful initial
exhibition for him at his Toronto gallery in 1962. Morriseau's
pictures drew from the Ojibwa pictorial tradition representing
animal spirits and *manidos*, such as his *Mishapihsoo* [175], which
presents the fearsome image of a twisting Underwater Panther
(see p. 60). Critics marveled at Morriseau's ability to combine
such evocative imagery with a broad modernist palette in a style
that suggested a kind of naive surrealism. Morriseau's work
was indeed unique and visionary. More importantly, however,
Morriseau inspired a broad movement of painting now known
as the Woodlands or Anishnabe style. Dozens of artists living in

175 *Mishapihsoo*, Norval Morriseau (Ojibwa), acrylic on brown paper, 1976. This powerful image of the Underwater Panther (see also figs 40 and 50) was based upon Morriseau's study of Ojibwa pictographs. Morriseau is the inspiration for the "Woodland" or "Anishnabe" school of Native painting.

small communities clustered around Manitoulin Island, Georgian Bay, and the northern Great Lakes country of Ontario and Michigan developed Morriseau's basic approach and style into community-based expressions of renewed cultural identity and spirituality. As painter Leland Bell explained to art historian Mary Southcott in 1979, "The land, the language, the culture, and spiritualism, these four things are interrelated. They are in balance. They are the foundation of our art."

Arts revivals proved to be powerful vehicles for community revitalization during the 1960s and 1970s. While the Inuit arts cooperatives and contemporary art on the Northwest Coast were mentioned briefly in previous chapters, it is important to understand their broad historic context and to note from the standpoint of today the enduring multi-generational potency of these community-based movements. As artist Marianne Nicholson (Kwakiutl, b. 1969), a resident of the village of Gwáyi or Kingcome Inlet, said during an interview recently, "The question of community constantly pops up in my work because here it is lived day to day."

The great success among contemporary artists in broadening their fields of endeavor has led to reappraisals and rediscoveries of artists active and yet relatively unknown in the past. Horace Poolaw (Kiowa, 1906–1984) lived in Anadarko, Oklahoma, the great hotbed of mid-twentieth-century Indian painting of his generation, but his artistic accomplishments never appeared at the exhibitions of the Philbrook Annual. Poolaw was a photographer "of the first rank," claimed Kiowa author N. Scott Momaday, but

176 *Lela Ware, Paul Zumwalt, and Trecil Poolaw*, photograph by Horace Poolaw (Kiowa), c. 1928. Poolaw's photographs chronicled the experiences of a community little seen by the outside world during the early twentieth century, showing images that often contrasted with more common stereotypes of Native life.

his mastery of non-traditional media kept him largely hidden from view outside his local circle up until recently. His photographs of family, friends, and local events, however, are powerfully authentic documents of mid-century American Indian life, filled with insight, irony, and gentle warmth [176].

For some artists, their own personal histories and those of their families and communities are inexorably intertwined in their work. Artist, critic, and activist Jolene Rickard (Tuscarora, b. 1956) descends from a family that includes Clinton Rickard, her grandfather and organizer of the Indian Defense League in 1926, great-grandmother and beadworker Florence Nellie Jones Chew, and other family members who stand at the forefront of a longstanding Tuscarora community-based movement to sustain the cultivation of indigenous corn. All of these relations have appeared in Rickard's artwork and writing [179]. Her photographs, photomontages, and installations recall and bring into the present her community's ongoing battles for survival and they remind us that, to quote Rickard, "in my community the last battle was last week." Rickard's imagery draws upon "thoughts, symbols, and visual ideas" more familiar to Native people than to outsiders. "I have to learn all of the specifics of other cultures in order to move freely in the world," she explains. "I want other people to take the responsibility of learning my symbols and thoughts."

Truman Lowe (Ho-Chunk or Winnebago, b. 1944) fabricates symbolic sculpture and structures, largely from wood, drawing upon experiences growing up in Black Falls, Wisconsin. Some of his family were basket makers and Lowe derives from that connection the joy of working with his hands. Emmi Whitehorse

177 Jaune Quick-to-See Smith (Flathead/Cree/Shoshone), *Celebrate*. Jack rabbit "tricksters" here stand for succeeding generations of resilient Native Americans, certainly worthy of celebration.

(Navajo, b. 1956) brings a very personal inventory of cultural images to her abstract paintings: designs from woven baskets and textiles, tools, markings, plants, the shapes of all things indelibly impressed on her memory from a life growing up among Navajo kin [180]. Jaune Quick-to-See Smith (Salish, Cree Shoshone, b. 1940) creates canvasses filled with free-association juxtapositions of ready-made images drawn from personal history and popular culture, combined with her own visual symbols [177]. Having been brought up with horses owned and traded by her father, Smith often uses the image of a horse to represent herself in her compositions. The many complex paintings and drawings created by Kay WalkingStick (Cherokee, b. 1935) range in concern from land, place, and a spiritual regard for the earth to issues of the body and sexuality [178]. WalkingStick feels equally comfortable drawing inspiration from the rugged mesas of Arizona or the verdant valleys of Italy. George Longfish (Seneca, Tuscarora, b. 1942), like WalkingStick, brings a cosmopolitan training to his painting in which he explores issues of Native identity and cultural representation [181].

Several artists have engaged with the ways in which popular media and academic discourse fabricate representations of American Indians and American Indian culture, and the consequences of these kinds of [mis]representations. The Columbus Quincentennial (1992) was a particularly fertile moment for these kinds of concerns, with the organization of several artist-driven critical projects. Artist and curator Jaune Quick-to-See Smith organized the traveling exhibition *The Submuloc Show/Columbus Wohs*, "a visual commentary on the Columbus Quincentennial from the Perspective of America's

178 Kay WalkingStick (Cherokee), *Dancing to Rome III*, charcoal on paper, 2000. For the past twenty years WalkingStick has worked within a diptych format, combining broadly conceived landscapes with more personal symbolism. Her work has recently been occupied with the joyful "dance" theme shown here.

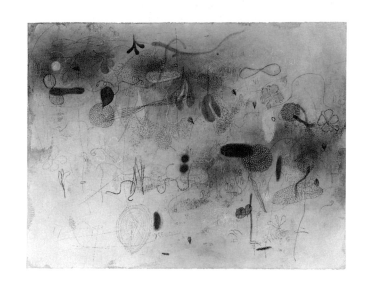

179 Jolene Rickard (Tuscarora), *Corn Blue Room*, installation at the Canadian Museum of Civilization and the National Museum of the American Indian, 1998. Rickard writes, "The corn literally feeds us. At the same time, we can center ourselves around it to feed us on the spiritual and cultural level."

180 Emmi Whitehorse (Navajo), *Meadow*, oil, chalk and paper on canvas, 1996. Whitehorse's gossamer symbols derive from the environment of her Navajo homeland.

181 George Longfish (Seneca/ Tuscarora), *Spirit Guide/Spirit Healer*, acrylic and pencil on paper, 1983. In this important transitional work of Longfish's, a vague figure with a feathered shield emerges within a largely non-representational composition.

First People," as the exhibition was subtitled. Shortly thereafter, in 1994, artist, art historian, and curator Gerald McMaster (Plains Cree, b. 1953) collaborated with the University of British Columbia Museum of Anthropology and curated *Savage Graces*, an exhibition of his own paintings and ready-made cultural artifacts (ranging from arrowheads to kitsch Indian postcards) as a powerful critique of the ways in which museums customarily represent American Indian culture. The project prompted the museum's director, Michael Ames, to ponder for us, "What happens to museums when their object becomes a speaking subject and 'asserts its presence?' Who is then revealed as the savage? And when the object regains a voice, what is left for the former subject to say?"

Native artists active at the beginning of the twenty-first century, working in a broad range of practices, have seized the apparatus of larger cultural discourse, the studio, the university, the gallery, the museum, and the verbal and written media that support them. But they are still represented primarily by museums specializing in Native American art. The larger histories of American art and American culture for the most part excludes them. The larger, far-from-resolved issues of cultural representation, sovereignty, land, and treaty rights persist with palpable consequences for Native people every day, yet they remain on the margins of a larger American consciousness at best. Of key importance to the reader of this book is an understanding that these issues and the art of Native America yesterday, today, and tomorrow, are inextricably linked. Whether personal or cultural expression, or both, whether in the past or in the future, Native artists vitalize their thought and our perception through their ability to create powerful objects and images.

Maps

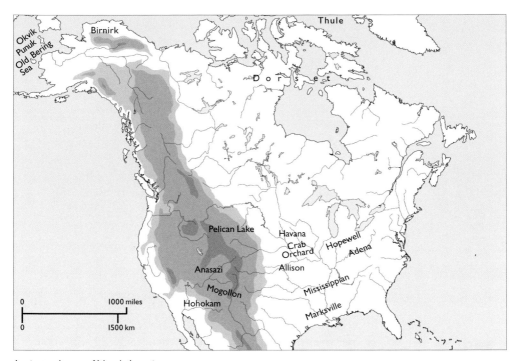

Ancient cultures of North America

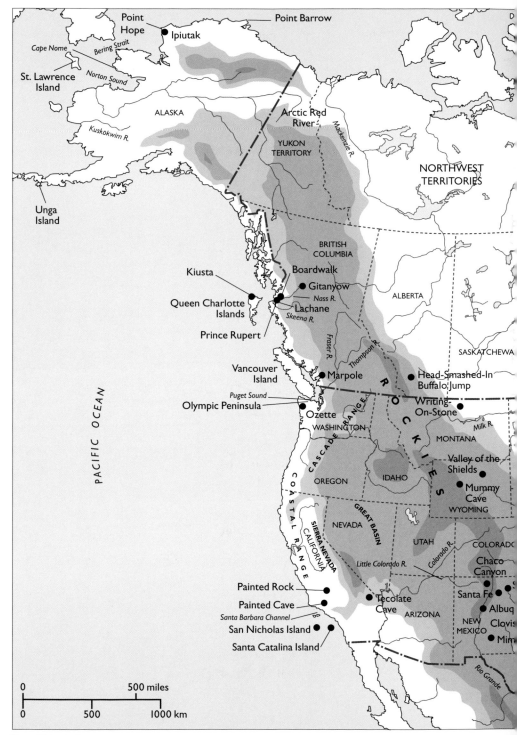

Sites of North America

Baffin Bay

GREENLAND

Povungnituk

Hudson Bay

LABRADOR

NEWFOUNDLAND

QUEBEC

NITOBA

PRINCE EDWARD ISLAND

ONTARIO

ake
/innipeg

NOVA SCOTIA

Saint Charles R.

Manitoulin
Island

Agawa

Great
Lakes

Georgian
Bay

Sault Sainte Marie

A   MINNESOTA

NEW YORK

Hudson R.

WISCONSIN

Andrews

MICHIGAN

PENNSYLVANIA

OTA

Pipestone

IOWA

Adena
Mound

OHIO

Mound City

KA

Illinois R.

INDIANA

Ohio R.

WEST
VIRGINIA

VIRGINIA

Chesapeake Bay

Springfield

Hopewell

ILLINOIS

Tremper

Cahokia

KENTUCKY

N. CAROLINA

ANSAS

Missouri R.

Indian Knoll

MISSOURI

TENNESSEE

S. CAROLINA

ARKANSAS

OKLAHOMA

Spiro

Etowah

GEORGIA

Anadarko

Moundville

Poverty Point

Mississippi R.

MISSISSIPPI

ALABAMA

TEXAS

St. Augustine

FLORIDA

LOUISIANA

Gulf of Mexico

ATLANTIC OCEAN

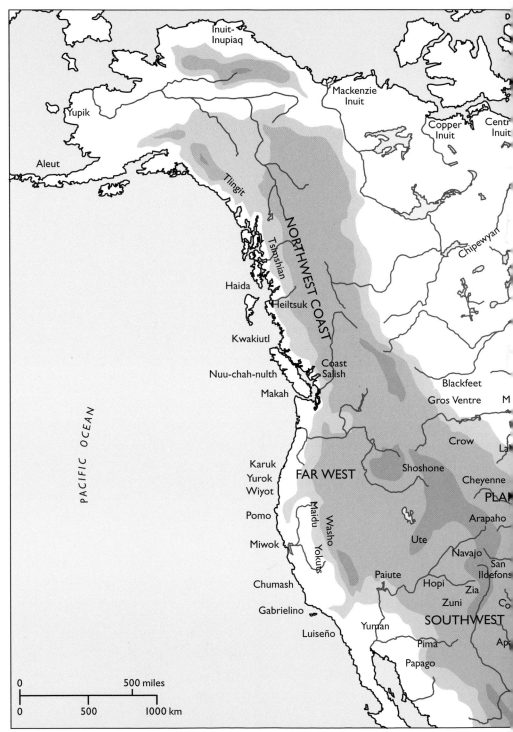

Tribes of North America

ARCTIC

Arctic
Quebec
Inuit

Naskapi

SUBARCTIC

Cree

Ojibwa

Odawa

Huron

Menominee

Fox

Winnebago

Potawatomi

Iroquois

Dakota

Iowa

Miami

EASTERN
WOODLANDS

Oto

Shawnee

Cherokee

Tuscarora

Osage

Quapaw

ANCIENT
WOODLANDS

Chickasaw

Caddo

Choctaw

Creek

Natchez

Seminole

ATLANTIC OCEAN

Chronology

13,000–8000 BC Paleo-Indian period, the period of the first North Americans, including Clovis and Folsom cultures. (The earliest dates are hinted at in the archaeological and geological record but remain hypothetical.)

11,500–1000 BC Clovis culture, the earliest well documented cultural pattern in North America

8000–6000 BC Early Archaic period

6000–3000 BC Middle Archaic period of the Eastern Woodlands region

c. 5000 BC Earliest evidence of grinding and polishing technology used to create grooved axes, atlatl weights, and other tools

3500 BC Earliest use of Head-Smashed-In Buffalo Jump in Alberta, Canada

3000–1000 BC Late Archaic Period of the Eastern Woodlands region

2200–1000 BC Arctic coast colonized by cultures of the Arctic Small Tool Tradition

c. 2000 BC Earliest pottery made in North America, a low-fired, fiber-tempered ware used in the Southeast

2000–1500 BC Earliest evidence of the use of cultivated corn in the North American Southwest

1600–1300 BC Earthworks built at the Poverty Point site, Louisiana

1000 BC–AD 200 Adena people build burial mounds in Ohio, Kentucky, and West Virginia

800 BC Earliest evidence of Dorset communities building houses in the central Canadian Arctic

520–320 BC Residents of the communities represented by the Lachane site, near Fort Rupert in British Columbia, use a carving style ancestral to the later "form-line tradition" of Northern Northwest Coast art

400 BC–AD 400 Villages with large plank houses of the Marpole phase built in southern British Columbia

300 BC Hohokam migrants from Mexico begin to colonize southern Arizona

300 BC–AD 700 Residents of communities located within the Bering Straits region develop Okvik and Old Bering Straits styles of walrus ivory engraving

200 BC–AD 400 Ohio Hopewell construct charnel houses and their subsequent burial mounds in southern Ohio. Several regional traditions participate in the exchange networks of the Hopewell Interaction Sphere.

c. AD 200 Mogollon tradition of pottery manufacture develops in southern New Mexico and adjacent Arizona

AD 300–1000 Birnirk and Punuk patterns of Arctic life established in the Bering Straits and northern Alaska

c. AD 600 Anasazi farmers of the Colorado Plateau (northern New Mexico and Arizona and southern Utah and Colorado) begin to manufacture pottery

c. AD 900 Earliest evidence of the Mississippian tradition of community organization in Mississippi valley

AD 986 Viking explorers based in Greenland reach North America

c. AD 1000 Thule peoples, descendant from the earlier Birnirk and Punuk traditions and the ancestors of the modern Inuit, begin to expand to the east, colonizing the northern Arctic Coast of North America all the way to Greenland

AD 1050 Chaco Canyon reaches its high point of population with nine great houses and many additional smaller communities. Pueblo Bonito, the largest structure, expands to 800 rooms.

AD 1150 High point of population at the Mississippian town of Cahokia, East St. Louis, Illinois. Monks Mound, North America's largest indigenous man-made structure, expanded to its final dimensions.

AD 1150 Earliest signs of settlement at the Hopi community of Oraibi, on the Third Mesa in northern Arizona

c. AD 1300 Construction of Mound C at the Etowah site, Cartersville, Georgia

c. AD 1300 Anasazi abandon the Colorado Plateau, gradually moving south to the ranges of modern Pueblo settlements

c. AD 1380 Re-burial rituals performed at the Craig Mound, Spiro site, in northeastern Oklahoma, which result in the "Great Cache" of engraved shell cups, copper cut-outs, wood and stone sculpture, and other categories of objects

AD 1492 Christopher Columbus's first voyage to America

1503 The tribes of Newfoundland establish trade relations with fishermen and whalers from Europe

1534 The Saint Lawrence Iroquois of the village of Stadacona, at the present site of Quebec, discourage Jacques Cartier from proceeding further up the St. Lawrence river, wishing to protect their trade interests as intermediaries between

the French and communities further west in the interior

1541 Paramount chief Tascaluza organizes the ambush and destruction of Hernando de Soto's army at Mabila in south-central Alabama, but the effort fails and as many as 2,500 Mississippian warriors are killed

1541 A translator and guide from the southern Plains known only as the "Turk" and the leaders of Pecos Pueblo in New Mexico conspire to misdirect Francisco Coronado and his army to "Quivira," characterized by them as a kingdom with abundant gold, in the hope that Coronado's army will become lost on the southern Plains

1607 Paramount chief Powhatan captures Jamestown colonist John Smith and attempts to forge a relationship by establishing Smith as a subordinate chief through an adoption ceremony in which his daughter, Pocahontas, pretends to save Smith's life

1610 Pedro de Peralta founds the town of Santa Fe, New Mexico

1621 The Pokanoket of eastern New England, encouraged by prospects for trade, sign a treaty of alliance with the fledgling Plymouth colony

1622 Powhatan Confederacy chief Opechancanough, exasperated with the British, goes to war and destroys a third of the Virginia colony

1623 The Dutch establish Fort Orange on the Hudson River, near present-day Albany, New York, and conduct trade directly with the Iroquois

1654 Wyandot and Odawa journey from Green Bay to Montreal in an enormous flotilla of birch-bark canoes filled with furs for trade

1675 Abnaki, Nipmuck, Narragansett, and Wampanoag join forces under the Wampanoag leader Metacom, known as King Philip to the colonists, and attack New England settlements in response to a Puritan plan to confine New England Indians to reservations

1680 After 80 years of colonial oppression, Pueblo communities revolt and expel the Spanish after a nine-day siege of Santa Fe. The territory is re-conquered in 1695 under the leadership of Spaniard Diego de Vargas.

1710 Mohawk leader Theyanoguin, known to the British as King Hendrick, travels to London with three others to meet with Queen Anne. Their portraits are painted by John Verelst.

1729 The French destroy Natchez villages in Alabama, putting an end to the last operative Mississippian chiefdom

1754 Blackfeet of the northwestern plains open direct trade with the Hudson's Bay Company

1763 Odawa leader Pontiac organizes a pan-tribal alliance against the British. Mackinac falls and Detroit is besieged.

1769 The Spanish establish a mission at San Diego, the first of many subsequent missions in California

1774 Nuu-chah-nulth and Haida trade furs with Spanish explorer Juan Pérez Hernandez, whose party are probably the first Europeans encountered by these communities

1795 After nearly a decade of conflict at the Ohio frontier, allied tribes of the Great Lakes region sign the Treaty of Greenville with the young United States, opening what will become the Northwest Territories to settlement

1799 The Tuscarora are given a small reservation near Lewiston, adjacent to Niagara Falls. Tuscarora artists later receive an exclusive concession to sell beadwork and other handcrafts to tourists visiting the American side of Niagara Falls in thanks for Tuscarora loyalty to the Americans during the War of the American Revolution.

1804–1806 Meriwether Lewis and William Clark, commissioned by President Thomas Jefferson, explore the Missouri river, descend the Columbia river to the Pacific, and return to the east to report on lands purchased from France

1818 Governor Vincente de Sola of California reports 64,000 Indians baptized, although 41,000 of them have died

1830 President Andrew Jackson signs into law the Indian Removal Act, requiring the forced removal of all Indian tribes of the east to reservations west of the Mississippi River

1834 Mato-Topé, a war chief of the Mandan, paints images of his exploits with watercolors on paper for artist Karl Bodmer and nobleman Prince Maximilian zu Wied during their visit to the chief's village on the upper Missouri River. Maximilian also brings a buffalo robe painted by Mato-Topé back to Europe.

1848 Ephraim George Squier and Edwin Hamilton Davis publish *Ancient Monuments of the Mississippi Valley* as the first publication of the young Smithsonian Institution (*Contributions to Knowledge*, volume 1). The volume includes topographic survey maps of Ohio Hopewell earthwork sites and Mississippian platform mounds.

1849 Hudon's Bay Company establishes a post at Fort Rupert, British Columbia, among the Kwakiutl

1851 Over 10,000 Sioux, Crow, Cheyenne, Arapaho, Assiniboine, Gros Ventre, and Arikira assemble at Fort Laramie in southeast Wyoming to hear United States officials ask for peace among the tribes in an effort to protect settlers in transit across the plains. The Fort Laramie Treaty that follows as a result of the negotiations promises the tribes annuity payments and compensation for settler's "depredations."

1868 After successfully closing the Bozeman Trail between Fort Laramie and Montana, Lakota leaders sign the second Fort Laramie Treaty, creating the "Great Sioux Reservation" that includes the Black Hills. George Armstrong Custer will lead an expedition into the Black Hills to search for gold in 1874, touching off renewed hostilities that will claim Custer's life in 1876.

1875 War leaders of several southern plains tribes are arrested and sent to prison at Fort Marion, Florida. During captivity, many, such as Zotom, Wohaw, Charles Ohettoint, and Cohoe, produce drawings that are very much prized today.

1879 US Congress approves a $20,000 appropriation to establish the Bureau of Ethnology, later named the Bureau of American Ethnology, and appoints John Wesley Powell director. That year Powell sends James Stevenson to the southwest, where he collects on a large scale for the Smithsonian Institution. Frank Hamilton Cushing, who accompanied Stevenson, remains at Zuni to pioneer the practice of participant ethnography.

1880 Trader Thomas Keam commissions from local potters, very likely including Hano potter Nampeyo, reproductions of Sikyatki and San Bernardo polychrome ceramics excavated from archaeological ruins located near the Hopi pueblos

1881–1882 Adrian Jacobsen collects artifacts in British Columbia at the behest of the newly founded ethnography museum in Berlin. Franz Boas, who will later become a prominent and foundational figure in American anthropology, will be inspired by these collections to pursue fieldwork among the Kwakiutl.

1884 The Indian Act voted into Canadian law includes a provision that specifies the practice of the potlatch as a punishable offense

1887 The General Allotment Act becomes federal law and over the next several decades two-thirds of Indian-owned land in the United States is lost to white settlement

1889 A Paiute man named Wovoka experiences visions in which ancestors show him a world restored to its condition before the arrival of the white man. Delegations from tribes throughout the west visit Wovoka to hear of his vision and to learn the religious rituals it inspires, known as the Ghost Dance. The next winter, over 300 Lakota Ghost Dance practitioners and their families are killed by federal troops at Wounded Knee, South Dakota.

1894 In the 12th Annual Report of the young Bureau of American Ethnography, Cyrus Thomas publishes a study that he believes offers definitive proof to the then-controversial notion that the ancient mound builders of the Midwest and Southeast are ancestors of modern American Indians

1897 Over 6,000 Lakota and guests assemble at the Rosebud reservation, South Dakota, for six days of Fourth of July celebrations. Although the government has discouraged traditional ceremonies, local officials are more permissive when the festivities are framed within this patriotic holiday. The Lakota stage sham battles (including a reinactment of the Custer fight), give-aways, adoption rituals, and other ceremonies.

1900 The Census reports that the population of American Indians in the United States had diminished to what will be the all-time low of 237,196. Thereafter, the population begins to increase.

1902 Students of teacher Esther Hoyt's classes at the San Ildefonso Mission School include future watercolorists Tonita Pena, Alfredo Montoya, and Awa Tsireh (Alfonso Roybal).

1904 Reservation officials organize the first Crow Agricultural Fair at the Crow reservation in Montana. "Crow fair" grows to be one of the largest annual inter-tribal powwows and festivals in North America today.

1905–1910 Hano potter Nampeyo, renowned for her Sikyatki-revival pottery, spends her summers at Hopi House on the south rim of the Grand Canyon, offering demonstrations and selling her creations to visitors

1915 Archaeologist Alfred Vincent Kidder begins excavations at Pecos, a Tiwa-Pueblo village site occupied between c. AD 1300 and 1838. His pioneering method of stratigraphic analysis will result in the first proposals for understanding chronological sequences of Anasazi history.

1919 Washo basket weaver Louisa Keyser is featured at the St. Louis Industrial Arts Exposition

1922 The Museum of New Mexico and the Santa Fe Indian School sponsor the first Southwest Indian Fair in Santa Fe, a prize-awarding competition and sale of southwest Indian arts that exists today as the Santa Fe Indian Art Market. The fair shows watercolors by Pueblo painters including Fred Kabotie, Awa Tsireh, and others who this same year are shown at the Society for Independent Artists exhibition at the Waldorf-Astoria Hotel in New York City.

1922 Agent William M. Halliday confiscates masks and other potlatch items, amounting to over 450 objects, from Kwakiutl Dan Cranmer's six-day potlatch at Village Island, British Columbia. Today, the Kwakiutl-run U'mista Cultural Center at Alert Bay has been able to reclaim almost all of the material from the several museums that made purchases from Halliday.

1931 Exposition of Indian Tribal Arts, an exhibition conceived to promote public interest in the work of living American Indian artists, opens in New York City and tours for the next two years throughout major American cities and abroad

1932 Julian Martinez and Awa Tsireh join with others to create murals in the cafeteria at the Santa Fe Indian School during the first year of The Studio School program run by Dorothy Dunn, teacher of fine and applied arts

1936 The Indian Arts and Crafts Board is created within the Department of Indian Affairs as a result of efforts by Commissioner of Indian Affairs John Collier, the reformist appointed by Franklin D. Roosevelt to oversee the "Indian New Deal"

1941 In a remarkable collaboration of the cultural elite and government policy, the Museum of Modern Art opens the exhibition "Indian Art of the United States," organized largely by René d'Harnoncourt as manager of the Indian Arts and Crafts Board. The show will have a profound impact on the work of New York artists Jackson Pollock, Adolph Gottlieb, and others.

1946 Acee Blue Eagle, Creek Pawnee painter and former head of the art department at Bacone College, wins first prize in the Woodland Division of the first Annual exhibition and competition for Native American arts at the Philbrook Museum, Tulsa, Oklahoma

1948 *Comrade in Mourning*, the marble memorial to Native Americans who died in World War II, by Chiricahua Warm Springs Apache sculptor Allan Houser, is dedicated at Haskell Institute, a government-funded Indian school in Lawrence, Kansas

1953 Kwakiutl carver Mungo Martin conducts a three-day potlatch to dedicate a full-size replica of the house in which he was born. He made the replica in Thunderbird Park, where he was employed as the chief carver of the totem pole preservation program to carve replicas of the many original totem poles installed in the park.

1953 The United States government initiates the policy of "termination" with the intent of eliminating all federal obligations to Indian tribes. By 1962 over 100 communities have lost their status as federally recognized tribes.

1962 The Institute of American Indian Art begins classes at the Santa Fe Indian School with Lloyd Kiva New as director

1962 Norval Morriseau, founder of the so-called Woodland School of American Indian painting, is debuted at the Pollock Gallery in Toronto, Ontario. The show is widely reviewed and attended, and all the paintings sell.

1969 Alcatraz Island, the former federal prison in San Francisco Bay, is occupied by over 400 American Indians demanding a center for Native American studies, an American Indian spiritual center, an ecological center, and a training school. This event inspires increased American Indian political activism.

1974 Vancouver Art Gallery opens "A Quarter-Century of Bill Reid Work," a retrospective of the Haida jeweler and sculptor

1977 Curator Ralph T. Coe and the Arts Council of Great Britain open the exhibition "Sacred Circles: Two Thousand Years of North American Indian Art" at the Hayward Gallery, London. Traveling to the Nelson Atkins Museum of Fine Arts in Kansas City, Missouri, in 1978, this is one of several large surveys of American Indian art organized by major art museums during the 1970s.

1988 The Lubicon Cree of Alberta, Canada, seeking recognition of long-standing land claims, organize a boycott of the exhibition "The Spirit Sings," a broad survey of Canadian Native art installed at the Glenbow Museum, Calgary, which opens in conjunction with the Winter Olympics. The Assembly of First Nations and the Canadian Museum Association organize a task force to examine museum ethics and responsibilities when organizing exhibitions dealing with Native American culture and history.

1989 The National Museum of the American Indian is created, transferring ownership and governance of the Museum of the American Indian, Heye Foundation, to the Smithsonian Institution

1990 The Native American Grave Protection and Repatriation Act is signed into law, protecting federal lands from excavation of human remains and defining categories of cultural artifacts to be repatriated from museums to tribes who can demonstrate affiliation

1994 The Columbus Quincentennial is marked by several publications, exhibitions, and events that examine and critique the legacy of the European discovery of the so-called "New World." Notable among them is the exhibition "The Submuloc Show/Columbus Wohs" curated by artist Jaune Quick-to-See Smith for Atlatl, a Native Arts organization based in Phoenix, Arizona.

1999 The year before his death, Ojibwa painter George Morrison is honored as senior artist at the first Eiteljorg Fellowship for Native American Fine Art, a program of biennial exhibitions and cash awards to artists inaugurated by the Eiteljorg Museum of American Indians and Western Art in Indianapolis, Indiana

2004 The Native-run National Museum of the American Indian is scheduled to open its museum on the National Mall in Washington, D.C.

Select Bibliography

1 Introduction

The term "survivance" is discussed in G. Vizenor, *Manifest Manners: Postindian Warriors of Survivance*, Wesleyan University Press, Hanover, 1994. The concept of an "aesthetic system" comes from S. Leuthold, *Indigenous Aesthetics: Native Art, Media, and Identity*, University of Texas Press, Austin, 1998. The use of Native terms and stereotypical representations of Native appearance to develop an American sense of national identity is the thesis of P. Deloria, *Playing Indian*, Yale University Press, New Haven, 1998. The best available overview of artist David Bradley's work can be found in D. Bradley, *Restless Native*, Plains Art Museum, Moorhead, Minnesota, 1991. Lewis Henry Morgan developed his ideas of social evolution in *Ancient Society: Researches in the Lines of Human Progress from Savagery through Barbarism to Civilization*, Holt, New York, 1877.
A history of the "Lord's Shirt" is detailed in P. M. Raczka, "Blackfoot Artists: Rights and Power," *American Indian Art Magazine*, vol. 5, no. 2, fall 1980, pp. 30–35. Kiowa cradle-making and its associated cultural values are explored in B. A. Hail (ed.), *Gifts of Pride and Love: Kiowa and Comanche Cradles*, Heffenreffer Museum of Anthropology, Brown University, Bristol, RI, 2000. The artistic biographies of Albert Edward Edenshaw and Charles Edenshaw are thoroughly researched and presented in R. K. Wright, *Northern Haida Master Carvers*, University of Washington Press, Seattle, 2001. A brief overview of George Morrison's artistic career is offered in D. W. Penney, "George Morrison," in B. Bernstein (ed.), *Contemporary Masters: The Eiteljorg Fellowship for Native American Fine Art*, Eiteljorg Museum of American Indians and Western Art, Indianapolis, 2000.

2 Ancient Woodlands

A broad, up-to-date overview of indigenous North American cultural history as revealed by archaeological research can be found in B. M. Fagan, *Ancient North America: The Archaeology of a Continent*, Thames & Hudson, London and New York, 3rd ed., 2000. The site report for the Titterington focus Airport site is published as D. C. Roper, *The Airport Site: A Multicomponent Site in the Sangamon River Drainage*, Illinois State Museum Research Series, Papers in Anthropology, no. 4, Springfield, 1978. Clarence B. Moore originally excavated the Indian Knoll site before 1916 and William S. Webb revisited the site in the 1940s. Webb's site report with an introductory analysis by Howard D. Winters has been reissued recently as W. S. Webb and H. D. Winters, *Indian Knoll*, University of Tennessee, Knoxville, 2001. D. S. Brose, J. A. Brown, and D. W. Penney, *Ancient Art of the American Woodland Indians*, Abrams, New York, 1985, offers a good overview of prehistoric Eastern Woodlands art and archaeology. The site report documenting the discovery of the Adena effigy pipe is W. C. Mills, "Excavations of the Adena Mound," *Ohio Archaeological and Historical Society Publications*, vol. 10, 1902, pp. 452–479. A good, concise summary of the burial mound evidence for Middle Woodland period mortuary ceremonies can be found in J. A. Brown, "Charnel Houses and Mortuary Crypts: Disposal of the Dead in the Middle Woodland Period," in D. S. Brose and N. Greber (eds.), *Hopewell Archaeology: The Chillicothe Conference*, Kent State University Press, Ohio, 1979. The discovery of the cache of Tremper mound effigy platform pipes is documented in W. C.

Mills, "Exploration of the Tremper Mound," *Ohio Archaeological and Historical Society Publications*, vol. 25, 1916, pp. 262–398.
A broad study that examines the circulation of objects and ideas throughout the "Hopewell interaction sphere" is D. W. Penney, *Hopewell Art*, University Microfilms, Ann Arbor, 1989. Significant site reports of major Ohio Hopewell sites consulted for this book include W. K. Moorehead, "The Hopewell Mound Group of Ohio," *Field Museum of Natural History, Anthropological Series*, vol. 6, 1922, pp. 73–184, and W. C. Mills, "Exploration of the Mound City Group," *Ohio Archaeological and Historical Society Publications*, vol. 31, 1922, pp. 423–584. More recent analysis of the Ohio Hopewell rituals in charnel houses, particularly the Hopewell site, is offered in N. Greber, "A Commentary on the Contexts and Contents of Large to Small Ohio Hopewell Deposits," in P. J. Pacheco (ed.), *A View from the Core: A Synthesis of Ohio Hopewell Archaeology*, Ohio Archaeological Council, Inc., Columbus, 1996. There have been several important studies of Hopewell exchange, both of artifacts and materials, such as S. I. Goad, *Exchange Networks in the Prehistoric Southeastern United States*, University Microfilms, Ann Arbor, 1978, which looked specifically at marine shell and copper, and M. F. Seeman, *The Hopewell Interaction Sphere: The Evidence for Interregional Trade and Structural Complexity*, Indiana Historical Society Prehistory Research Series, vol. 5, no. 2, Indianapolis, 1979. The origins of the Mississippian cultural system are addressed in a collection of essays and studies found in B. D. Smith (ed.), *The Mississippian Emergence*, Smithsonian Institution Press, Washington, D.C., 1990. Among the abundant and often confusing literature about Cahokia, the most recent and up-to-date interpretations can be found in T. E. Emerson, *Cahokia and the Archaeology of Power*, University of Alabama Press, Tuscaloosa, 1997, and C. J. Bareis and J. W. Porter (eds.), *American Bottom Archaeology*, University of Illinois Press, Urbana, 1984. More detailed studies about major Mississippian sites and thematic essays about Mississippian art and culture are collected in P. Galloway (ed.), *The Southeastern Ceremonial Complex: Artifacts and Analysis*, University of Nebraska Press, Lincoln, 1989. Moundville and Spiro receive detailed treatment in V. J. Knight and V. P. Steponaitis (eds.), *Archaeology of the Moundville Chiefdom*, Smithsonian Institution Press, Washington, D.C., 1998, and J. A. Brown, *The Spiro Ceremonial Center*, Memoirs of the University of Michigan Museum of Anthropology, vol. 29, Ann Arbor, 1996. J. A. Brown and P. Phillips, *Pre-Columbian Shell Engravings from the Craig Mound at Spiro, Oklahoma*, pts. 1 and 2, Peabody Museum of Archaeology and Ethnology, Harvard University, 1978, 1984, provides an exhaustive catalogue of these important objects. D. H. Dye and C. A. Cox (eds.), *Towns and Temples Along the Mississippi*, University of Alabama Press, Tuscaloosa, 1990, focuses on Mississippian towns in the immediate Mississippi valley. C. M. Hudson, *Knights of Spain, Warriors of the Sun: Hernando de Soto and the South's Ancient Chiefdoms*, University of Georgia Press, Athens, 1997, is particularly valuable in the way it ties together archaeological research with the historic documentation of de Soto's travels through the Mississippian Southeast.

3 Eastern Woodlands

A broad overview of Iroquois history before and after contact with Europeans is offered in D. R. Snow, *The Iroquois*, Blackwell Publishers, Cambridge, MA, 1994. More focused essays about the dynamics and consequences of contact, including some detail about the relations between Jamestown and the

Powhatan chiefdom, can be found in W. W. Fitzhugh (ed.), *Cultures in Contact: The Impact of European Contacts on Native American Cultural Institutions*, A.D. 1000–1800, Smithsonian Institution Press, Washington, D.C., 1985. George Hamell explores the ways in which European material culture was reconsidered and reconfigured in accordance with Native cultural values in "Strawberries, Floating Islands, and Rabbit Captains: Mythical Realities and European Contact in the Northeast during the Sixteenth and Seventeenth Centuries," *Journal of Canadian Studies*, vol. 21, no. 4, pp. 72–94. A brief history of the royal cabinet of curiosity of France is offered in A. Vitart, "From Royal Cabinets to Museums: A Composite History," in W. R. West et al., *Robes of Splendor: Native American Painted Buffalo Hides*, New Press, New York, 1993. E. M. Maurer, "Presenting the American Indian: from Europe to America," in *The Changing Presentation of the American Indian: Museums and Native Cultures*, National Museum of the American Indian, Washington, D.C., 2000, surveys the early practices of European collecting more broadly. A. W. Whiteford, "The origins of Great Lakes beaded bandolier bags," *American Indian Art Magazine*, vol. 11, no. 3, summer, 1986, pp. 32–43, discusses the historical development of this distinctive form of shoulder bag. Early collections assembled by British military officers are surveyed in T. J. Brasser, *"Bo'jou, Neejee!" Profiles of Canadian Indian Art*, National Museum of Man, Ottawa, 1976, and R. B. Phillips, *Patterns of Power: The Jasper Grant Collection and Great Lakes Indian Art of the Early Nineteenth Century*, The McMichael Canadian Collection, Kleinburg, ON, 1985. The broader issue of the relationships between collecting practices and the responses of Native artists, more specifically the Huron of Lorette, are dealt with in R. B. Phillips, *Trading Identities: The Souvenir in Native North American Art from the Northeast, 1700–1900*, University of Washington Press, Seattle, 1998. The availability of Mohawk moccasins at Niagara Falls is mentioned in M. M. Quaife (ed.), *John Long's Voyages and Travels in the Years 1768–1788*, Lakeside Press, Chicago, 1922. A brief discussion of Menominee quillwork is included in W. H. Keating, *Narrative of an Expedition to the Source of St. Peter's River*, Cox and Bayles, London, 1825. The visit to the Ojibwa "atelier" near Sault Sainte Marie is recorded in J. G. Kohl, *Kitchi-Gami: Life Among the Lake Superior Ojibway*, 1860; Minnesota Historical Society Press, St. Paul, 1985. An overview of early nineteenth-century Great Lakes formal clothing and the techniques of its decoration can be found in D. W. Penney, *Art of the American Indian Frontier: The Chandler/Pohrt Collection*, University of Washington Press, Seattle, 1992. The specific history of the Seminole or Creek shirt is from P. Bolz and H.-U. Sanner, *Native American Art: The Collections of the Ethnological Museum Berlin*, Staatliche Museen zu Berlin, 1999. The distinctive craft of decorating birch bark with porcupine quills is surveyed in S. Graham and C. Feest, *Ottawa Quillwork on Birchbark*, Harbor Springs Historical Commission, Harbor Springs, MI, 1983. Statements from Ojibwa women about the sources of their floral beadwork designs come from B. Coleman, *Decorative Designs of the Ojibwa of Northern Minnesota*, Catholic University of America Press, Washington, 1947. The oral traditions relating to the Agawa Rock paintings were collected in S. Dewdney and K. E. Kidd, *Indian Paintings of the Great Lakes*, University of Toronto Press, Toronto, 1962. Statements about the significance of war clubs are offered in A. D. Raudot, "Memoir concerning the different Indian nations of North America," in W. V. Kinietz, *The Indians of the Western Great Lakes*, University of Michigan Press, Ann

Arbor, 1965. Johann Georg Kohl's conversation with a young Ojibwa man about the designs engraved on his club come from Kohl's memoir, cited above. The artist Paul Kane met the Ojibwa pipe carver and made a drawing of the pipe, as related in his memoir, *Wanderings of an Artist among the Indians of North America*, 1859; Dover Publications, New York, 1996. A good survey of the historical statements about the significance of spoons and labels is compiled in B. C. Prisch, *Aspects of Change in Seneca Iroquois Ladles*, A.D. 1600–1900, Rochester Museum and Science Center, Research Records no. 15, Rochester, 1982.

4 Southwest

L. S. Cordell, *Prehistory of the Southwest*, Boston, Academic Press, 2nd ed., 1997, offers the most up-to-date thinking about southwestern prehistory. A more focused discussion about the historical development of pottery is in S. Peckham, *From This Earth: The Ancient Art of Pueblo Pottery*, Museum of New Mexico Press, Santa Fe, 1990. Discussions about the provenance of several important early Anasazi ceramics, including those illustrated in this book, can be found in R. H. Lister and F. C. Lister, *Anasazi Pottery*, Maxwell Museum of Anthropology and University of New Mexico Press, Albuquerque, 1978. There is a great deal to be learned about the significance of pottery both within Anasazi communities and as a tool for archaeological research in B. J. Mills and P. L. Crown (eds.), *Ceramic Production in the American Southwest*, University of Arizona Press, Tucson, 1995, and M. Hegmon, *The Social Dynamics of Pottery Style in the Early Puebloan Southwest*, Crow Canyon Archaeological Center, Occasional Paper no. 5, Cortez, Colorado, 1995. Chaco Canyon and Hohokam are treated as regional cultural systems in P. L. Crown and W. J. Judge (eds.), *Chaco and Hohokam: Prehistoric Regional Systems in the American Southwest*, School of American Research Press, Santa Fe, NM, 1991. A broader archaeological and art historical survey of Anasazi culture is J. J. Brody, *The Anasazi: Ancient Indian People of the American Southwest*, Rizzoli, New York, 1990. A fairly up-to-date synthesis of the art historical and archaeological research on the Mimbres valley is S. A. LeBlanc, *The Mimbres People: Ancient Pueblo Painters of the American Southwest*, Thames & Hudson, London and New York, 1983. The early kiva paintings with images of Kachinas are discussed in J. J. Brody, *Anasazi and Pueblo Painting*, School of American Research Press, Santa Fe, NM, 1991. A case for tying together kiva paintings, painted designs on ceramics, and changes in community and kiva layout as evidence for the development of Kachina ritualism is developed in E. C. Adams, *The Origin and Development of the Pueblo Katsina Cult*, University of Arizona Press, Tucson, 1991. An overview of historic and contemporary Kachina ritual is offered in P. Schaafsma (ed.), *Kachinas in the Pueblo World*, University of New Mexico Press, Albuquerque, 1994. Biographies and artistic practices of contemporary Kachina doll carvers are compiled in H. Teiwes, *Kachina Dolls: The Art of Hopi Carvers*, University of Arizona Press, Tucson, 1991. The best concise sources for the history of Pueblo and Navajo textiles are still K. P. Kent, *Pueblo Indian Textiles: A Living Tradition*, School of American Research Press, Santa Fe, NM, 1983, and K. P. Kent, *Navajo Weaving: Three Centuries of Change*, School of American Research Press, Santa Fe, NM, 1985. Jonathan Batkin explores the early curio trade in the Southwest in "Tourism is Overrated: Pueblo Pottery and the Early Curio Trade, 1880–1910," in R. B. Phillips and C. B. Steiner (eds.), *Unpacking Culture: Art and Commodity in Colonial and Postcolonial Worlds*,

University of California Press, Berkeley, 1999. A masterful study of the practices of ceramic production on the Hopi Mesas over the last 150 years is L. L. Wyckoff, *Designs and Factions: Politics, Religion, and Ceramics on the Hopi Third Mesa*, University of New Mexico Press, Albuquerque, 1985. The most recent artistic biography of the influential potter Maria Martinez is R. L. Spivey, *The Legacy of Maria Poveka Martinez*, Museum of New Mexico Press, Santa Fe, 2003. A broader view of the pan-generational nature of pottery-making in the Southwest is S. Peterson, *Pottery by American Indian Women: The Legacy of Generations*, National Museum of Women in the Arts, Washington, D.C., 1997. The history of Navajo silverwork is discussed in A. H. Whiteford et al., *I Am Here: Two Thousand Years of Southwest Indian Arts and Culture*, Museum of New Mexico Press, Santa Fe, 1989.

5 Plains
Although somewhat controversial, many of us have a great deal of confidence in the archaeological and linguistic interpretations of Plains history compiled in K. H. Schlesier (ed.), *Plains Indians, A.D. 500–1500: The Archaeological Past of Historic Groups*, University of Oklahoma Press, Norman, 1994. A very sensible approach to the difficult topic of Plains rock art, and one that is relied upon heavily in this book, is found in J. D. Keyser and M. A. Klassen, *Plains Indian Rock Art*, University of Washington Press, Seattle, 2001. The story of Saukamappee's battle experiences is recorded in D. Thompson, *David Thompson's Narrative of his Explorations in Western America 1784–1812*, R. Glover (ed.), Publications of the Champlain Society, Toronto, 1962. Bull Lodge's account of how he acquired his shield and its powers is in G. P. Horse Capture (ed.), *The Seven Visions of Bull Lodge*, Bear Claw Press, Ann Arbor, MI, 1980. An interpretation of the shield that belonged to the Cheyenne warrior, Little Rock, is found in M. Kan and W. Wierzbowski, "Notes on an Important Southern Cheyenne Shield," *Bulletin of The Detroit Institute of Arts*, vol. 57, no. 3, 1979, pp. 125–133. Details about No Two Horns's shield are in E. M. Maurer (ed.), *Visions of the People: A Pictorial History of Plains Indian Life*, Minneapolis Institute of Arts, Minneapolis, 1992. The Ghost Dance and Ghost Dance garments are discussed in G. P. Horse Capture et al., *Wounded Knee: Lest We Forget*, Buffalo Bill Historical Center, Cody, WY, 1990. The history of Little Bluff's tipi is offered in J. C. Ewers, *Murals in the Round: Painted Tipis of the Kiowa and Kiowa-Apache Indians*, Smithsonian Institution Press, Washington, D.C., 1978. Little Shield's ledger book is discussed in J. C. Berlo (ed.), *Plains Indian Drawings 1865–1935: Pages from a Visual History*, Harry N. Abrams, New York, 1996, and Zotom's drawings are discussed in E. Wade and J. T. Rand, "The Subtle Art of Resistance: Encounter and Accommodation in the Art of Fort Marion," in that volume. The seminal study of drawings made by the Fort Marion prisoners is K. D. Petersen, *Plains Indian Art from Fort Marion*, University of Oklahoma Press, Norman, 1971. The archaeological and early historic use of catlinite is discussed in M. Mott, "The relations of historic tribes to archaeological manifestations in Iowa," *Iowa Journal of History and Politics*, vol. 36, no. 2, 1938, pp. 227–314. Joseph Nicollet's eventful trip to the catlinite quarry is recounted in his memoir, "Expedition to Pipestone Quarry June 9–July 20, 1838," in E. C. Bray and M. C. Bray (eds.), *Joseph Nicollet on the Plains and Prairies*, Minnesota Historical Society, St. Paul, 1976. The art of the anonymous pipe carver is examined in J. C. Ewers, "Three effigy pipes by an Eastern Dakota master carver," *American Indian Art Magazine*, vol. 3, no. 4, 1978, pp. 51–55, 74. Picking Bones's story and a discussion of the Cheyenne quilling society appears in G. B. Grinnell, *The Cheyenne Indians: Their History and Ways of Life*, Yale University Press, New Haven, 1923, University of Nebraska Press, Lincoln, 1972, 2 vols. The Lakota rite of *Isnati Awicalowampi* is discussed in J. R. Walker, *Lakota Belief and Ritual*, University of Nebraska Press, Lincoln, 1980. Cedar Woman's account of the Arapaho sacred workbags appears in A. L. Kroeber, *The Arapaho*, University of Nebraska Press, Lincoln, 1983. Northern Arapaho cradles were explored by R. Gilmore in "The Northern Arapaho cradle," *American Indian Art Magazine*, vol. 16, no. 1, 1990, pp. 64–71. More archival detail revealing the identity of a Northern Arapaho sacred workbag keeper responsible for the cradles appears in M. C. Bol, "Identity recovered: portrait of a Northern Arapaho quillworker," in J. M. Szabo (ed.), *Painters, Patrons, and Identity: Essays in Native American Art to Honor J. J. Brody*, University of New Mexico Press, Albuquerque, 2001. The Spotted Tail shirt is illustrated and discussed in J. D. Horse Capture and G. P. Horse Capture, *Beauty, Honor, and Tradition: The Legacy of Plains Indian Shirts*, National Museum of the American Indian, Washington, D.C., 2001. The dress that may or may not have been collected during the Lewis and Clark expedition is discussed in C. McLaughlin, *Arts of Diplomacy: Lewis and Clark's Indian Collection*, University of Washington Press, Seattle, 2003. The Lakota title of *Ongloge Un* or "Shirt Wearer" is discussed in C. Wissler, *Societies and Ceremonial Associations in the Oglala Division of the Teton-Dakota*, American Museum of Natural History Anthropological Papers, vol. 11, part 1, New York, 1912. The importance of Fourth of July celebrations and their attendant give-aways as a strategy of Lakota cultural survival is given thorough treatment in A. Greci Green, *Performances and Celebrations: Displaying Lakota Identity, 1880–1915*, University Microfilms, Ann Arbor, 2001.

6 Far West
Thorough but basic overviews of California prehistory and ethnography are available in R. F. Heizer (ed.), *Handbook of North American Indians: California*, vol. 8, Smithsonian Institution Press, Washington, D.C., 1978. A more modern updating of California prehistory and rock art in particular is found in B. M. Fagan, *Before California: An Archaeologist Looks at Our Earliest Inhabitants*, AltaMira Press, Lanham, MD, 2003. The Miwok chief's basket is discussed in S. A. Barrett and E. W. Gifford, *Miwok Material Culture*, Bulletin of the Public Museum of the City of Milwaukee, vol. 2, no. 4, 1933. Lilliam Smith's study of the Chumash "coin" baskets is "Three inscribed Chumash baskets with designs from Spanish colonial coins," *American Indian Art Magazine*, vol. 7, no. 3, summer 1982, pp. 62–68. The relationship between the artist Louisa Keyser and her patrons, the Cohns, is examined in M. Cahodas, "Louisa Keyser and the Cohns: mythmaking and basket making in the American West," in J. C. Berlo (ed.), *The Early Years of Native American Art History: The Politics of Scholarship and Collecting*, University of Washington Press, Seattle, 1992. A thorough artistic biography of Elizabeth Hickox in the larger context of northern California ethnohistory is offered in M. Cohodas, *Basket Weavers for the California Curio Trade: Elizabeth and Louise Hickox*, University of Arizona Press, Tucson, 1977. A broad regional study of Paiute and Mono basket makers is offered by C. D. Bates and M. J. Lee, *Tradition and Innovation: A Basket*

History of the Indians of the Yosemite-Mono Lake Area, Yosemite
Association, Yosemite National Park, CA, 1990.

7 Northwest Coast

The most up-to-date interpretation of Northwest Coast
prehistory is K. M. Ames and H. D. G. Maschner, *Peoples of the
Northwest Coast: Their Archaeology and Prehistory*, Thames &
Hudson, London and New York, 1999. Basic archaeological and
ethnographic research is reviewed in W. Suttles (ed.), *Handbook
of North American Indians: Northwest Coast*, vol. 7, Smithsonian
Institution, Washington, D.C., 1990. Many of the Fraser River
seated figure effigy bowls are illustrated and discussed in
W. Duff, *Images: Stone B.C.*, University of Washington Press,
Seattle, 1975. The Hagwilget stone clubs are examined in
W. Duff, "Stone clubs from the Skeena River area," and D. N.
Abbott and J. C. H. King, "A 'Hagwilget' club from England," in
D. N. Abbott (ed.), *The World is as Sharp as a Knife: An Anthology
in Honour of Wilson Duff*, British Columbia Provincial Museum,
Victoria, 1981. More focused essays addressing the prehistoric
art of the Northwest coast, including material from the Ozette
site, are found in R. L. Carlson (ed.), *Indian Art Traditions of the
Northwest Coast*, Simon Fraser University, Burnaby, BC, 1982.
The Archibald Menzies club is illustrated and discussed in J. C.
H. King, *First Peoples/First Contacts: Native Peoples of North
America*, British Museum, London, 1999. The Wixha memorial
poles and their history appear in M. Barbeau, *Totem Poles of the
Gitksan, Upper Skeena River, British Columbia*, 1929, National
Museum of Man, Ottawa, 1973. Aldona Jonaitis's interpretation
of the Rain Screen is found in A. Jonaitis, *Art of the Northern
Tlingit*, University of Washington Press, Seattle, 1986. A
discussion of the Raven Barbecuing Hat appears in S. A. Kaplan
and K. J. Barsness, *Raven's Journey: The World of Alaska's Native
People*, University Museum, University of Pennsylvania,
Philadelphia, 1986, and with more detail in L. Shotridge,
"War Helmets and Clan Hats of the Tlingit Indians," *University
Museum Journal*, vol. 10, 1919, pp. 43–48. The identity of the
artist responsible for the Whale House posts is discussed in
B. Herem, "A historic Tlingit artist: the trail of his world and its
modern recreation," *American Indian Art Magazine*, vol. 15, no. 3,
summer 1990, pp. 48–55. The basic primer of "form line
design" is B. Holm, *Northwest Coast Indian Art: An Analysis of
Form*, University of Washington Press, Seattle, 1965. Bill Holm
hinted at the identity of Heiltsuk carver Richard Carpenter in
"Form in Northwest Coast art," in *Indian Art Traditions of the
Northwest Coast*, cited above. Further discussion of Richard
Carpenter's biography and works appears in M. Black, *Bella
Bella: A Season of Heiltsuk Art*, University of Washington Press,
Seattle, 1997, and additional artists are identified and discussed
on the basis of their form line paintings in B. McLennan and K.
Duffek, *The Transforming Image: Painted Arts of Northwest Coast
First Nations*, University of British Columbia Press, Vancouver;
University of Washington Press, Seattle, 2000. My statement
that the images on Chilkat blankets are not crests stems from
M. Halpin, "The structure of Tsimshian totemism," in J. Miller
and C. M. Eastman (eds.), *The Tsimshian and Their Neighbors of
the North Pacific Coast*, University of Washington Press, Seattle,
1984. The basic source for historic accounts of Tlingit
shamanism is G. T. Emmons and F. de Laguna, *The Tlingit Indians*,
American Museum of Natural History, New York; University of
Washington Press, Seattle, 1991. Aldona Jonaitis explores the
iconography of Tlingit shamans' masks in "Sacred art and
spiritual power: an analysis of Tlingit shamans' masks" in Z. P.

Mathews and A. Jonaitis (eds.), *Native North American Art
History: Selected Readings*, Peek Publications, Palo Alto, CA,
1982. A thorough overview of Tlingit shamans' art with a
discussion of the National Museum of the American Indian
mask illustrated in this book can be found in A. Wardwell,
Tangible Visions: Northwest Coast Indian Shamanism and its Art,
Monacelli Press and Corvus Press, New York, 1996. The
"emaciated shaman dagger" is discussed in S. Brown, *The Spirit
Within: Northwest Coast Native Art from the John H. Hauberg
Collection*. Rizzoli, New York; Seattle Art Museum, Seattle, WA,
1995. The Boas quote comes from texts provided by the
U'mista Cultural Center, Alert Bay, British Columbia. The
modern history of the Kwakiutl potlatch is treated in A. Jonaitis
(ed.), *Chiefly Feasts: The Enduring Kwakiutl Potlatch*, American
Museum of Natural History, New York; University of
Washington Press, Seattle, 1991. Willie Seaweed's artistic
biography is the subject of B. Holm, *Smoky-Top: The Art and
Times of Willie Seaweed*, University of Washington Press, Seattle,
1983. Masterful discussions of Haida argillite carving, Albert
and Charles Edenshaw, and Simeon *sdiihldaa* can be found in
R. K. Wright, *Northern Haida Master Carvers*, University of
Washington Press, Seattle, 2001. Bill Reid's life and work is
the subject of D. Shadbolt, *Bill Reid*, Douglas and McIntyre,
Vancouver; University of Washington Press, Seattle, 1998.

8 Arctic and Subarctic

Area surveys of Arctic prehistory and ethnography can be
found in D. Damas (ed.), *Handbook of North American Indians:
Arctic*, vol. 5, Smithsonian Institution, Washington, D.C., 1984. A
well-illustrated survey of engraved walrus ivory from the Bering
Straits is offered in A. Wardwell, *Ancient Eskimo Ivories of the
Bering Strait*, Hudson Hills, New York, 1986. The whaling kit
owned by the Sledge Island *umialik* is illustrated and discussed
in S. A. Kaplan and K. J. Barsness, *Raven's Journey: The World of
Alaska's Native People*, University Museum, University of
Pennsylvania, Philadelphia, 1986. A thrilling account of a recent
Point Barrow whaling expedition can be found in B. Hess,
"The gift," in J. C. H. King and H. Lidchi (eds.), *Imaging the Arctic*,
British Museum, London, 1998. The Ipiutak and Aleut masks
are illustrated and discussed in H. B. Collins et al., *The Far
North: 2000 Years of American Eskimo and Indian Art*, National
Gallery of Art, Washington, D.C., 1973. The Ekven site shaman's
burial is mentioned and many of the objects are illustrated in
W. W. Fitzhugh and A. Crowell (eds.), *Crossroads of Continents:
Cultures of Siberia and Alaska*, Smithsonian Institution Press,
Washington, D.C., 1988. Modern and historic Yupik masks and
performances receive thorough treatment in A. Fienup-
Riordan, *The Living Tradition of Yup'ik Masks*, University of
Washington Press, Seattle, 1996. See also W. W. Fitzhugh and
S. Kaplan, *Inua: Spirit World of the Bering Sea Eskimo*, Smithsonian
Institution Press, Washington, D.C., 1982. Nick Charles's
statements and artistic biography can be found in A. Fienup-
Riordan et al., *The Artists Behind the Work*, University of Alaska
Museum, Fairbanks, AL, 1986. Notes on carving appear in E. W.
Nelson and W. W. Fitzhugh, *The Eskimo About Bering Strait*,
Smithsonian Institution Press, Washington, D.C., 1983. Happy
Jack and other ivory carvers of Nome are discussed in D. J. Ray,
Artists of the Tundra and the Sea, University of Washington Press,
Seattle, 1961. Recent carving among the Canadian Inuit is
discussed in M. von Finckenstein (ed.), *Celebrating Inuit Art
1948–1970*, Canadian Museum of Civilization, Hull, QC, 1999.
Lucy Kownak's and Emily Nipishna's statements appear in a

thorough study of Inuit clothing offered in Judy Hall et al., *Sanatujut: Pride in Women's Work: Copper and Caribou Inuit Clothing Traditions*, Canadian Museum of Civilization, Hull, QC, 1994. Alexander MacKenzie's quote appears in Judy Thompson's study of Athapascan clothing traditions, *From the Land: Two Hundred Years of Dene Clothing*, Canadian Museum of Civilization, Hull, QC, 1994. Naskapi hunting coats are analyzed in D. K. Burnham, *To Please the Caribou: Painted Caribou Skin Coats worn by the Naskapi, Montagnais, and Cree Hunters of the Quebec-Labrador Peninsula*, University of Washington Press, Seattle, 1992. The spiritual associations of their painted designs are discussed in F. G. Speck, *Naskapi: The Savage Hunters of the Labrador Peninsula*, University of Oklahoma Press, Norman, 1935. The history of Sub-Arctic floral embroidery, which includes Mary Agnes Bonnetrouge's *mukluks*, is thoroughly discussed in B. A. Hail and K. C. Duncan, *Out of the North: The Subarctic Collection of the Haffenreffer Museum of Anthropology*, Haffenreffer Museum of Anthropology, Brown University, Bristol, RI, 1989.

9 Artists of the Modern and Contemporary World

Plamondon's portrait of Zacharie Vincent is discussed in F. Gagnon, "Antoine Plamondon, Le dernier des Hurons (1838)," *The Journal of Canadian Art History*, vol. 12, no. 1, 1989, pp. 68–79. The life and art of Earnest Spybuck are the subject of L. A. Callander and R. Slivka, *Shawnee Home Life: The Paintings of Earnest Spybuck*, Museum of the American Indian, New York, 1984. James Howard's description of the Shawnee war dance appears in J. H. Howard, *Shawnee! The Ceremonialism of a Native American Tribe and Its Cultural Background*, Ohio University Press, Athens, 1981. The presentation of young Hopi and San Ildefonso painters on the national stage is the subject of D. W. Penney and L. Roberts, "America's pueblo artists: encounters on the borderland," in W. J. Rushing (ed.), *Native American Art in the Twentieth Century*, Routledge, London and New York, 1999. For another revealing look at the Pueblo watercolorist exhibition in New York, see E. H. Cahill, "America has its 'Primitives,'" *International Studio*, vol. 75, no. 299, 1922, pp. 80–83. The best and most detailed history of this early episode in Native American painting is J. J. Brody, *Pueblo Indian Painting: Tradition and Modernism in New Mexico, 1900–1930*, School of American Research Press, Santa Fe, NM, 1997. A pioneering study of twentieth-century Native American painting is D. M. Fawcett and L. A. Callander, *Native American Painting: Selections from the Museum of the American Indian*, Museum of the American Indian, New York, 1982. The "Studio School" and its artists are examined in B. Bernstein and W. J. Rushing, *Modern by Tradition: American Indian Painting in the Studio Style*, Museum of New Mexico Press, Santa Fe, 1995. The Philbrook contributions to the "American Indian fine arts movement" are detailed in L. L. Wyckoff (ed.), *Visions and Voices: Native American Painting from the Philbrook Museum of Art*, Philbrook Museum of Art, Tulsa, OK, 1996. A recent artistic biography of Allan Houser is W. J. Rushing, "Allan Houser, American hero," in W. J. Rushing (ed.), *After the Storm: the Eiteljorg Fellowship for Native American Fine Art, 2001*, Eiteljorg Museum of American Indians and Western Art, Indianapolis, IN, 2001. A thorough examination of the genesis of the Institute of American Indian Arts and its relationship to United States Indian policy is J. L. Gritton, *The Institute of American Indian Arts: Modernism and U.S. Indian Policy*, University of New Mexico Press, Albuquerque, 2000. Good, basic biographies of many important Native

American artists can be found in R. Matuz (ed.), *St. James Guide to Native North American Artists*, St. James Press, Detroit, 1998: the Fritz Scholder quote is from that source. George Morrison's artistic autobiography is G. Morrison and M. F. Galt, *Turning the Feather Around: My Life in Art*, Minnesota Historical Society Press, St. Paul, 1998. The significance of Joe Herrera's later work is discussed in W. J. Rushing, "Authenticity and subjectivity in post-war painting: concerning Herrera, Scholder, and Cannon," in M. Archuleta and R. Strickland (eds.), *Shared Visions: Native American Painters and Sculptors in the Twentieth Century*, New Press, New York, 1991. A good insider's overview of the larger issue of twentieth-century Native American art is offered in G. Longfish, "The twentieth century: 'who's going to ride your wild horses?'" in D. W. Penney and G. Longfish, *Native American Art*, Hugh Lauter Levin, New York, 1994. The important work of T. C. Cannon is reviewed in J. Frederick, *T. C. Cannon: He Stood in the Sun*, Northland Press, Flagstaff, AZ, 1995. The Oxendine quote comes from L. E. Oxendine, "23 contemporary Indian artists," *Art in America*, July–August 1972, pp. 58–69. The sources of Norval Morriseau's painting are discussed in R. Phillips, "'Messages from the past': oral traditions and contemporary woodlands art," in Canadian Museum of Civilization (ed.), *In the Shadow of the Sun: Perspectives on Contemporary Art*, Canadian Museum of Civilization, Hull, QC, 1993. Interviews with artists of the "Woodland School" appear in M. E. Southcott, *The Sound of the Drum: The Sacred Art of the Anishnabec*, Boston Mills Press, Erin, ON, 1984. A brief discussion of Kwakiutl artist Marianne Nicholson appears in A. Walsh, "Marianne Nicholson, Kwakwaka'wakw," in B. Bernstein (ed.), *Contemporary Masters: The Eiteljorg Fellowship for Native American Fine Art*, vol. 1, Eiteljorg Museum of American Indians and Western Art, Indianapolis, IN, 1999. A moving essay about Kiowa photographer Horace Poolaw, written by Kiowa author N. Scott Momaday, is "The photography of Horace Poolaw," *Aperture; Strong Hearts: Native American Visions and Voices*, no. 139, summer 1995, pp. 14–19. Photographer and artist Jolene Rickard's own words appear in an interview in P. C. Smith, "Jolene Rickard: Corn Blue Room; unplugging the hologram," G. McMaster (ed.), *Reservation X: The Power of Place in Aboriginal Contemporary Art*, Canadian Museum of Civilization, Hull, QC; University of Washington Press, Seattle, 1998. An introduction to the work of Winnebago artist Truman Lowe is offered in J. Complo, *Haga (Third Son): Truman Lowe*, Eiteljorg Museum of American Indians and Western Art, Indianapolis, IN, 1992. The catalogue for the important Columbus Quincentennial exhibition is J. Q. Smith (ed.), *The Submuloc Show/Columbus Wohs: A Visual Commentary on the Columbus Quincentennial from the Perspective of America's First People*, Atlatl, Phoenix, AZ, 1992. The catalogue for the Gerald McMaster exhibition is G. McMaster et al., "Savage Graces: 'after images,'" *Harbor Magazine of Art and Everyday Life*, vol. 3, no. 1, winter 1993–1994.

List of Illustrations

Measurements are given in centimeters, followed by inches, height before width before depth, unless otherwise stated.

51 x 21 (20⅛ x 8¼). Musée de l'Homme, Paris

40 Odawa bag, 1820–50. Goodhart, Emmet County, Michigan. Vegetal fiber, animal wool yarn, 17.2 x 21 (6¾ x 8¼). The Detroit Institute of Arts, Detroit, 81.39. Photo Dirk Bakker

41 Black buckskin bandolier bag. Collected by Lord Jeffrey Amherst, 1758–63 (Ojibwa?). © The Field Museum, Chicago, #A99654

42 Menominee (?) knife case. 1800–30. Wisconsin. Blackened buckskin, vegetal fiber, porcupine quills, 28.9 x 13 (11⅜ x 5⅛). The Manoogian Collection, Taylor, Michigan

43 *Iroquois Woman*, French or English artist, late 18th century. Watercolor. Frank H. McClung Museum, University of Tennessee, Knoxville. Photo Dirk Bakker

44 Miami skirt, 1820–40. Peoria, Indiana. Wool fabric, silver brooches, silk ribbon, 141 x 135 (55½ x 53⅛). Collection of Cranbrook Institute of Science, Bloomfield Hills, Michigan. Photo © Robert Hensleigh

45 Creek shoulder bag, 1830s or 1840s. Georgia or Alabama. Wool fabric, cotton fabric and thread, silk ribbon, glass beads, 135.2 x 18.7 x 19.4 x 10.2 (53¼ x 7⅜ x 7⅝ x 4). The Detroit Institute of Arts, Detroit, 1988.29. Photo Dirk Bakker

46 Ojibwa sash, *c.* 1850. Michigan. Glass beads, cotton thread, wool yarn, 72.4 (177.8 with fringe) x 4.8 (28½ [70 with fringe] x 1⅞). Detroit Historical Museum, Detroit (Chandler-Pohrt no. 39). Photo Dirk Bakker

47 Seminole shirt of printed calico, early 19th century. 110 (43¼). Ethnological Museum, Berlin, IV B 247

48 Quill box, Yvonne Walker Keshick "Falling Leaf," Little Traverse Bay Band of Odawa Indians, 1990s. Courtesy Yvonne Walker and Tribal Expressions, Illinois

49 Ojibwa family, late 19th century. Michigan State University Museum, East Lansing. Photo D. F. Barry

50 Pictographs at Agawa Rock, Lake Superior, Ontario

51 Unknown Iroquois artist, ball head club. Wood, 49.5 (19½). Denver Art Museum Collection: Gift of Mrs Effie Parkhill, 1951.300. Photo © by Denver Art Museum. All rights reserved

52 Ojibwa gunstock club, early 19th century. Upper Michigan. Wood, iron blade, 63.5 (25). The Detroit Institute of Arts, Detroit, 2000.2. Photo Dirk Bakker

53 Miami pipe bowl, *c.* 1700s. Peru, Indiana. Catlinite, 7.9 x 6.7 (3⅛ x 2⅝). The Detroit Institute of Arts, Detroit, 81.265. Photo Dirk Bakker

54 Pipe bowl carved by Aubonwaishkum (Ojibwa), from Manitoulin Island, collected 1920. Black stone, 16.1 x 6.6 x 2.9 (6⅜ x 2⅝ x 1⅛). With permission of the Royal Ontario Museum, Toronto © ROM, NS38457 Pipe Bowl ROM2003-_937

55 Iroquois spoon, 1800s. Maple, 14 x 8.3 x 4.5 (5½ x 3¼ x ¾). Thaw Collection, Fenimore Art Museum, Cooperstown, New York. Photo John Bigelow Taylor, NYC

56 Crooked knife, late 19th century. Great Lakes region. Wood, steel blade, rawhide, 23.5 (9¼). The Detroit Institute of Arts, Detroit, 1986.20. Photo Dirk Bakker

57 Mesquakie feast bowl, 19th century. Tama, Iowa. Maple, 35.9 x 42.5 (14⅛ x 16¾). The Detroit Institute of Arts, Detroit, 81.643. Photo Dirk Bakker

58 Pictograph at Sutherland Wash, Arizona. Photo courtesy Nile Root

59 Basketmaker III bowl. Tohatchi Flats, Navajo Reservation, New Mexico, *c.* AD 600–700. La Plata black-on-white, 8.7 x 19.1 (3⅜ x 7½). University of Colorado Museum, Boulder, Earl H Morris Memorial Pottery Collection

60 Black-on-white *ollas*. Navajo Reservation, Arizona, AD 700–900. Left 41 x 37.2 (16¼ x 14⅝), right 43.4 x 36.7 (17⅛ x 14½). University of Colorado Museum, Boulder, UCM 9449 and UCM 9448

61 Mimbres bowl, AD 1000–1150. New Mexico. Fired clay, 26.7 x 10.2 (10½ x 4). The Detroit Institute of Arts, Detroit, 76.87. Photo Dirk Bakker

62 Anasazi Fourmile polychrome jar, AD 1325–1400. New Mexico. Fired clay, 23.4 x 23.4 (9¼ x 9¼). The Detroit Institute of Arts, Detroit, 1999.1394. Photo Dirk Bakker

63 Pueblo Bonito, Chaco Canyon, New Mexico. Photo Mick Sharp

64 *left* Plan of the great kiva at Casa Rinconada, Chaco Canyon. After Ferguson and Rohn

64 *right* The great kiva at Casa Rinconada, Chaco Canyon. National Park Service, USA

65 Hohokam shell frog, Martinez Hill site, Arizona. Marine shell. Arizona State Museum, University of Arizona, Tucson

66 Casa Grande, Hohokam. Smithsonian Institution, Washington, D.C.

67 Oraibi pueblo, Hopi, Arizona, *c.* 1890. School for American Research, Collection of the Museum of New Mexico, Santa Fe. Photo Ben Wittick

68 Awatovi, Test 14, room two, right wall design 6. Illustration Louie Ewing

69 Fred Kabotie, *Zuni Shalako*, *c.* 1928–32. Gouache on tan paper, 14.8 x 23 (5¾ x 9). Indian Arts Research Center, School for

American Research, Santa Fe, New Mexico. Mary Cabot Wheelwright Gift, 1934

70 Zuni 'One Horn' Kachina doll, purchased 1930s. Zuni, Arizona. Wood, cotton fabric, hair, feathers, shell pendants, 38.1 (15). The Detroit Institute of Arts, Detroit, 1997.2. Photo Dirk Bakker

71 Hopi Hemis Kachina doll, 1930s. Arizona. Painted wood, 47.6 (18¾). The Detroit Institute of Arts, Detroit, 1997.23. Photo Dirk Bakker

72 Alvin James Jr. (Hopi), Hemis Kachina doll, 1970s. The Detroit Institute of Arts, Detroit, 1995.99

73 Painted cotton blanket *c.* AD 1250. Hidden House site, Anasazi. Cotton, 162.6 (64). Arizona State Museum, University of Arizona, Tucson. Photo E. B. Sayles

74 Chief's blanket, Navajo, *c.* 1850. The Manoogian Collection, Taylor, Michigan

75 Navajo early classic-style poncho, 1840–60. 171.4 x 127 (67½ x 50). Southwest Museum, Los Angeles, Gift of Charles Fletcher Lummis, 457.G.3

76 Hubbell trading post, Ganado, Arizona, *c.* 1900. School for American Research, Collection of Museum of New Mexico, Santa Fe. Photo Ben Wittick

77 Cochiti and Tesuque figurines, *c.* 1880. Museum of New Mexico, Santa Fe, neg. no. 16293. Photo Ben Wittick

78 Jar, Laguna Pueblo, 1880–1900. University Museum, University of Pennsylvania Museum, Philadelphia, 45-15-103

79 Painted pottery jar, black-on-orange. Attributed to Nampeyo. Hopi, early 20th century. 39.5 (15½). Museum für Volkerkunde, Vienna

80 Maria and Julian Martinez, storage jar, 1930s. San Ildefonso. Fired clay, 38.1 x 49.9 (15 x 19⅝). The Manoogian Foundation, Taylor, Michigan

81 Navajo bracelets, 1900–30. Silver with turquoise inlay. Courtesy Toby Herbst, Santa Fe

82 Ghost Dance dress, *c.* 1890, Southern Arapaho. Tanned elkhide, pigment, eagle feathers, 137.2 x 137.2 (54 x 54). Buffalo Bill Historical Center, Cody, Wyoming, Chandler-Pohrt Collection, Gift of Mary J. and James R Jundt, NA.204.4

83 Pictographs of figures with large shields. Valley of the Shields. Drawing courtesy James D. Keyser

84 Pictograph of warriors fighting. Writing-On-Stone site, southern Alberta. Provincial Museum of Alberta, Edmonton, Canada

85 Shield, Cheyenne, Little Rock, Arkansas, mid-1880s. The Detroit Institute of Arts, Detroit, 76.144

86 No Two Horns, shield, *c.* 1870. Leather

with pigment, 45.1 (17¾). Denver Art Museum Collection: Gift of C. W. Douglas, 1932.237. Photo © Denver Art Museum. All rights reserved

87 Unknown artist, pictographic robe, late 1700s. Buffalo hide. Musée de l'Homme, Paris, MH 86.17.1

88 Little Shield, *Pawnee Riffle* (sic), before 1868. Pencil and ink, 8.3 x 14 (3¼ x 5½). St. Louis Mercantile Library, St. Louis, Missouri, 78.038.2.20

89 No Two Horns (He Nupa Wanica), Hunkpapa Lakota, *Scene of War Exploits*, 1900–15. Paper, pigments, 20.3 x 25.4 (8 x 10). State Historical Society of North Dakota, Bismark, Collected by The Reverend Aaron McGaffey Beede at Fort Yates, Standing Rock Reservation, North Dakota

90 No Two Horns (He Nupa Wanica), Hunkpapa Lakota, horse effigy, 1900–20. Wood, leather, pigment, metal, hair, 76.2 (30). State Historical Society of North Dakota, Bismark, 867.234.180

91 Zotom, *On the Parapet of Fort Marion Next Day After Arrival*, 1876–77. Pencil and colored pencil, 21.6 x 27.9 (8½ x 11). The National Cowboy and Western Heritage Center, Oklahoma City, Arthur and Shifra Silberman Collection 95.2.633

92 Unknown artist, pipe bowl, Santee Sioux, 1830s or 1840s. National Museum of Natural History, Smithsonian Institution, Washington, D.C., 26.22

93 Cradle, *c.* 1880, Arapaho, Wyoming. Sack cloth, rawhide, dew claws, porcupine quills, 81.3 x 33 x 28 (32 x 13 x 11). Buffalo Bill Historical Center, Cody, Wyoming, NA.11.47

94 Man's shirt, collected by Charles G. Sawtail (Second Lt. 6th Calvary), Fort Laramie, 1855; belonged to Spotted Tail (Sinte Gleska), Brule Sioux. National Museum of the Amerian Indian, Smithsonian Institution, 17.6694

95 Side seam dress, Upper Missouri, Lewis and Clark Expedition. Peabody Museum of Archaeology and Ethnology, Harvard University, Cambridge, Massachusetts

96 Northern Cheyenne knife case, *c.* 1860. Fort C. F. Smith, Montana Territory. Buffalo rawhide, buckskin, glass beads, 25.4 x 7.6 (10 x 3). The Detroit Institute of Arts, Detroit (Chandler-Pohrt no. 94), 2000.31

97 Crow knife case, *c.* 1890. Montana. Rawhide, buckskin, glass beads, 31.8 (45.7 with fringe) x 11.4 (12½ [18 with fringe] x 4½). The Detroit Institute of Arts, Detroit (Chandler-Pohrt no. 129), 2000.5

98 Crow parfleche, *c.* 1880, Montana. Buffalo, rawhide, pigment, 60.3 x 39.4 (23¾ x 15½). The Detroit Institute of Arts (Chandler-Pohrt no. 100), 1988.51

99 Beadwork display of Joseph and Edith Claymore (Lakota), Standing Rock Reservation, *c.* 1900–10. State Historical Society of North Dakota, Bismarck. Photo Frank Fiske

100 Pictographs of big horn sheep on the rocks of the Coso mountains of Inyo County, 550 BC–AD 950. © William D. Hyder 1989

101 Blythe geoglyphs, Blythe, California. Photo Bureau of Land Management, Arizona

102 Paintings at Painted Cave, Santa Barbara County, San Marcos Pass, California, Chumash. © William D. Hyder

103 Chumash pipe, found on San Nicholas Island, California. Gabrielino culture, AD 1400–1600. Steatite, shell beads, asphalt. The Detroit Institute of Arts T1987.145. Collection of Gordon Hart

104 Miwok feast basket, late 1800s. Field Museum of Natural History, Chicago

105 Baskets of acorn mush, Southern Maidu, photographed 1900–10. Field Museum of Natural History, Chicago

106 Callipene and Lena Brown (Southern Miwok), June 1901. Photo D. H. Wulzen

107 Pomo feather basket, Deppe Collection, collected 1837. Ethnological Museum, Berlin, Inv.-Nr. Ca 77

108 Jump Dance basket. Hupa, 19th century. Northern California. Willow, conifer root, beargrass, maidenhair fern, feathers, deerskin. Southwest Museum, Los Angeles

109 Horn purse, Morek, California, Unknown Yurok artist, late 19th or early 20th century. Antler, pigment, 3.5 x 12.1 x 3.5 (1⅜ x 4¾ x 1⅜). The Brooklyn Museum of Art, Museum Expedition 1905, Museum Collection Fund, 05.588.7436. Photo Justin Kerr

110 Hupa participants in the Jump Dance at Pekwon, a Yurok town on the Klamath River, 1893. National Archives of Anthropology, Smithsonian Institution, Washington, D.C., NAA 43114-A

111 Mission hat. 36 (14⅛). British Museum, London. Ethno Van.196

112 Ana Maria Marta, coiled basket with Spanish inscription and royal coat of arms, 1822. Ventureño Chumash. 16 x 40.5 (6¼ x 16). Lowie Museum of Anthropology, University of California, Berkeley

113 Louisa Keyser, 'Beacon Lights' coiled basket, Washoe, Carson City, Nevada, 1904–05. Willow, western redbud, bracken fern root, 28.6 x 40.6 (11¼ x 16). Thaw Collection, Fenimore Art Museum, Cooperstown, NY, T751. Photo John Bigelow Taylor, NYC

114 Elizabeth Hickox, basket with a lid, *c.* 1914. California, Wiyot. Redwood root, maidenhair fern, porcupine quills, 16.5 x 14 (6½ x 5½). Montclair Art Museum, Montclair, New Jersey. Gift of Mrs. Henry Lang in memory of her mother, Mrs. Jasper R. Rand, 1914.27 A-B

115 Carrie Bethel (Mono Lake Paiute), coiled basket, 1930s. Yosemite Valley, central California. Sedge root, redbud, bracken fern root, willow, 81.9 (32¼). Yosemite Museum, Yosemite National Park YM-66820

116 Blue heron effigy pestle, Marpole site, 400 BC–AD 400. Photo Roy Carlson

117 Whale bone club, Boardwalk site, Prince Rupert Harbor, British Columbia, *c.* 500 BC. Canadian Museum of Civilization, Gatineau, Quebec, MCC/CMC No. 588-926

118 *Chitoolth* or whale bone club. Collected 'New Georgia' by Archibald Menzies in 1792–94. Whalebone inlaid with abalone shell, 57.5 (22). Field Museum of Natural History, Chicago, 14851

119 Stone club with head of sandhill crane. Hagwilget, Bulkley Canyon, British Columbia, *c.* 500 BC–AD 1. British Columbia Provincial Museum, Victoria

120 Oil dish in the shape of a reclining figure, Ozette site. Courtesy Richard D. Daugherty

121 Chief's house in Kitwancool Village, *c.* 1910. British Columbia Archives, Victoria, A-06907

122 Rain wall screen, Whale House, Klukwan village, Alaska. Tlingit. Alaska State Library, Juneau, Alaska PCA 87-13

123 Raven Barbecuing Hat, early 19th century. Wood, deerskin, ermine, spruce root, iron nail, bird beak, 52 (20½). University Museum, University of Pennsylvania, Philadelphia, NA 8502

124 Bentwood chest, attributed to a carver of the Nisga'a Tsimshian, Nass River region, British Columbia, active 1800s. © The Field Museum, Chicago, #A108396 1. Photo Ron Testa

125 Captain Richard Carpenter, or Du'k!wayella (Heiltsuk), chief's seat, before 1900. Northern Kwakiutl. Wood, 225 x 112.5 x 76.5 (88⅝ x 44¼ x 30⅜). Royal British Columbia Museum, Victoria, 1856

126 Robe Naaxein, Chilkat robe. Tlingit, *c.* 1890. Mountain goat wool, yellow cedar bark and natural dyes, 170 x 131 (66⅞ x 51⅝). Seattle Art Museum, Hauberg Collection 83.229. Photo Paul Macapia

127 Pattern board for Chilkat robe, Tlingit, *c.* 1890. Spruce wood, pigment and paint, 53 x 95 (20⅞ x 37⅜). Seattle Art Museum, Gift of John H. Hauberg. Photo Paul Macapia

128 Shaman's mask, Tlingit, before 1850. Wood, opercula, and red, black and blue-green pigment, 33 (13). National Museum of the American Indian,

Smithsonian Institution, 9/8032. Purchased from Emmons, 1919

129 Oystercatcher rattle, Tlinglit. Hoonah. Wood, abalone, rawhide, ermine skin, and red and black pigment, 30 (11¾). British Museum, London, 1944.Am.2.125

130 Guardian figure, Tlingit, *c.* 1820–40. American Museum of Natural History, New York

131 Dagger Ixti'ku gwal'aa, Shaman's Thrust, Tlingit, Klukwan village, Saayeina'aat, *c.* 1770. Iron, copper, and buckskin, 10.5 x 54.6 x 0.3 (4⅛ x 21½ x ⅛). Seattle Art Museum, Gift of John H. Hauberg. Photo Paul Macapia

132 Hamatsa crooked beak mask, Willie Seaweed (Kwakiutl/Nakwaxda'xw), Kingcome Inlet, British Columbia, 1940s. Wood, cedar bark, paint, 94 (37). Royal British Columbia Museum, Victoria

133 Bullhead mask, Hopetown, carved before 1901. Wood, rope, 89 x 54.5 (35 x 21⅜). American Museum of Natural History, New York 16/8942, AMNH 1902–46. Collected by George Hunt, 1902

134 Sailors, Haida, *c.* 1845, Queen Charlotte Islands. Argillite, ivory, 47 x 20 (18½ x 7¾). Shaw Collection, Fenimore Art Museum, Cooperstown, New York, T187. Photo John Bigelow Taylor, NYC

135 Argillite chest, Charles Edenshaw (Haida), *c.* 1900–10. Royal British Columbia Museum, Victoria, cat. no. 10622, neg. no. CPN 10622

136 Mask representing an elderly man, Simon Stilthda (*sdiihldaa*), Haida, before 1889. Royal British Columbia Museum, Victoria, 10670

137 Bill Reid (Haida), box with lid, 1971. Gold, 10. x 94 x 8.2 (3⅞ x 37 x 3¼). Canadian Museum of Civilization, Gatineau, Quebec, CMC VII-B-1574a,b

138 Robert Davidson, *Raven Stealing the Moon*, 1977. Haida, Queen Charlotte Islands. Silkscreen on paper, 58.1 x 27 (22⅞ x 10⅝). Field Museum of Natural History, Chicago, 14851

139 Floating or flying polar bear, Dorset culture, AD 100–1000. Walrus ivory. Canadian Museum of Civilization, Gatineau, Quebec, MCC/CMC No. 590-3293

140 Winged object, Okvik, 300–1 BC. Walrus ivory. Detroit Institute of Arts, Detroit 1983.7

141 Whale-shaped box, Sledge Island, found 1912. University Museum, University of Pennsylvania, Philadelphia, NA 4780

142 *Umiak* seat, whale fetish. Sledge Island, Seward Peninsula, found 1912. Wood, inlaid with wooden pegs, variegated stone inset under whale from the back. 27 (10⅝). University Museum, University of Pennsylvania, Philadelphia, NA 4778

143 Hunting hat, collected on Norton Sound in 1886. Wood, ivory, 33 (13). Canadian Museum of Civilization, Gatineau, Quebec, IV.E.92

144 Burial mask, Ipiutak site, near Point Hope, Alaska, AD 1–800. Walrus ivory. American Museum of Natural History, New York, 60.1.7713

145 Baby walrus, Ipiutak site, near Point Hope, Alaska, AD 1–800. Walrus ivory. American Museum of Natural History, New York, 60.1.7665

146 Human mask, found in an archaeological deposit, Delarof Harbor, Unga Island. Wood with traces of pigment, stained with modern preservative, 30.5 (12). National Museum of Natural History, 13082, Arctic Studies Center, Smithsonian Institution, Washington, D.C.

147 Masked dancers performing in the *qasgiq* in Qissunaq, Alaska, 1946. Photo Alfred Milotte, Milotte Collection, Alaska State Museum, Juneau, neg. no. 1098

148 Kuskokwim river mask, muskrat, *c.* 1900. 70.5 (27¾). National Museum of the American Indian, Smithsonian Institution, 9/3403

149 Story knife, collected at Kongiganak, on Kuskokwim Bay. Engraved ivory with black pigment, 36.1 (14¼). National Museum of Natural History, Smithsonian Institution, 127403

150 Unknown, tusk with scrimshaw, 19th century. Walrus tusk. Gift of the University of Tulsa, Ellis Soper Collection, The Philbrook Art Museum, Tulsa, Oklahoma, 1995.24.268

151 Engraved walrus tusk, Happy Jack, Nome, Alaska, early 20th century. Front and back view. Carnegie Institute, Pittsburgh, PN CMNH 23102-15445

152 Joe Talirunili, *Migration*, *c.* 1975. Gray stone, skin, cotton thread, wood, 34.5 x 29 x 20.6 (13⅝ x 11⅜ x 8⅛). Canadian Museum of Civilization (IV-B-1644)

153 Attirak of Baker Lake, *c.* 1920. Hudson's Bay Company Archives, Archives of Manitoba. 1987/363-E-250-4

154 Woman's parka, Caribou Inuit (Padlimuit), 1938. Eskimo Point, Hudson Bay, Northwest Territories, Canada. Caribou fur, wool cloth, glass beads, caribou hide, caribou teeth, 121.9 (48). Royal Ontario Museum, Toronto

155 Summer outfit, late 19th century, Caribou hide, sinew, porcupine quills, silver-willow seeds. Tunic 115 (45¼), moccasin-trousers 121 (47⅝), hood 30 (11¾), mittens 26 (10¼), knife sheath 30 (11¾). Canadian Museum of Civilization, Hull, CMC VI-73 A-F

156 Tailored coat (back view), painted with curvilinear (double curves) and rectilinear designs. Naskapi, collected in 1825. Paint on leather, 97 (38⅛). Museum für Völkerkunde und Schweizerisches, Basel

157 Pouch, Swampy Cree, Hudson Bay, before 1840. Canadian Museum of Civilization, Gatineau, Quebec, MCC/CMC No. 575-626

158 Metis-Cree octopus bag, *c.* 1840. Red River region, Manitoba. Buckskin, caribou hide, porcupine quills, 39.4 x 19.1 (15½ x 7½). The Detroit Institute of Arts, Detroit, 81.59

159 Fire-bag, Cree of Metis, 1850s. Haffenreffer Museum of Anthropology, Brown University, 87-142

160 Man's jacket, early 20th century. Collected by H. A. Connoy, possibly at Arctic Red River, Northwest Territories, acquired 1911. Moosehide, black velvet, ermine skin, multicolored glass beads, silk ribbon (ties), 73 (28¾). Canadian Museum of Civilization, VI-S-4

161 Mary Agnes Bonnetrouge, *mukluks*, 1985. Fort Providence, Northwest Territories. Moose hide, caribou fur, porcupine quills, 28 x 19 x 33 (11 x 7½ x 13). Haffenreffer Museum of Anthropology, Brown University, 85-645

162 Zacharie Vincent, photograph painting a self-portrait, 1870s or 1880s. Photo Université de Montréal Division des archives, Collection Baby, P0058 1Fp,06718

163 Zacharie Vincent (Huron of Lorette), *Self-Portrait*, mid-19th century. Oil on canvas. Musée de La Civilisation, dépôt du Séminaire de Québec, no. 1991.102

164 Earnest Spybuck (Shawnee), *War Dance and Gathering Scene*, *c.* 1910. Watercolor on paper, 43.8 x 62.9 (17¼ x 24¾). Museum of the American Indian, Heye Foundation, New York, 2/5614

165 Fred Kabotie (Hopi), *Mixed Kachina Dance*, *c.* 1919. Pencil and watercolor on paper, 10.8 x 25.5 (4¼ x 10). School for American Research, Santa Fe, Indian Arts Collection Fund no. 1985.20.2, Gift of Mr. & Mrs. Oliver Seth, 1985

166 Crescencio Martinez (San Ildefonso), *Buffalo Dancers*, *c.* 1916. Watercolor, 37.2 x 54 (14⅝ x 21¼) (image); 57.2 x 72.4 (22½ x 28½) (sheet). Philbrook Museum of Art, Tulsa, Oklahoma, 1981.5

167 James Silverhorn (Kiowa), *Preparing for a War Expedition*, *c.* 1887. Pencil and crayon, 24.8 x 34.3 (9¾ x 13½). Marion Koogler McNay Art Museum, San Antonio, Gift of Mrs Terrell Bartlett, 1962.1.1

168 Stephen Mopope, *The Procession*, undated. Watercolor on board, 48.7 x 61.6 (19⅛ x 24¼) (image), 48.7 x 61.6 (19 3/16 x 24¼) (sheet). Philbrook Museum of Art, Tulsa, Oklahoma, 1958.20

169 Dick West (Dr. Walter Richard West), *Cheyenne Sun Dance, the Third Day*, 1949. Watercolor, 54.1 x 89.2 (21⅜ x 35⅛)

(image); 62.6 x 89.2 (24⅝ x 35⅛) (sheet). Philbrook Museum of Art, Tulsa, Oklahoma, 1949.20

170 Allan C. Houser, *Drama on the Plains.* Alabaster, 21.8 x 27 x 8.8 (8⅝ x 10⅝ x 3½). Buffalo Bill Historical Center, Cody, Wyoming; William Weiss Contemporary Art Fund; 16.77

171 Oscar Howe (Yanktonai Sioux), *Ghost Dance,* 1960. Casein on paper, 47 x 61 (18½ x 24). In the collection of the Heard Museum, Phoenix, Arizona, Copyright Adelheid Howe, 1983

172 George Morrison (Ojibwa), *Red Rock Crevices. Soft light. Lake Superior Landscape,* 1987. Acrylic and ink on canvas on board, 16.5 x 29.2 (6½ x 11½). Collection Tweed Museum of Art, University of Minnesota, Duluth, Alice Tweed Tuohy Foundation Purchase

173 Fritz Scholder (Luiseño), *Santana, Kiowa, c.* 1968. Oil on canvas

174 T. C. Cannon (Caddo/Kiowa), *Self-Portrait in the Studio.* Oil on canvas, 182.9 x 132.1 (72 x 52). Courtesy Estate of T. C. Cannon

175 Norval Morriseau (Ojibwa), *Mishapihsoo,* 1976. Canadian Museum of Civilization, Gatineau, Quebec, MCC/CMC No. K95-37

176 Horace Poolaw, "Lela Ware, Paul Zumwalt and Trecil Poolaw," c. 1928. Mountain View, Oklahoma. National Museum of the American Indian, Smithsonian Institution, Washington D.C., P26509

177 Jaune Quick-to-See Smith (Flathead/Cree/Shoshone), *Celebrate.* Courtesy the artist

178 Kay WalkingStick (Cherokee), *Dancing to Rome III,* 2000. Charcoal on paper, 63.5 x 127 (25 x 50). Courtesy the artist and June Kelley Gallery, NYC

179 Jolene Rickard (Tuscarora), *The Corn Blue Room: Iroquois White Corn,* 1998. Installation, 1828.8 x 762 (720 x 300). Courtesy the artist

180 Emmi Whitehorse (Navajo), *Meadow,* 1996. Oil, chalk and paper on canvas, 101.6 x 129.5 (40 x 51). Courtesy the artist

181 George Longfish (Seneca/ Tuscarora), *Spirit Guide/Spirit Healer,* 1983. Acrylic and pencil on paper, 101.6 x 76.2 (40 x 30). Heard Museum, Phoenix, Arizona, HM.IAC2218

Every effort has been made to trace the copyright holders of the images contained in this book, and we apologize in advance for any unintentional omissions. We would be pleased to insert the appropriate acknowledgment in any subsequent edition of this publication.

Index

Page numbers in *italic* refer to illustrations